The New Americans
Recent Immigration and American Society

Edited by
Carola Suárez-Orozco and Marcelo Suárez-Orozco

A Series from LFB Scholarly

Language, Race, and Negotiation of Identity
A Study of Dominican Americans

Benjamin H. Bailey

LFB Scholarly Publishing LLC
New York 2002

Library of Congress Cataloging-in-Publication Data

Bailey, Benjamin H.
  Language, race, and negotiation of identity : a study of Dominican
Americans / Benjamin H. Bailey.
     p. cm. -- (The new Americans)
  Includes bibliographical references (p.   ) and index.
   ISBN 1-931202-24-9 (alk. paper)
   1. Dominican Americans--Ethnic identity--Case studies. 2.
Dominican
Americans--Race identity--Case studies. 3. Dominican
Americans--Languages--Case studies. 4. Categorization
(Psychology)--Case studies. 5. High school students--Rhode
Island--Providence--Social conditions. 6. United States--Ethnic
relations--Case studies. 7. United States--Race relations--Case
studies. 8. Discourse analysis--United States. 9. Providence
(R.I.)--Ethnic relations. 10. Providence (R.I.)--Race relations. I.
Title. II. New Americans (LFB Scholarly Publishing LLC)
   E184.D6 B35 2002
   305.868'72930745--dc21

2002003270

ISBN 1-931202-24-9

Printed on acid-free 250-year-life paper.

Manufactured in the United States of America.

To Julia

Contents

Chapter 1
Introduction

Chapter 2
Community, Field Site, Methods, and Principal Subjects

Chapter 3
Linguistic Resources of Dominican Americans

Chapter 4
Second Generation Identities and Language in a Racialized America

Chapter 5
Dominican American Understandings of Race and Social Identity

Chapter 6
The Interactional Negotiation of Race by an African-descent Dominican American

Chapter 7
Individual Patterns of Language Use and Implications for Ethnic/Racial Identities

Chapter 8
Concluding Remarks

CHAPTER 1
Introduction

1.1 Introduction

This monograph analyzes the language and identities of Dominican second-generation[1] immigrant high-school students as they negotiate ethnic and racial categories in Providence, Rhode Island. Dominican second-generation ethnic/racial identities are often ambiguous because the ethnolinguistic terms in which members of the second generation think of themselves are frequently at odds with the phenotype-based[2] racial terms in which they are seen by others in the United States. Up to 90% of Dominicans have African[3] ancestry, which would make them African American by American "one-drop" rules of racial classification (Davis 1991). Members of the second generation, however, do not think of themselves as "Black" or "African American"--or "White"-- but rather as "Dominican," "Spanish," or "Hispanic." Everyday enactment of a second-generation Dominican, or Dominican American, identity thus involves resistance to American racial categorization, a fundamental form of social organization in the United States.

Through interviews, discourse analysis of naturally occurring, video-recorded talk, and description of linguistic forms, I show that language is central both to the ways Dominican American high school students see themselves and the ways that others see them. Dominican Americans explicitly define their race in terms of language, rather than phenotype, explaining that they *speak* Spanish, so they *are* Spanish. In the United States, African-descent phenotype has historically preceded all other criteria, e.g. national origins, language, or religion, for social classification, and African-descent immigrants have generally merged into the African American population by the second generation (Bryce-Laporte 1972). Unlike these other African-descent groups, Dominicans

1

are maintaining a distinctive, non-Black ethnolinguistic identity in the second generation. The many second-generation Dominican high school students who are phenotypically indistinguishable from African Americans regularly show that they can "speak Spanish" in order to counter others' assumptions--in both intra- and inter-ethnic contexts-- that they are "Black." Many of their peers, including non-Hispanics, accept this Spanish speaking as evidence of non-Black identity. In many contexts, Dominican Americans are thus reversing the historical precedence of African descent over ethnolinguistic identity for social classification.

At the same time that Dominican American high school students use their Spanish language to resist American Black/White categorization, however, their English language varieties frequently contribute to categorization as Black. Their extensive adoption of African American Vernacular English syntax, lexicon, and interactional practices, combined with African-descent phenotype, make many individuals situationally indistinguishable from African Americans, even to other Dominican Americans.

This ambiguity of identity and this agency of individuals in identity negotiations are particularly salient among adolescents in multi-lingual, multi-ethnic immigrant high school contexts such as the one described here. Large, urban public schools veil the linguistic and cultural practices that are so evident in immigrant homes and communities, which results in a social arena in which individuals' ethnic/racial identities can be uncertain. In this ambiguous context, the verbal play and trying-out of identities that is typical of adolescence involves the explicit straddling and challenging of ethnic/racial boundaries.

The language and identities of the Dominican second-generation in Providence reflect their social reality of growing up in Dominican families with Dominican social networks, but residing and going to school in a low-income, multi-ethnic American inner-city. This socialization results in language and identities that are not just "Dominican" and "American" but distinctively inner-city Dominican American. At the same time that such teen-agers adopt language, dress, and musical fashions associated with low-income African American urban youth, for example, they maintain Dominican linguistic and cultural practices in other spheres of their lives, e.g. by speaking Spanish at home and with adult relatives, attending Spanish-language religious services, and going to Caribbean Hispanic nightclubs where they dance to *merengue, bachata,* and *salsa* music.

Dominican American language is not a result of diglossia (Ferguson 1959) in which linguistic forms and code use are highly predicted by social domains (Fishman, Cooper and Ma 1971), but a situation of hybrid, syncretic (Hill and Hill 1986), or 'heteroglossic' (Bakhtin 1981) language use. The linguistic resources used to constitute Dominican American identities include not monolithic codes of English and Spanish, but forms drawn from multiple varieties of each, e.g. Standard Providence English, Non-Standard Providence English (e.g. "yous guys"), African American Vernacular English (e.g. "He be working"), Standard Dominican Spanish, and Regional Non-Standard Dominican Spanish (e.g. /puelta/ for *puerta* ['door'] and /poike/ for *porque* ['why']). Linguistic forms with diverse social provenances and associations are often juxtaposed in ways that are treated as unmarked by participants. African American Vernacular English (hereafter, AAVE) syntactic patterns and vocabulary can thus be alternated or combined with Spanish forms and institutionally prestigious English forms, for example, as in the following segment of speech by a female, high school junior:

> That's one thing I l- I love the way [institutionally prestigious English] *como l*-[Spanish] the American be doing sandwich, they be rocking [AAVE syntax and vocabulary] them things, yo, they put everything up in there, yo.

Dominican American language includes not just the alternation of forms associated with diverse varieties, but the use of distinct, convergent forms resulting from language contact, e.g. word and phrasal calques (Otheguy et al. 1989) and syntactic transference and convergence (Clyne 1967, 1987).

This broad linguistic repertoire (Gumperz 1964) reflects and helps constitute the multiple facets of individuals' identities and the repertoire of identities (Kroskrity 1993) available to the Dominican American community (Bailey 2000a). Dominican Americans are not a monolithic group, and their identities include competing folk-racial, ethnolinguistic, national, and regional allegiances and ascriptions. Analysis of situated discourse shows that individuals use multiple Spanish and English resources to enact identities in ways that often belie simple "we/they" dichotomies (Gumperz 1982) and one-to-one correspondences between code and social affiliation (e.g. Fishman 1989). AAVE syntax and lexicon, for example, can be used among bilingual speakers to express specifically Dominican national/ethnic pride, as in the phrase, "DR ['Dominican Republic'] in the house," uttered by a male, high school junior.

The meanings locally attributed to linguistic forms are intimately intertwined with local Dominican American structural position--low-income[4], of African-descent phenotype, Hispanic, and immigrant. The second generations' structural position leads to solidarity with other non-Whites experiencing the same discrimination and same set of disadvantages, particularly African Americans and other Hispanics. Unlike their parents, many in the second generation define their race not just as Dominican, but also as "Hispanic" or "Spanish," categories which do not exist as such in the Dominican Republic. Also unlike their parents, the Dominican second generation do not deny their African ancestry or disparage African Americans, who are their peers and friends at school.

Social meanings and identities are locally and interactionally negotiated rather than prescribed by linguistic forms or code choice, and individuals vary in the aspects of identity they treat as most salient to them. Some Spanish forms, for example, are seen as indexing (Silverstein 1976) rural Dominican origins which are associated with poverty and lack of education, and are a source of embarrassment to many teen-agers. While the second generation view Spanish language positively, more recent teen-aged immigrants who have less facility with English are seen as backward and not cool. African American Vernacular English forms, in contrast, are treated by many as indexes of a hip, non-White youth identity. Forms associated with White American speech, in turn, are stigmatized as indexing lack of solidarity and loyalty to roots. Students consciously avoid "talking White" in some situations for fear of social censure, and some make mocking use of registers and speaking styles associated with White Americans.

This monograph uses micro-cultural data to analyze the identities of the Dominican second generation, but with consistent reference to macro-social constellations such as race, ethnicity, and socioeconomic class. Micro-social approaches to identity have focused on the dynamics of ethnic identity and identification among individuals, the role of ethnicity in everyday life, and the activities involved in ethnic boundary maintenance. Macro-social approaches have emphasized the historical and geographic roots of ethnic groups, the related ethnic content of the groups, and the power relations in society that result in ethnic hierarchies (Mittelberg and Waters 1993).

Immigration makes especially clear the relationships between macro-social constellations such as race, and individual negotiation of them through language (Bailey 2001). From a macro-social perspective, immigration results in the juxtaposition of peoples with different social realities resulting from distinct social histories. Thus, the available macro-social categories in the Dominican Republic organize the identities of Dominican out-migrants, i.e. the ways that they think of themselves, while the social categories available in America determine the identity options for immigrants upon arrival. Dominican immigrants experience these disparities in macro-social categories at the micro-social level of everyday lived experience. Differences between America and the Dominican Republic in historical social conditions, e.g. forms of economic development during and after slavery, are reflected in differences between the two countries in contemporary social organization. These differences are then confronted and negotiated by individual migrants in their everyday lives after immigration.

The first-generation is often shielded from such macro-social contrasts and their meanings because of linguistic isolation and social networks (Milroy 1987) that are limited to immigrants and co-ethnics. Although the second-generation receive their early socialization in Dominican family networks, they encounter popular American discourses on language, race, ethnicity, and identity in their American neighborhoods, schools, and part-time jobs. They must negotiate an American social reality with understandings and interpretive frameworks that are partly the result of Dominican social history. The work of these individual actors, particularly their assertion of an ethnolinguistic identity, in turn, forms part of a new American social reality, with implications for the constitution of American social categories. When existing patterns of social relations and meanings are merely reproduced at the micro-level, it is difficult to discern the agency of individual social actors. The juxtaposition of social realities and contestation of meanings resulting from migration, in this case, make especially clear the agency of individual social actors because they are not merely reproducing pre-existing categories and meanings but turning "common-sensical" (in the Gramscian sense) beliefs on their heads. The ongoing struggles of Dominican Americans with ambiguous ascriptions of identity in everyday life thus contribute to the transformation of existing social categories as well as the constitution of new ones where they might otherwise not have existed.

1.1.1 Organization of the book

In the remainder of this chapter, I address three, interrelated theoretical issues which are illuminated by the identity negotiations of the Dominican second generation: implicit purity in linguistic and racial category formation in the United States (Section 1.2); non-linear processes of acculturation among post-1965 immigrants to the United States (Section 1.3); and the relationships between structural constraints and the agency of individual social actors in constituting ethnic/racial identities through language (Section 1.4).

In Chapter 2, I briefly describe the Providence, Rhode Island, Dominican community and Central High School, the primary research site. I then introduce, one-by-one, the six principal subjects of the study. The language use and negotiations of identity of these six individuals form the core data of the book. In Chapter 3, I describe the multi-variety and hybrid linguistic repertoire of the Dominican second generation. This hybridity of linguistic forms is particularly salient in their speech because they switch between distinct languages (Spanish and English) and among varieties associated with significant social difference and distance. This broad repertoire reflects the social history of the Dominican community, e.g. immigration and economic and ethnic/racial segregation of neighborhoods and schools in the United States.

Chapter 4 considers the effects of economic, linguistic, and ethnic/racial inequality on the linguistic negotiation of identities. The identity options that young Dominican Americans face, as well as the linguistic choices that they make, are shaped by the social hierarchies that exist in the United States. Dominican American high school students must navigate among social worlds and situations in which the relative prestige of particular forms and identities are not fixed, but rather are shifting and locally negotiated.

In Chapter 5, I contrast traditional Dominican and American frameworks for understanding Black and White race. Second-generation Dominican understandings of race are shown to reflect both traditional Dominican *and* traditional United States notions of race. Because members of the first generation generally retain a Dominican frame of reference, first- and second-generation Dominicans' understandings of racial identities and politics can be sharply at odds. The distinctive nature of Dominican second-generation identities is illustrated by comparing their identity negotiations to those of second-generation African-descent immigrants who are not from Spanish-speaking countries.

In Chapter 6, I analyze a single student's use of language and negotiation of ethnic/racial identities during one high school class. Through skillful use of multiple language varieties, this student is able to situationally highlight Dominican, American, and African-descent facets of his Dominican American ethnolinguistic identity. At the same time that language gives him the freedom to highlight ethnolinguistic facets of identity, however, language is also used to impose restrictive identities as his classmates repeatedly invoke his African-descent phenotype.

Chapter 7 focuses on individual variation within the categories "Dominican American" and "Dominican American language." While such categories are analytically useful, they can imply a homogeneity that privileges analytical constructs over the data themselves, i.e. the experiences and language of particular individuals. Individual Dominican Americans vary significantly in language use, phenotype, and life experiences, with the result that individuals face different issues of social identity with different linguistic tools to negotiate them. Finally, in Chapter 8, I review implications of this study for our understandings of ethnic/racial formation processes and the roles of language in ethnic/racial identity negotiations.

1.2 Implicit Purity in Linguistic and Racial Categories

Dominican American negotiation of identities through language tells us much about racial formation--"the sociohistorical process by which racial categories are created, inhabited, transformed, and destroyed" (Omi and Winant 1994:55)--in the contemporary United States. Dominican American use of Spanish and convergent Spanish/English forms to enact Dominican/Spanish/Hispanic identities in Providence,

Rhode Island, decenters deeply naturalized ways of thinking about what it means to be "Black" or "White," and reveals incipient transformation of such categories. Such phenotype-based categories are already superseded by ethnolinguistic identity claims in many local Providence contexts, the result of the everyday enactment of identity by Dominican Americans and other African-descent Hispanics.

Dominican American enactment of Dominican or Hispanic identities challenges deeply naturalized American notions of identity and difference. Although academics over the last decades have increasingly emphasized that American notions of race are local, mutable, and contradictory socio-political constructions, race is rarely perceived or challenged as such by Black and White Americans in everyday life. Outside of academic discourse, most Americans treat individuals of African ancestry as "Black" and individuals of only European ancestry as "White." Such categories organize the American social world, e.g. through residential patterns, marriage partner choices, church memberships, and overall social hierarchy, and they are treated by both Black and White Americans as useful guideposts to understanding social reality (Smedley 1993, Omi and Winant 1994). These categories popularly represent and assume "profound and unbridgeable difference" (Smedley 1993:21) between individuals assigned to different categories.

United States constructions of linguistic and racial categories rest on implicit notions of purity. Social and linguistic categories, e.g. "African American" and "English," suggest uniformity, masking internal variation and the diachronic change that is characteristic of both available social categories (e.g. Lee 1993) and language (e.g. Thomason and Kaufman 1988). Implicit homogeneity of categories is particularly evident in the racial category African American. African descent in America has historically been a totalizing criterion for social categorization, preceding all ethnic or other descent criteria. Despite an ostensibly biophysical basis for the category Black, the "one-drop" rule of racial classification has meant that anyone with an African ancestor has been defined on that basis, even if the majority of an individual's ancestors came from other phenotype-racial groups, e.g. Europeans and Native Americans (Davis 1991).

Intertwined with purist constructions of language and race is an assumed primordial unity among language, race, and ethnic/national identity. This assumed unity--explicitly claimed and celebrated by

European philosophers von Herder (Gal 1989:355) and, earlier, by Condillac (Aarsleff 1982:30-31; Woolard and Schieffelin 1994)-- implicitly underlies Western social and linguistic categorization systems.

Dominican Americans undermine highly naturalized categories because their language, phenotypes, and enacted identities flout United States assumptions about purity of categories and the unity of language, race, and identity. Dominican American enactment of ethnolinguistic identity highlights contradictions in the category African American particularly clearly because African-descent ethnicity in the United States has historically been treated as *equivalent* to race (Waters 1991). As a result, immigrants of African descent have historically been invisible to the wider society as a distinct group, and have merged into the African American population by the second generation (Bryce-Laporte 1972).

The Spanish language of Dominican Americans makes their Hispanic ethnicity salient, which directly problematizes the popular American construction of Black identity as both race *and* ethnicity (Bailey 2000b). While most Dominican Americans are clearly of African descent, they are also clearly Spanish speakers, which is a popularly perceived criterion for membership in the group "Hispanic." Unlike many other African-descent immigrants who have defined themselves as "Black" by the second generation (e.g. Waters 1994, Woldemikael 1989), Dominican Americans are maintaining a distinct ethnolinguistic identity.

Dominican American undermining of phenotype-based racial categorization is not just a function of their Spanish language, but of the *hybridity* of their language. Their alternation of Spanish and English forms is precisely what draws attention to their distinctive identities, rather than simply their use of one language variety or another. Members of the first generation, for example, do not face the same ambiguity experienced by the second generation because their limited English proficiency marks them to a degree as outside of the historical American Black/White categories. Similarly, individuals who lose Spanish language in the second and third generations have difficulties maintaining a distinct, non-Black ethnolinguistic identity in their everyday interactions. Second generation bilinguals, in contrast, are able to enact American language identities as well as Spanish language ones. The explicit and salient heteroglossia (Bakhtin 1981) of

Dominican Americans--drawing on forms from discrete codes and distinctive social varieties of language--embody and recreate a social world which defies purist and monolithic social and linguistic categories.

Dominican Americans also confound constructed categories of purity in terms of phenotype and personal and family networks. Over 70% of the Dominican population are of African *and* European descent, with smaller groups of just European and just African descent. The numerically dominant and socially unmarked phenotype in the Dominican Republic is precisely one that embodies African and European ancestry. This lack of observation of a color line undermines the differences and boundaries constructed between Black and White races[5] in the United States. By asserting a common ethnic identity despite diverse phenotypes, Dominican Americans subvert the myths of difference characteristic of phenotype-race in the United States.

Dominican Americans regularly confront the dominant United States notions of race because so many are seen by others in ways, based on both phenotype and language, that are fundamentally different from the ways they see themselves. Rejection of phenotype-based racial ascription is often explicit: "They ask me, 'Are you Black?' I'm like, 'No, I'm Hispanic.'" Such everyday contestation of racial categories is a local form of social action that reveals the historical, contingent, and political nature of race.

Dominican American assertion of an identity that is not Black or White, although occurring in everyday contexts, has broader sociopolitical implications. It is an act of resistance in the face of dominant American discourses on race, and it represents a retention of symbolic power. Power resides not only in control of material resources, but also in control over symbolic discourse, the ways in which the world is represented and categories made. Racial categorization and hierarchy are increasingly maintained through relatively symbolic means rather than through the *de jure* coercion prevalent during slavery, Jim Crow, and pre-Civil Rights times (Omi and Winant 1994).

Scholars have referred to symbolic discourses (i.e. ways of representing and thinking about social relations) that mask domination and insidiously reproduce themselves, by a variety of names: Hegel and Marx's ideology/false consciousness (Marx 1976), Gramsci's hegemony (Sassoon 1987; Williams 1977), Foucault's discourse (e.g.

Foucault 1972, 1980), and Bourdieu's symbolic domination/violence (Bourdieu 1977, Bourdieu and Passeron 1977). Such symbolic power is difficult for members of a society to confront because it resides in shared understandings of the world, what Gramsci calls "common sense" (Sassoon 1987). Dominican American assertion of identity directly conflicts with "common sense" understandings of the world, e.g. that individuals of African descent are "Black," and it models a social reality that undermines the dominant one. Everyday enactment of Dominican/Spanish identity through language thus represents a retention of symbolic power and decentering of American racial classification.

Dominican American notions of their racial identity not only undermine essentialist notions of race, but also reveal the narrow focus of some modern, constructionist social science treatments of race. Omi and Winant (1994:55), for example, define race as a "concept which signifies and symbolizes social conflicts and interests by referring to different types of human bodies." The idea that race refers only to "different types of human bodies" is not shared by all American groups. While phenotype is the *dominant* symbol of racial identity in America today (and is understood by many as being equivalent to race), language is the defining criterion of racial identity among Dominican Americans. Analysis of Dominican American notions of race--which are based more on ethnolinguistic heritage--thus contextualizes contemporary academic theories of race, showing them to be historically, geographically, and culturally specific rather than universal.

Dominican American negotiation of race highlights the ways that race inhabits social structure and shapes Dominican American acculturation, even as Dominicans resist dominant racial definitions as applied to them. Race is not just an issue of subjective cultural meanings, as might be understood from the commonplace phrase "social construction," but an issue that is deeply rooted in social structure and institutions. Although Dominican Americans reject their classification as Black or White, they are deeply affected by racial structuring of American society, particularly through residential and school segregation and economic inequality. Dominican Americans in South Providence grow up with relatively little contact with White Americans and with middle- and upper-income Americans. Socialization in this low-income, multi-ethnic, non-White, heavily immigrant, urban environment shapes the language and options for identities of the second generation.

Although the Dominican second generation in South Providence do not think of themselves in terms of Black or White, they learn to think of themselves as expressly *non-White*, regardless of phenotype, and they experience significant solidarity with other non-Whites, particularly Hispanics and African Americans, who are their neighbors and peers at school. This non-White identity is expressed in part through African American style English, which has positive in-group connotations for many low-income, non-White youth in Providence. This urban, non-White language style can even serve as a unifying language for Hispanics who speak identical, urban forms of English, but who speak different regional varieties of Spanish, e.g. Guatemalan, Colombian, or Dominican Spanish, based on their families' origins.

Purism has dominated Western thought about language for hundreds of years, and perceived interlanguage influences have frequently been considered akin to mongrelization and degeneration (Hill and Hill 1986:55). Dominican American language displays a hybridity--through code- and variety-switching and convergent forms-- that is disparaged by dominant classes of both Spanish and English speakers. As an in-group form it proposes and embodies an understanding of the world that includes Dominican ethnolinguistic heritage and socialization in a low-income, urban environment in a racially, ethnically, and economically hierarchical society. This urban youth form of language can contribute to reproduction of the very marginalization that led to it. Individuals make detailed social evaluations of each other based on language usage (e.g. Lambert et al. 1960), and the forms characteristic of Dominican American youth speech are frequently disparaged by the dominant society. Use of such disparaged forms can lead to negative evaluations by many of the gate keepers, e.g. White school teachers, that Dominican American students encounter, particularly since the stigmatized forms are used by non-White individuals about whom gatekeepers may already entertain negative stereotypes.

Dominican American enactment of identity highlights the sociohistorical, processual nature of racial formation. Language is central to Dominican American resistance to American racialization practices, and successful Dominican American enactment of non-Black identities suggests incipient transformation of the Black/White dichotomy in America, particularly as the non-White immigrant population grows. Dominican American ethnolinguistic self-definition, which is activated both intra- and inter-ethnically, challenges deeply naturalized American notions of race and even some modern, constructionist social science analyses. At the same time that they successfully resist many American Black/White racial meanings, Dominican American language, lives, and identities are shaped by hierarchical American racial structure.

1.3 Acculturation among Children of the New Immigration

The negotiation of identities by the Dominican second generation can tell us much about the theoretical trajectories of acculturation available to contemporary non-White immigrants to America, who are primarily from Latin America, the Caribbean, and Asia. Many popular and academic assumptions about immigrant acculturation and assimilation are based on the experiences of European immigrants from 1880-1920, but their patterns of acculturation were very different from the ones documented here among Dominican Americans. In the "straight-line" theory of assimilation derived from the 1880-1920 immigration (Warner and Srole 1945), immigrants become assimilated to an unmarked, White American identity as they become temporally and generationally removed from immigrant origins. Dominican second-generation acculturation in Providence, Rhode Island, however, is to a distinctive urban, low-income, non-White, Dominican American identity, rather than toward a White, middle class identity. Dominican American trajectories of acculturation thus directly refute the straight-line theory of assimilation. Their patterns highlight the fact that "acculturation" and "assimilation" in straight-line theory assume idealized cultural processes that are disconnected from structural constraints such as racial hierarchy and segregation and correlated economic inequality.

At the same time that Dominican American acculturation refutes straight-line theory, it also refutes the opposite of straight-line theory, the speedy assimilation of non-White immigrants to impoverished native non-White groups (Gans 1992, Portes 1995, Portes and Zhou 1993, Portes and Rumbaut 1996). Such a theoretical trajectory of acculturation fails to take into full account the Dominican cultural meanings and organization that the Dominican second generation preserve despite discrimination and economic obstacles in America. Members of the second generation situationally use their Dominican Spanish language to highlight boundaries between themselves and longer established non-White American groups, even as their shared structural position contributes to solidarity in many contexts.

The multiple and hybrid trajectories of second-generation Dominican acculturation are nowhere more evident than in everyday Dominican American language, which includes elements associated with diverse class and racial groups. Syncretic second-generation linguistic practices reflect and reconstitute a distinctive identity that is both urban American and Dominican immigrant. "Acculturation" implies a cultural change in a direction *toward* ("ac-" meaning "toward") a specific group or end, but while Dominican American language and identities are influenced by multiple other groups, they remain distinct from any other one group.

Socialization in a thriving Dominican community in South Providence contributes to the constitution and reproduction of a distinctive Dominican American identity. Portes (Portes and Zhou 1993, Portes 1995) has suggested the positive socioeconomic effects that acculturation in, and to, such an enclave can have, especially for individuals who face obstacles based on race or ethnicity in the White mainstream. The current study shows that socialization in such an enclave also has powerful effects on language use and the interrelated sense of identity in the second generation. This community level of socialization and language maintenance in America is central to resisting pressure from other American groups to acculturate to phenotype-based identities.

1.3.1 Approaches to Immigrant Identity and Acculturation in the United States: Assimilation

Until the 1980's, studies of immigrant ethnicity in America focused largely on the experiences of the waves of European immigrants who arrived in America between 1880 and 1920 and successive generations of their descendants. The large number of these immigrants and their trajectories of socioeconomic success across generations have informed both popular and social scientific assumptions about immigration, acculturation, and ethnicity. The most central assumption from this specific history is that ethnic assimilation and socioeconomic mobility occur linearly as individuals become further temporally and generationally removed from their immigrant-origins (Srole and Warner's (1945) straight-line theory). Causation of assimilation is implicitly attributed to the passage of time and generations, and the historical and social specificity of the conditions in which this assimilation occurs are backgrounded.

During the heightened immigration associated with the 1880-1920 period, many doubted that the largely Southern and Eastern European newcomers would ever assimilate to the culture of the dominant groups, who were of predominantly Northwestern European origin. Such groups as Italians, Slavs, and Jews were described as being of a different race than Northwestern European-Americans, or of an inferior species (Waters 1990:2). Social differences between these immigrants and European Americans who were already in America were perceived as insurmountable. Immigrant ethnics lived in segregated neighborhoods, and a constant influx of compatriots kept immigrant languages, cultural practices, and identities flourishing until the 1920's when immigration was cut off by the federal government.

As generations of academics and writers have since chronicled, the descendants of these European immigrants did adapt, assimilate, and overwhelmingly gain full acceptance into American life. Today they hold positions of power throughout society, in government, business, and professions. The ethnicity that was once so salient has become nearly invisible in the third-, fourth-, etc. generations. Discrimination and residential segregation waned at the same time that linguistic and cultural distinctiveness of immigrant enclaves faded as immigration restrictions prevented new co-ethnics from arriving. Individuals began to live, go to school, make friendships, and marry outside of the ethnic group, i.e. they assimilated (Gordon 1964).

This immigrant assimilation and success was not simply the result of the passage of time, however, but rather the result of specific social, economic, and historical forces. The fact that these immigrants were European, for example, was central to the assimilation of their descendants, who count as White. As European-descent Americans, successive generations did not face the discrimination or segregation that non-European have historically faced in this country. As linguistic and cultural practices associated with European immigrants waned across generations, there were few markers to distinguish descendants of these immigrants from other European-descent Americans.

Specific historical social policies and economic conditions also help explain the socioeconomic successes of the 1880-1920 immigrants and their descendants. The abrupt restriction on immigration in the 1920's, for example, decreased low-wage competition for immigrants and their offspring who were already in this country, granting them a measure of economic power. The growing industrial economy of the early 1900's afforded secure blue-collar jobs that could be obtained by immigrants who didn't speak English and hadn't been educated in American schools. This thriving industrial economy also provided well-paying blue-collar jobs that allowed incremental upward mobility from generation to generation even without education (Portes and Zhou 1993). When later generations did achieve higher levels of education, often in the third- and fourth-generations (Gans 1992), the unprecedented economic growth after World War II afforded new opportunities for economic success and comfort.

The model of assimilation based on 1880-1920 European immigration fails to explain the historical experiences of many non-Europeans in America. African Americans, Native Americans, and Chicanos, for example, have been in this country for centuries, allowing more than enough generations for cultural assimilation and socioeconomic success to occur based on straight-line theory of assimilation. Many members of such groups, however, have retained distinctive social identities and have not enjoyed the socioeconomic successes enjoyed by Americans of solely European descent.

Failure to attend to the specific social histories of various groups, e.g. forms of incorporation into the United States and American racial structuring, leads to invidious and invalid comparisons. Group deficiencies among non-Whites, rather than structural disadvantages and differences, become popular and sometimes academic explanations for ongoing segregation, maintenance of distinctive identity, and relative poverty, for example. Deficiencies in the theory of assimilation and the American ideology of socioeconomic opportunity are thus presented as deficiencies in the groups whose realities do not match the theory.

1.3.2 The New Immigration

Dominican immigrants to America are part of the *New Immigration*, which is made up primarily of immigrants from Latin America, the

Caribbean, and Asia. The watershed event defining the New Immigration was the enactment of changes in American immigration law in 1965. Highly restrictive immigration quotas that were based on nationality and that favored Northwestern European countries were abandoned in favor of increased quotas based on hemisphere, not country. In addition, quotas were lifted entirely for "family reunification," i.e. immigrants who were already in the United States and who met certain criteria could be joined by close relatives. Those who were given visas as part of such family reunification could then eventually sponsor *their* close relatives, resulting in elaborately linked webs of large numbers of immigrants (Kraly 1987). The result of these changes in immigration law was a new wave of immigration beginning in the late 1960's that represents the largest influx of immigrants to America since the 1880-1920 period.

The new *second* generation, the children of these immigrants, were projected to reach over 28 million before the year 2000, thus outstripping the previous peak of second-generation immigrants, which occurred in the 1940's (Portes 1996:2). This second generation group represents about ten percent of the overall United States population, and a much higher percentage of American youth. By the year 2035, it is estimated (Sanjek 1998:1) that fewer than one-half of children in the United States under age 18 will be White. The trajectories of acculturation of the new second and third generations will thus determine to a large degree the nature of American society.

This post-1965 immigration is "new" not only in that it is more recent than the 1880-1920 immigration, but also in that it is different. Most of the new immigrants do not come from Europe, so most do not count as White, and they arrive to a much different economic context than those earlier migrants arrived to. These differing macro-social factors may not only invalidate linear-temporal models of assimilation, but may reverse the predictions of such models. In one scenario proposed by Gans (1992), non-White, low-income immigrants will assimilate not to middle-class White American status, beliefs, and practices, but to impoverished American non-White groups. During periods of economic stagnation, such assimilation could take place in one generation, thus not only turning straight-line theory on its head, but also accelerating the process of acculturation. In an economy that increasingly requires education for well-remunerated work, for example, poor second-generation immigrants who have acculturated

out of their parents' immigrant jobs face downward mobility if they do
not achieve academically:

> second-generation decline is likely to produce an early
> convergence between the present American poor and some
> second-generation poor, for if immigrant parents are unable or
> unwilling to enforce strict school...discipline, if language
> problems cannot be overcome, or if the youngsters...see that
> their occupational futures are not promising, they may begin
> to get low grades, reject schooling and eventually drop out or
> get themselves pushed out of the school system. (Gans
> 1992:183)

Assimilation to marginalized ethnic and folk-racial groups may be
encouraged by the seductive freedoms available to youth in America
that are not available in countries of origin (Gans 1992:187). The
freedoms to choose friends, date without chaperones, and develop
personal interests and activities are frequently more attractive to
second-generation adolescents than the delayed gratification associated
with work, education, and eventual achievement of social mobility,
which is preached by many first-generation parents. These freedoms
can work against upward mobility if they contribute to drug use, gang
membership, poor school performance, or early pregnancy that hinders
further education.

Portes and Zhou (1993) suggest that the direction of assimilation of
the second generation has not necessarily been reversed, but rather has
become "segmented," i.e. the trajectories of acculturation of members
of the second generation will vary and fall into three distinct types. The
basic question is *to which* American groups new immigrants
acculturate. Portes and Zhou (1993:82) predict three possible
trajectories of assimilation: 1) Children of immigrants of higher
education and social class will be likely to use education as a means to
social and economic mobility, approximating the traditional notion of
linear assimilation and upward mobility over time. 2) Others will
assimilate to marginalized, impoverished ethnic/racial groups already
in the United States. 3) Still others will maintain strong, multiple
relationships and solidarity within the immigrant community,
maintaining the community's values and experiencing economic
stability or some upward mobility.

Although Dominican Americans can follow the first trajectory in terms of achieving socioeconomic mobility, few Dominican Americans can assimilate to White American identities. Over 85% of Dominicans are of African ancestry, and no African-descent group has ever assimilated to an unmarked ethnic/racial status in America. Notions of Black/White race remain a fundamental social organizing principle in America, and individuals who count as Black are regularly subjected to discriminatory treatment, regardless of class status (Feagin 1991). The majority of Dominican Americans will not be able to enjoy the privileges that status as White brings, regardless of how acculturated they become.

The second possible trajectory of acculturation predicted by Portes and Zhou (1993) for the new second generation--assimilation to marginalized, impoverished ethnic/racial groups already in the United States--is occurring among Dominican Americans in Providence in limited spheres of their lives. The concentration of Dominican immigrant households in the low-income urban center of Providence puts the second generation in close contact with impoverished native-born groups (as well as other immigrants), and the acculturation of the second generation is largely toward these groups, notably African Americans and other Caribbean Hispanic Americans. The Dominican American second generation, for example, extensively adopt dress and musical fashions commonly associated with urban African American youth, and the English of many young Dominican Americans shares linguistic and stylistic features with varieties of AAVE. This acculturation is evident in only limited spheres of the second generations' lives, however. The same teen-agers who use AAVE, listen and dance to hip hop music, and meet with African American friends at Burger King also speak Spanish at home and with extended family, attend Spanish-language Mass, eat fried plantains and rice and beans, and dance to *merengue, salsa,* and *bachata* at Caribbean Hispanic clubs. Although the second-generation acculturate in some domains to marginalized native-born groups, they do *not assimilate* to them in the second generation. Distinctive identity is apparent in self-ascriptions, ascriptions by others in local contexts, cultural practices, and language.

Portes and Zhou (1993:83) predict a third potential trajectory of assimilation for new immigrants, one that includes "deliberate preservation of the immigrant community's values and tight solidarity."

Acculturation thus depends not just on characteristics of individuals and the receiving society but also on the nature of the immigrant ethnic community in which it takes place. Flourishing immigrant communities model options for acculturation and identity that are not a reaction to disparagement by the dominant groups in America. Such communities can recreate institutions and attitudes from the home country, inculcating youth with a common cultural memory based on shared language and customs. Portes (1995) calls such ethnicity--based on continuation of cultural practices from the home country--"linear" ethnicity. He contrasts linear ethnicity with "reactive" ethnicity, which is based on experiences of discrimination in the United States and characterized by opposition to an oppressive, White-dominated mainstream:

> Linear ethnicity...gives rise to an entirely different outlook based on the partial recreation of institutions brought from the home country. The emergence of immigrant churches, schools, restaurants, shops, and financial institutions patterned in the mold of the old country reinforces the first-generation stance in two ways: first, by creating a social environment that validates its norms and values; second, by creating opportunities within the immigrant community that are absent in the outside. (Portes 1995:257)

Maintaining strong ties within an immigrant/ethnic enclave can thus represent a successful strategy for maximizing material and psychological resources (Portes and Zhou 1993).

This community level of social analysis helps to explain the maintenance of a distinctive identity among Dominican Americans in Providence, including their resistance to American phenotype-racial classification. There are structural pressures that encourage the second generation to identify strongly with other disadvantaged groups: Dominican Americans and many native-born non-White Americans in South Providence share a social reality that includes grossly inadequate schools, neighborhoods with high rates of drug use and crime, ethnic/racial discrimination, and poverty, and many Dominican Americans are viewed by outsiders as undifferentiated from African Americans. In view of these pressures, a vigorous ethnic community that maintains a common cultural memory, reinforcing Dominican norms and beliefs, is central to maintenance of a distinct identity. It provides a Dominican cultural framework in which to define oneself ethnolinguistically rather than by phenotype, and the size and distinctive language of the community contribute to "Dominican" and "Spanish" being recognized as valid local alternatives to phenotype-based categories.

The Dominican American trajectory of acculturation refutes the linear-temporal model of assimilation, in which assimilation to an unmarked White American identity results from the passage of time and generations. Such a model idealizes cultural processes, disconnecting them from the structural constraints of racial discrimination and correlated economic inequality. Acculturation of the Dominican second generation is directly limited and channeled by structural inequality in America. At the same time, Dominican American acculturation in Providence shows that the preservation of cultural and linguistic practices and understandings can keep the second generation distinct from longer-established groups, despite commonalties in phenotype, neighborhoods, and experiences of discrimination. Specific features of Dominican second-generation acculturation, e.g. resistance to phenotype-based identification through accentuation of ethnolinguistic identity, can thus suggest frameworks for understanding the acculturation of non-White children of the New Immigration more generally.

1.4 Agency vs. Structural Constraint in Identity Enactment

Dominican American negotiation of identity highlights the reciprocal relationships between individuals' linguistic resources and activities and the historical and structural forces that permeate their lives. Dominican Americans claim and successfully enact varying identities through language, demonstrating the social agency of individuals. This agency is particularly striking in resistance to Black/White racial ascription, which is the type of social identity ascription over which individuals have historically had least control. Individual agency is also clearly constrained and channeled by the macro-social structures and meanings that suffuse everyday life. Not all Dominican American claims of identity, e.g. as non-Black, as Dominican, or as American, represent successful enactment of those identities. In everyday talk and interaction, the validity of identity claims is negotiated, and only those identities that are validated or ratified by others are unequivocally constituted. Claims of race, ethnicity, or other social category memberships that depart from others' Gramscian "common sense" understandings of those categories can be denied. Macro-social or structural constraints on identity claims are thus exercised at the local level in everyday encounters.

Analysis of the identity options available to Dominican Americans tells us much about the relationships among power, specific types of identities, and the range of choices individuals have in claiming identities. The majority of Dominican Americans meet the dominant groups' criteria for classification in two categories, African American and Hispanic. Both of these categories are very salient in everyday life in that 1) both are based on criteria that are publicly available and can thus be unilaterally treated as relevant by others, 2) both are associated to a high degree with individuals' behavior, including language. As described above, these categories have traditionally been seen as mutually exclusive, creating ambiguity in the identities that are ascribed to Dominican Americans.

This ambiguity has important implications for Dominican American ethnogenesis and social categories in America more generally. While it is clear that larger-scale social constellations, e.g. racial categories, affect individuals' behavior, such larger scale phenomena are themselves constituted through social action and relations at a smaller scale (Giddens 1984). Dominican American resistance to categorization as African American highlights the contradictions and inadequacy of such received social categories and contributes to the transformation of existing categories, as well as the constitution of new ones. The ongoing struggle of Dominican Americans in Providence to assert their distinctive identity in everyday life has already increased the number and types of locally available social categories for individuals of African descent.

1.4.1 Theoretical Approaches to Social Identity

Over the last thirty years social scientists have increasingly interrogated received notions of ethnicity and race. While race and ethnicity are popularly seen as primordial, natural categories, social scientists now emphasize that such categories are socially constructed. From this social science perspective, racial and ethnic categories are folk-categories, the result of specific social and historical forces in particular times and places, rather than natural categories that capture the essence of individuals or groups.

Underpinning many constructionist approaches to social identity is the notion of social processes involving members themselves. Barth (1969), for example, emphasizes not what is internal to the group ("ethnic content"), but the boundaries that groups construct between themselves. His formulation of ethnicity as a function of boundary maintenance serves to denaturalize what are often implicitly treated as primordial social differences. It foregrounds the social reality of individual actors in that it is their judgments and activities, rather than an analyst's lists of ethnic/racial features, that serve to constitute categories. According to Barth (1969:14):

> It is important to recognise that although ethnic categories take cultural differences into account, we can assume no simple one-to-one relationship between ethnic units and cultural similarities and differences. The features taken into account are not the sum of 'objective' differences, but only those which the actors themselves regard as significant....some cultural features are used by the actors as signals and emblems of differences, others are ignored, and in some relationships radical differences are played down and denied.

Ethnic (and other social) groups are thus not defined by the sum of objective differences between groups, but rather by the differences that are made to matter by members and non-members and used to create, reconstitute, or highlight boundaries.

Language has played a changing role in the study of ethnicity as theoretical emphases in the social sciences have shifted from structure to social process and practice (Ortner 1984). Through the 1960's, for example, ethnicity was often defined in terms of the "ethnic content," including language, of a group (Isajiw 1974). In such content-based definitions of ethnicity, the presence or absence of various linguistic, cultural, and racial diacritica determine ethnicity.

With increased interest in actual practices of individuals has come a shift in conceptions of the role of language in ethnicity. Face-to-face interaction is a constitutive form of sociality and thus a means to understanding the construction and reproduction of larger-scale social constellations (Garfinkel 1967). From this perspective, language does not define ethnicity by its presence or absence, but rather is a tool that social actors use in the construction and reproduction of ethnicity. The analyst can thus gain understandings of social processes from examining language use. The central question is how social actors use language to achieve, maintain, challenge, or deny certain social relations and categories (Gumperz and Cook-Gumperz 1982).

If identity is a process and achievement rather than a fixed attribute, and if individuals have social agency, identity, in theory, should be fluid, and individuals should be able to choose what identities to enact. Such a formulation, however, neglects the macro-social constellations that are part-and-parcel of micro-level activities:

> Ethnic constructionists are the most visible critics of primordialists. Yet, some of their work is overly focused on discourse and fails to recognized fully that ethnicity is invented in the course of cultural, political, and economic struggles....The repeated insistence in the constructionist literature on the fluidity of ethnicity illustrates the limitations of a narrow, discursive focus. Ethnicity is constructed; hence, it follows in principle that ethnicity is fluid, but this fluidity is limited by hegemonic processes of inscription and by the relations of forces in society. (Alonso 1994:392)

While identity is clearly a social construction rather than a fixed attribute, it is not boundlessly fluid. Available social categories are the result of historical social processes, and negotiation of identity takes place within limits.

In face-to-face interaction, fluidity and choice of identity are constrained by the historical social relations that are actualized in present-day received categories. These received categories shape the ways that individuals are seen and classified by others. Since boundaries delineating social groups are double boundaries (Royce 1982), comprising a boundary that is enacted or identified from within and another one from without, successful constitution of an identity involves congruent self-ascription and other-ascription. Macro-social categories, even if they represent folk-understandings as with phenotype-racial categories, organize the range of social groups to which individuals are assigned by others. Alonso (1994) locates "hegemonic forms of inscription" outside of discourse, but social history and hierarchy are omnipresent as everyday "common sense" understandings of the world in face-to-face interaction. These understandings are situationally activated in discourse and serve as guideposts for social ascription.

1.4.2 Identity Types and Constraint on Individuals

Dominican Americans face greater constraint in their claims of identity than many other groups because of the *types* of identity ascribed to them by others. The term "ethnicity" implies a class of similar phenomena, but ethnic (and racial) categories in the United States are based on widely divergent criteria and have widely divergent implications in everyday life. Ethnic categories are based on such disparate criteria as historical national origin (Italian Americans), religion (Jews), colonial history/linguistic status (Hispanic), and phenotype (African American). These different types of categories, grouped under one rubric, vary widely 1) in the degree to which they are associated with individual language and behavior and 2) the degree of choice that individuals have as to whether or not their membership in a category will be invoked or treated as relevant by others (cf. Mittelberg and Waters 1993).

At one end of the continuum are symbolic ethnics (Gans 1979, Waters 1990) such as third-generation Italian-Americans who have affective ties to their ancestral country of origin but whose Italian ethnicity is not directly relevant to their everyday activities. Such ethnicity does not play a primary role in such decisions as where to live or whom to choose as a marriage partner, for example. Symbolic ethnics have the freedom to invoke this ethnicity when they choose, e.g. at ethnic festivals, and it is not necessarily apparent to others that they possess it. The defining feature of symbolic ethnicity is its voluntary nature, i.e. the control that the symbolic ethnic has over his or her ascription of identity. A type of ethnicity with greater prominence in everyday life is represented by practicing American Jews from Reform and Conservative groups. Among this group, ethnicity may affect choice of marriage partners, for example, and membership may be apparent to outsiders because of practices such as attending Friday services or observing non-Christian holidays. Members have situationally varying control over whether or not others know of this identity and whether others treat it as a relevant identity.

Two other ethnic categories--ethnolinguistic minority and phenotype-racial minority--affect everyday life more deeply and present fewer identity options for members than the preceding types of ethnicity. Unlike the symbolic Italian-American, for example, members of these groups have little control over the salience to others of these identities: members of these groups cannot unilaterally hide them. Language minority immigrants' status as non-native speakers of English is immediately obvious to those with whom they have contact, and this status can be invoked by anyone who hears the individual speak. Even more salient and intrusive than ethnolinguistic minority status is non-White folk-racial status, particularly for individuals of African descent. Such racialized ethnicity affects individuals' everyday lives because it is immediately apparent to others, and it is popularly associated with specifically ethnic individual behavior. Not only do outsiders unilaterally invoke and treat as relevant these language minority and phenotype-based identities, they can then interpret individuals' behavior in terms of pre-existing stereotypes for individuals of those social categories.

The types of ethnicity commonly available to Dominicans in America--ethnolinguistic minority and folk-racial minority--are the most visible to outsiders and the types popularly most associated with individual patterns of behavior. The Dominican first generation has little control over ascription of ethnolinguistic identity because their English (or lack of English) reveals that they are non-native speakers, and their everyday use of Spanish suggests that they are Hispanic. Dominicans who grow up in America, as native English speakers, have more control over others' ascriptions of their ethnolinguistic identity. They have the option of speaking either Spanish or English, thereby invoking or making relevant different facets of their identities. For Dominican Americans who are socialized in American inner cities, however, the English varieties they control include many features that are popularly associated with marginalized African Americans and Hispanics. Even speaking English can result in assignment by dominant groups to a disparaged ethnolinguistic minority and/or non-White status.

The ascriptions of identity over which Dominican Americans have least control are based on phenotype. Unlike other types of ethnic identity, e.g. language minority status or affective ties to an ancestral out-migrant country, phenotype does not "diminish" with acculturation across generations. While European second-generation immigrants who are native English speakers can identify or be identified as unmarked, middle-class White Americans, the second-generation of phenotype-racial minorities can be identified as non-White minorities regardless of acculturated speech, dress, behavior, and social networks. While ethnicity is a social construction that is achieved, rather than given, individuals cannot enact identities without regard to the macro-social categories available in society, which *others* use to classify and identify them. The available American social categories for classifying Dominicans highly constrain Dominicans' choices of identities.

Individual Dominican Americans thus claim identities from a limited set of options. A useful way of conceptualizing the simultaneous freedom and constraints of identity choice is Kroskrity's (1993:207) "repertoire of identity." Individuals have the ability to pick from among a *limited* set of identities, their repertoire, the scope of which will vary by individual and social group. The received identities variously available to individual Dominican Americans in Providence--Dominican, American, African American, White American, Hispanic--are not uniformly available to members of the group, and no one member can enact all of them. The ethnicity of a group is thus understood not as a singular, unitary identity, nor as a boundless category, but as the set of identities that can be successfully achieved by members of that group. Agency of individuals as well as sociohistorical constraints and conditions are compatible with such a model.

The identities available to Dominican Americans as a group are available to individuals based largely on sociocultural knowledge, e.g. proficiency in varieties of English and Spanish, and by phenotype. Only those individuals who speak native-like Spanish can successfully enact a Dominican identity across situations, e.g. with recently immigrated friends and relatives, and only those who speak native-like English can successfully enact American identities across situations. The identities that are available to the second-generation in non-Hispanic contexts depend largely on phenotype. Some native English speakers can successfully enact a White American identity, while many can enact an African American identity. The majority can enact a racially ambiguous identity in everyday encounters that is non-White but not unequivocally Black. Although the initial criterion used to define Dominican Americans--children of immigrants from the Dominican Republic--properly suggests certain group commonalties, any notion of Dominican American identity must encompass a range or repertoire of identities.

While the available categories of identity and the criteria for membership in them are shaped by social history, Dominican American identities are also claimed and enacted in response to more micro-level conditions. In the company of newly immigrated relatives, Dominican Americans find themselves labeled as *americanos* ['(White) Americans'], for example. On standardized test forms and in demographic analyses they typically count as "Hispanic." When outside of Caribbean Hispanic communities, many Dominicans count as African Americans, most count as a non-White minority, and some count as White Americans. Dominican American identities are thus a function of social conditions and processes, both large scale and local, that make particular facets of their identities relevant.

1.4.3 Multiple, Conflicting Ascriptions and Ambiguity of Identity

The diversity within the Dominican American community and the lack of congruence in identity ascription among Dominican immigrants and receiving groups highlight the multiple and situational nature of Dominican American identities. Because there are no objective criteria for defining ethnic identity--it is a function of self-ascription and other-ascription--group identity is ambiguous when there is a lack of accord among members and non-members. The social boundaries and identities recognized by the dominant group(s) carry official authority, but are no more valid from a social scientific perspective than any other ascribed identity. Even the very criteria for social classification are subjective, and different groups can contest the particular characteristics that matter in given circumstances, whether language, phenotype, religion, etc. In heterogeneous, class societies there are many groups, with varying perceptions, whose recognition of group boundaries and their meanings may diverge from those of the dominant group(s).

Mittelberg and Waters (1992:416) identify a theoretical receiving group, the "proximal host," as particularly significant for the identity development of immigrants. The proximal host is "the [American]

group to which the wider society would assign the immigrant...[and] define as the immigrant's co-ethnics." When the identities assumed by the immigrants are congruent with the identities recognized by the dominant society and proximal host, a familiar pattern of incorporation into society occurs. When a Pole immigrates to an ethnic enclave in the United States, for example, he/she is associated with the Polish and Polish-Americans in that enclave both by enclave members and the dominant society. Both the immigrants and various groups in the receiving society use Polish national origin and/or language as the distinguishing elements of Polish identity. The fact that Polish language is spoken only in Poland encourages an unambiguous national/linguistic/ethnic category. The Polish immigrant and/or immediately subsequent generations thus assume a Polish-American identity, an identity which accords with the identities ascribed to him/her by various outside groups (Mittelberg and Waters 1993).

Unlike the case of the hypothetical Polish immigrant, for whom there is one unambiguous proximal host, there are several potential proximal hosts for Dominicans. Readily apparent American co-ethnics for Dominican immigrants include Dominican Americans, Hispanics, and African Americans. None of these categories is uniformly used by the immigrants themselves, the dominant society, and proximal hosts, however. For the dominant society, for example, "Dominican" is not a salient or widely recognized social/ethnic category. The Dominican Republic is small and economically less-developed, it has only a short history of immigration to America, and it shares its national/ethnic language with many other countries. Although the category "Hispanic" is widely and officially recognized, it is an umbrella term that includes groups who have relatively little in common with Dominicans. The category of Hispanic includes individuals who can belong to any of several phenotype-based racial categories, e.g. White, Black, and Native American, who come from a range of countries with widely varying social histories, and who have been incorporated into America under widely varying conditions. Finally, African Americans fit as co-ethnics of most Dominicans in terms of historical one-drop rules of folk-racial categorization, but not in other ways. Dominicans, for example, are Spanish-speaking immigrants, they do not think of themselves as "Black" or as having a meaningful degree of African heritage, and significant numbers of Dominicans have little or no African ancestry.

The multiple potential proximal hosts for Dominicans create ambiguity at several levels. Each of these receiving groups, for example, treats different characteristics of Dominican immigrants as relevant for establishing solidarity or co-ethnicity, i.e. as relevant for social categorization. For African Americans, for example, African phenotype is significant for establishing co-ethnicity, and those Dominicans who are phenotypically indistinguishable from African Americans are perceived to share a significant social attribute. According to Dominican American consultants in Providence, Dominicans of more African phenotype are treated with greater solidarity by African Americans than other Dominicans. The Spanish language of Dominicans, however, serves to differentiate them from African Americans and leads many Hispanics to recognize them as co-ethnics. Dominican phenotypes can serve as a basis for solidarity with some Hispanics, but not others. Puerto Ricans, for example, share the European and African ancestry of Dominicans, but Guatemalans in America are of predominantly Mayan and European ancestry. Dominican American high school students in Providence differentiate sharply between themselves and Guatemalan Americans and cite phenotype as a salient difference between groups.

Two axes for evaluating social characteristics--a) relevance as criteria for social categorization, and b) positive or negative valence of the characteristic--can crosscut each other in different ways for different groups. Both African Americans and European Americans treat African ancestry as significant for social classification, but they assign different values to it. Apparent African ancestry is a source of pride for many African Americans, while it is a source of stigma in the eyes of many European Americans. Both of these treatments of African ancestry contrast with the Dominican perspective. Dominicans differ from both groups in terms of the first axis--relevance for social categorization--because African descent is not a significant criterion for ethnic classification in the Dominican Republic. On the axis of subjective social valence, Dominicans are in accord with European Americans for whom African ancestry is seen as a source of stigma and not pride or solidarity.

There is thus a lack of accord among the dominant society, Dominican immigrants, and various potential proximal hosts as to how--and on what bases--Dominican Americans should be categorized. This lack of accord has important implications for Dominican American ethnogenesis and social categories in America more generally. Although social categories are popularly perceived to be natural categories, they represent particular points in specific histories of social relations and struggles. Over time, changes occur in the available social categories as well as criteria for assignment to them at the macro-level, as is evident in the evolution of categories in the American census (e.g. Lee 1993). While it is clear that larger-scale social phenomena, e.g. racial categories, affect individuals' social actions, such larger scale phenomena are themselves constituted through social action and relations at a smaller scale. When there is strong resistance to forms of categorization at the local level, and when this resistance makes clear the contradictions and inadequacy of available categories, change in categories is more likely to occur at a larger scale. The ongoing struggle of Dominican Americans with ambiguous ascriptions of identity in everyday life can thus contribute to the transformation of existing social categories as well as the constitution of new ones where they might otherwise not have existed.

1.5 Conclusions

Syncretic Dominican second-generation language reflects both Dominican cultural/linguistic heritage and American inner-city socialization. This hybridity of language contravenes the implicit purity of received United States social and linguistic categories. In combination with diverse Dominican phenotypes, this hybrid language also undermines assumed unity of language/race/identity, particularly in the construction and reproduction of the categories African American and Hispanic. It is this assumed unity of language/race/identity in the category African American that enables Dominican Americans to use Spanish language to resist ascription to it.

The negotiation of identity among Dominicans who fit only ambiguously into historical American social categories illuminates the reciprocal relationships between micro-level practices and macro-social constellations such as ethnic and racial categories. While the constraints inherent in these categories shape the language and identities of Dominican Americans, their everyday contestation of the ways in which they are classified is subtly shaping the available categories. Communicative behavior links the work of individual social actors and these larger-scale social categories in ways that can be documented and analyzed. The daily affirmation of a Dominican identity among the African-descent second generation has already made the category "Dominican," rather than "Black," a recognized term for an African-descent group in many parts of Providence, Rhode Island, even among non-Hispanics. Analysis of Dominican American negotiation of identity can thus tell us much about the larger social processes of which it forms a part, racial formation in America and acculturation of the new immigrant second generation.

CHAPTER 2

Community, Field Site, Methods, and Principal Subjects

2.1 The Providence Dominican Community

Fieldwork for this study took place in Providence, Rhode Island, from August 1996 to July 1997, with January 1997 spent in Santiago, Dominican Republic. In this chapter, I introduce the Providence Dominican community, describe the main site and methods, and introduce the six principal subjects.

Dominican settlement in Providence is concentrated in the contiguous neighborhoods of Washington Park, Elmwood, southern South Providence, and the West End. At the time of this fieldwork, community leaders estimated the Dominican population of Providence to be over fifteen thousand. Census data from 1990 put the Dominican population of Providence at 7,973, but that figure almost certainly represents an undercount for that year[6], and it doesn't include immigrants arriving in the early 1990's, a period of increased migration resulting from economic crises on the island (Grasmuck and Pessar 1996).

Although the Dominican community of Providence, Rhode Island, is concentrated in one area of the city and contains many family networks[7], it is an imagined community (Anderson 1983) in the sense that most members of it will never know each other. It is defined by its multiple social, economic, and familial links to the Dominican Republic. These links are maintained by a regular bi-directional flow of goods, ideas, and people and through the daily reproduction of linguistic and cultural practices from the island.

The main streets running through the heavily Dominican neighborhoods, Elmwood Avenue, Cranston Street, and, particularly, Broad Street, are lined with Dominican-owned and operated businesses serving the Dominican and Hispanic population: bodegas ['corner groceries'], international telephone calling centers, Spanish/Dominican CD and cassette stores, liquor stores, remittance wiring services, travel agents, freight and courier services, accountants, clothing boutiques, nightclubs, *botanicas* ['herbal/alternative medicine shops'], temporary employment agencies, Dominican bus-lines and taxi companies, etc. Providence media and politicians have recognized Dominican immigrants as having revitalized, through entrepreneurship, what had been blighted, boarded-up thoroughfares.

The names of Dominican businesses along these streets reflect regional and national identities, e.g. "Dominican Taxi Company," "Quisqueya [the indigenous name for the island] Liquors," "Dominican Supermarket," and "Cibao Market." Broad Street is the symbolic heart of the Dominican community, and on the annual Dominican Independence Day Festival at a nearby park, traffic on the street comes to a standstill as revelers wrapped in Dominican flags dance atop vehicles to competing car audio systems playing the latest *bachatas* and *merengues*.

Three Spanish-language AM radio stations were serving Providence at the time of fieldwork, and radios in Dominican homes and businesses were invariably tuned to these stations when first-generation adults were present. There was some Spanish programming on a local UHF TV station in addition to national cable stations, and several Spanish-language newspapers appeared sporadically. Several large Catholic Churches that once served Irish and Italian immigrants in South and Western Providence now offer Mass primarily in Spanish. Smaller Spanish-language Evangelical churches operate out of other churches and storefronts. The first generation can thus shop, find employment, socialize, take a bus or taxi, receive many social services, listen to the radio, and attend Church--i.e. conduct their lives--in a Dominican/Spanish world.

According to 1990 census data, the Dominican unemployment rate in Providence was 17.4%, 38.5% of households were below the federal poverty line, and the median household income was $17,533. First generation Dominican immigrants have limited vocational options because of language barriers, non-transferable qualifications, and lower overall educational levels in the Dominican Republic. Although Dominican immigrants to the U.S. are well-educated by Dominican standards, they are not well-educated by U.S. standards because the average levels of education in the United States are much higher. The percentage of Americans graduating from high school is almost twice as high as in the Dominican Republic, and the percentage graduating from college is nearly three times as high (Grasmuck and Pessar 1996:282, 291).

2.2 Central High School

The main research site for observation, interviewing and video-recording was Central High School, a Providence city school of 1350 students, which is over 20% Dominican. Roughly 60% of the student body is Hispanic, with Puerto Ricans and Guatemalans comprising the second and third largest Hispanic groups. About sixteen percent of the students are Black (including many immigrants), 16% are Southeast Asian, primarily first- and second-generation Cambodian and Laotian refugees, and about 5% are White American.

Central is one of four major high schools in the city of Providence system, a system that tracks its high-achieving students into one academic-magnet school. Central High School has the problems typical of many inner city public schools. Almost ninety percent of the students are categorized as poor based on federal guidelines, and more than half of the students officially enrolled in the 9th grade drop out by the 11th grade.[8] In 1997, only 11 students at Central High School scored over 900 combined on the SAT. Attendance is poor and many of the teachers appear demoralized and make little effort to reach students. The Providence leader of the National Association for Advancement of Colored People (NAACP) repeatedly called for Central High School to be closed down. A 1997 front-page feature article on Central High School in the Providence daily newspaper began with the following despairing characterization[9]:

> If there is anything more bleak than the environment outside Central High School--ubiquitous obscenity-laced graffiti, crumbling concrete steps, young people bunking class,

smoking cigarettes--it is within the walls of the state's poorest-
performing high school.

2.3 Methods and Data

Data collection methods included participant observation in high
school, family, and community contexts, 1-2 hour interviews of high
school and college students, and videotaping of six principal subject
high school students in the course of a school day and in one non-
school context.[10] Interviews of students were organized around a
questionnaire that addressed issues of language use and ethnic/racial
identity growing up in Providence, including peer and family social
networks and perceptions of different ethnic groups. Interviews were in
English, except for a sample of spoken Spanish that was recorded for
each student. Interviews of high school students were done during
school hours, after school on school grounds, in homes, and at a Friday
night Spanish language Catholic youth group at a South Providence
church. Portions of these recorded interviews were transcribed, and
segments of these transcripts are presented throughout this paper.

   Contact with students at Central High School was initially made
through the Cuban American vice-principal, who introduced me to
various ESL, bilingual education, and Spanish for native-speakers
teachers. These teachers let me take Dominican immigrant students out
of class for interviews. I soon found that students who had first come to
America after about age 10 were more *Dominican* than Dominican
American in language, culture, and perceptions. They were Spanish
dominant, had almost solely Spanish speaking friends, defined
themselves not as minority Americans but rather as Dominican
nationals, and saw their stay in America as a temporary sojourn. Their
limited English proficiency and Dominican/Hispanic social networks
prevented them from confronting dominant American discourses on
race and ethnicity. Regardless of degree of African-descent phenotype,
such recent immigrants didn't report being mistaken for African
American, and many seemed confused--and some insulted--when I
asked them if they had been perceived as anything but Dominican. This
led me to restrict my sample of subsequent consultants to those who
had come to America before age 10 and were English dominant.

   From among these students, I asked individual students who had
been forthcoming in interviews if I could videotape them during the

course of a school day and in one non-school context. I made an effort to select students who had experienced ascription as African American as well as students who hadn't, and to include both males and females. The six students, five juniors and one sophomore, represent some of the variability I found among Dominican American students at Central High School. They include four females and two males. Two of the students were born in the United States, and four others came to the United States between ages five and eight. Five considered themselves fluent Spanish speakers. Three reported being perceived to be African American with at least some regularity. Two were almost certainly college-bound. Two had parents on welfare or disability, three had parents who did factory work, and one had a father who is a self-employed carpenter. The father of one student attended some college in the Dominican Republic, but only one or two of the other parents and step-parents finished high school. One student spent a high school year in the Dominican Republic, and another spent part of a high school year there, but both had problems adjusting and returned. Five of the six had no intention of ever living long-term in the Dominican Republic.

Prior to videotaping, I interviewed each of the six students on multiple occasions, totaling two to four hours, and I accompanied them to class during part of their school day. The six students were then videotaped throughout the school day, going to classes and interacting with teachers and friends (parents gave permission on school-mandated release forms). Between classes I followed students with camera in hand, and during classes I positioned the camera on desks. During tests, silent reading, or other longer periods of verbal inactivity, I turned the camera off. In addition, each student was videotaped in at least one non-school, largely Spanish-speaking context. These included preparing and eating dinner at home, attending Friday night Catholic youth group, playing Nintendo with a recently-immigrated cousin, holding a baby-shower for a younger sister, and attending dance practice for a Dominican cultural festival. Each student was thus videotaped for between four and eight hours.

The tapes were logged and sections transcribed, yielding over 200 pages of logs and transcripts. Four of the six video-recorded subjects assisted with transcription of tapes and interpretation of the language and interaction on them. Segments of talk and interaction transcribed from videotape appear in Chapters 3, 4, 6, and 7.

2.4 Introducing the Six Principal Subjects

What follows is a brief introduction to the six students who were videotaped and served as primary consultants.[11] These descriptions include information on place of birth/age at immigration, household composition, parental education levels, trajectory of educational success, and vocational aspirations. This information is summarized in a table following discursive introductions to the students. The names--pseudonyms--of these six principal subjects will appear frequently in this monograph in examples of patterns of language use (Chapters 3, 6, and 7) and as consultants describing experiences of growing up Dominican American (Chapter 4).

Isabella (age 16)

Isabella was a junior who was very active in school activities and organizations and was almost certainly college-bound. She was junior class secretary, a member of the student senate, Vice-President of the Future Business Leaders of America, and one of several leaders of a non-violence group that gave presentations in school and community settings. She had entered a program as a high school freshman that guaranteed her admission to the University of Rhode Island if she took the appropriate college-preparatory courses and participated in academic and community activities with other members of the program. She also participated in Educational Talent Search, an program that organized visits to various colleges and counseled students on the college application process. She was more talkative than other students in class, and appeared to be at ease both with the faculty at Central and with her peers.

Isabella was born in Barahona, Dominican Republic, and had lived there until she was six, coming to the United States for the second half of first grade. She and her brother had stayed with her maternal grandmother for three years while their mother had come to the United States to join their father. Her parents separated soon after she arrived in Providence, and she had had little contact with her father, who had returned to the Dominican Republic. She lived with her mother, who was on AFDC, an 18-year-old brother who had recently dropped out of high school, and her 8-year-old half-brother. Her mother had no relatives in Providence and Isabella had relatively little contact with the many aunts and uncles there from her father's side of the family.

Isabella spoke only Spanish to her mother, who spoke no English, and primarily English to her two brothers.

Isabella talked about becoming a high school history teacher and then going into politics. She was worried about her family's financial situation and the number of years her education would take before she could contribute substantially to her mother's financial security. Federal legislation had just been passed that would deny AFDC to legal immigrants like her mother, and Isabella was not sure how her family would make ends meet. Her mother compared living in America to being in hell--she missed her family, hated the cold, and had had many financial problems--but she wanted her children to be educated there. It was expected that they would repay her for her sacrifices by supporting her comfortably in the Dominican Republic after they had finished their educations. The fact that Isabella's older brother had fathered a child and stopped school before receiving a diploma put added pressure on her.

Her non-violence training and presentations, and her summer jobs brought her into contact with people from different ethnic/racial and class backgrounds. During the summer, for example, a community block grant sponsored her administrative work in the development office of a major Providence hospital, and the summer after I met her she received a scholarship to go to non-violence workshops in Nashville, Tennessee for several days.

Alejandro (age 16)

Alejandro was born into an upper-middle class family in Santiago, Dominican Republic, and came to the United States at age eight, later than the other five students. When I met him, he had not been back to the island in the eight years since he had left, but he was planning to spend the next summer there. Unlike the other five students, who had no plans of ever residing full-time in the Dominican Republic, he was not sure if he was going to stay in America. At several times during his school years in America, a family return to the Dominican Republic had seemed imminent. When I asked whether his family owned or rented their house, Alejandro said that they rented, but that they owned a house in Santiago. In another context he noted that they had had two maids, a car, and two motor scooters in the Dominican Republic, and that his uncle was a doctor. For Alejandro, more than the other five principal subjects, the Dominican Republic was not just a place of origin and a symbol, but also a place that could become his home.

Alejandro's parents were relatively well educated--his father had completed some college, and his mother had completed the 11th grade, but stopped schooling when she got pregnant. They emphasized education to him, and said that they would do what they could to pay for college. He was unsure whether he would try to attend college in the United States or the Dominican Republic. This ambiguity had discouraged him from participating in pre-college programs at his high school that would have assured him of admission to a Rhode Island college.[12]

The composition of his household had changed frequently over the previous few years. He had two older sisters, 18 and 20, who had recently moved out, but they had also spent an earlier year of high school in the Dominican Republic. Their father had sent them there to stay with their grandmother as punishment for fighting at school and regularly skipping class. Neither finished high school when they returned, which was a disappointment to their father. Alejandro's father moved between the two countries, working on a house in Santiago during periods of unemployment in America, which freed Alejandro from his father's relatively stricter discipline. At times Alejandro's maternal grandmother resided with them. Alejandro spoke only Spanish with his parents and grandmother, and a mixture of Spanish and English with his sisters.

In school, Alejandro was often a class-clown who exasperated teachers by walking a fine line between obviously disruptive behavior and subtle mocking of authority that set his classmates to laughing. He responded well to teachers and administrators who recognized his intelligence and took a personal interest in him, e.g. by talking with him about his behavior one-on-one rather than just punishing him, or by calling his parents. A former 'A' student, he was receiving numerous C's and D's his junior year. He said that he wanted to do well in school and study criminal law eventually, but that classes were boring. He felt that many teachers picked on him unjustly and that some of his White teachers were unfair to him because of his racial/ethnic background.

Alejandro was more sensitive than other Dominican American students to discrimination he faced in America, not only in school, but also at work and in public spaces. He thought that the few White workers at his Burger King job were favored by managers, even though the managers were primarily African American. He had regular verbal confrontations with clerks and security guards in stores, malls, movie theaters, and roller-skating rinks, where he said that he and his friends were singled out for surveillance and questioning due to ethnicity/race. He grouped "Spanish" and "Black" together in distinction to "White" in such phrases as "we Spanish and Black," in talking about such experiences of discrimination, and he was highly critical of some of his cousins who had grown up in a suburb of Providence and "acted White" and superior.

Maria (age 15, sophomore)

Maria was born in New York City, and moved to Providence when she was eight years old. Her mother had migrated to New York at age eleven and received her GED there. Her biological father was half-Puerto Rican and half-Dominican, but she avoided talking about him, referring instead to her stepfather as her "real" father. Despite being born in America to a mother who received a significant amount of her socialization in America, Maria had maintained more Spanish language than many of her American-born peers. Because of family difficulties when she was young, for example, she lived with her Spanish-dominant grandmother rather than her English-dominant mother. When she was thirteen, she went to the Dominican Republic for a year, attending seventh grade there and living with her great-grandmother, which greatly improved her Spanish. Her mother met Maria's stepfather there, and he came back to the United States with them. Both her mother and stepfather have family in the Dominican Republic who are successful in business, but both work in factories in Providence. Maria's mother is a fluent English speaker, but her stepfather speaks little after having spent eight years in America. Maria lived with her mother, stepfather, 12-year-old brother, and two young half-sisters. She speaks more Spanish than English to her mother and English with her siblings, except in front of her stepfather when she speaks Spanish. She said it would be disrespectful to speak English in front of him (cf. Zentella 1997: 85).

Maria had attended four different schools in the preceding three years, a Catholic junior high school, an alternative tutoring program for students at risk of dropping out of school, an English-language school in the Dominican Republic for one-month, and Central High School. She reported that she was supposed to attend the flagship Providence college-preparatory public high school, but that she didn't want the pressure and stress that caused students from there to drop out. She seemed comfortable at Central although she was bored and not challenged by most of her classes. She was interested in becoming a criminal defense lawyer or a singer. One of her uncles in the Dominican Republic was a lawyer, and she had admired Johnny Cochran in the O.J. Simpson trial. At her Catholic school, she had felt discriminated against by the White students and nuns, and had publicly confronted both students and teachers as racist, leading to her eventual withdrawal from the school.

Maria identifies herself unequivocally as Dominican, but she also expresses solidarity with Puerto Ricans, perhaps in part because of her Puerto Rican ancestry on her biological father's side of the family, her years in New York City, and her American birth. She explicitly recognizes the binary racial categorization system of America into Black and White, and asserts that Dominicans and Hispanics are seen in the same category as African Americans. She explained that White people think everything they do is better than what non-Whites do, and she expressed resentment at the stares Whites direct at her family when they eat in restaurants in predominantly White neighborhoods.

The Catholic Church is an extremely important institution in Maria's life. As she related to a friend at school, *Yo vivo en la iglesia* ['I live in the church']. Because of the demographics of the Catholic population in South Providence, her church is a Spanish language and heavily Dominican institution. She sings in the choir, attends and acts as student leader of a Friday night Spanish language religious training group, attends Mass, and works answering the phone several evenings a week in the rectory.

Janelle (age 17)

Janelle was born in New York City but lived in a small town outside of New Paltz, NY until age 9, when she and her family moved to Providence. She lived with three half-siblings, aged nine, ten, and fifteen, and her mother and stepfather. Her mother, who had finished the 8th grade in the Dominican Republic, worked in a jewelry factory, and her stepfather was a carpenter who had a successful business making and installing kitchen counters. A 20-year-old sister had already moved out of the house and lived with her recently immigrated husband and two children.

Janelle was doing well in school, receiving almost all A's and B's her junior year, and she planned to attend college, perhaps to pursue a career in business. Her older sister, whom she admired, was taking classes at the local community college and planned to transfer into a four-year college, but no one else in her family had gone to college. She had taken the PSAT, but didn't know her scores because she hadn't gone to the guidance office to get them by the end of the school year.

Janelle had fewer ties to the Dominican Republic than the other five students, and had less fluency in Spanish. She had been to the island only once, when she was four years old, and she was unfamiliar with the places and institutions there that people talked about. Her Dominican friends teased her and called her a "bootleg" Dominican, suggesting that she was inauthentic as a Dominican because of her lesser degree of Spanish fluency, her lack of knowledge about the island, and the fact that she had spent so little time there. She reported that she spoke a considerable amount of English to her mother and stepfather although they usually answered and addressed her in Spanish. In my observations, she spoke only Spanish to them. She spoke primarily English with her siblings, although she began to speak more Spanish with her older sister after her sister married a recently immigrated Dominican and established a Spanish-speaking household.

Janelle took advantage of social programs targeted to inner-city teens. She participated in a leadership program organized by the city, and her summer job as a secretary in a hospital was sponsored by a bloc grant for her low-income neighborhood. She was hired in part based on her bilingual abilities, and she was worried about whether her Spanish would be good enough for the job.

Frangelica (18)

Frangelica came to the United States at age 5, from a poor, rural, agricultural background. When I met her, she was living with her father and her paternal grandfather, although she was often alone as they spent increasingly long periods of time in the Dominican Republic. During these times she spent much of her time with her upstairs neighbor, a Guatemalan immigrant and her Anglo-American husband. She had grown up with her mother, a sister five years younger, and two half-siblings who were seven and fourteen years younger. Her younger sister, who was thirteen, was expecting a baby that spring. Her mother received disability payments for mental illness and was an alcoholic.

Her father was also on permanent disability, having injured his leg in a fall.

Frangelica maintained strong ties to the island in part because of having fallen in love while spending the summer with relatives two years earlier. She had moved in with her boyfriend there shortly after meeting him, and then returned the next spring to spend another month with him. She was trying to get him a visa to come to the United States, and I helped her to fill out the immigration forms. She planned to marry him the next summer and spoke repeatedly about details of the planned wedding.

Although she maintained strong Spanish and ties to the island, she had told her parents that she wasn't going to return there. She was appreciative of the infrastructure in American--paved streets, electricity, 911, and running water, and the rights and economic opportunities she had in America. She thought that the poor were discriminated against more intensely in the Dominican Republic and had fewer rights. She said that if you were first in line in America you would be served first, whereas you could be first in line in the Dominican Republic, and the upper class would still get first priority.

Frangelica did not have many friends at school, and she treated school in a very business-like way. In her own words, "I just go to school, go home, do my work, do what I have to do." She was organized and disciplined about meeting minimal requirements for each class, but she was not enthusiastic about school, and several of her teachers treated her as if she were stupid. She talked of going to college at the University of Rhode Island and becoming a social worker or working in social services. She worked five hours each evening at a factory making displays for jewelry and would have worked more if she could have gotten more hours.

By spring of her junior year she had broken up with her long-distance boyfriend and was pregnant from a 26-year-old recent Dominican immigrant, whom she would marry the following August.

Wilson (17)

Wilson came to Providence at the beginning of second grade to join his father, who had separated from Wilson's mother and come to the United States five years earlier. He had lived until then with his mother and older half-sister on the outskirts of Santo Domingo. His father remarried in America, to an Italian-American, and Wilson spent his elementary and junior high school years in Cranston, a primarily white and heavily Italian-American municipality adjoining Providence. He returned to the Dominican Republic to live with his mother for his freshman year of high school, but found that his American education, in English, was an obstacle to succeeding in school there. His father spent part of that year in the Dominican Republic but returned when he realized the extent of the problems with public services such as water and electricity and the poor economic prospects, and he brought Wilson back with him.

Wilson spoke English at home while his father was married to his stepmother but reverted back to Spanish after she and his father divorced. Wilson's father was a self-employed carpenter. He had completed the eighth grade in the Dominican Republic but read about history, geography, and religion in both English and Spanish. When Wilson was young, his father practiced Spanish reading and writing with him to encourage him to preserve and build on his Spanish skills.

The friendships he had developed in the Dominican Republic served him in Providence in that several friends and relatives emigrated at the same time that he left. His closest friends in Providence were several young men to whom he was linked through his year in the Dominican Republic.

Wilson liked working with his hands and was interested in attending a local technical institute, possibly to learn about computer repair. He displayed little interest in his schoolwork, missed many days of classes, and was failing several subjects in the spring of his junior year.

Table 1: Summary Table of Principal Subjects

Isabella
Age: 16
Lived with: Mother
Parental education: Middle School
Age at arrival in United States: 6
Educational achievement: Four-year college-bound
Vocational aspirations: High school teacher/Politician

Alejandro
Age: 16
Lived with: Mother and Father
Parental education: Some college
Age at arrival in United States: 8
Educational achievement: Formerly A's; C's-D's
Vocational aspirations: Lawyer

Maria
Age: 15
Lived with: Mother and Stepfather
Parental education: High school
Age at arrival in United States: United States-born
Educational achievement: formerly A's; B's-F's
Vocational aspirations: Lawyer or singer

Janelle
Age: 17
Lived with: Mother and Stepfather
Parental education: Middle school.
Age at arrival in United States: United States-born
Educational achievement: Four-year college-bound
Vocational aspirations: Businesswoman

(Table 1, continued)

Frangelica
Age: 18
Lived with: Sometimes alone; sometimes with Father
Parental education: Elementary school
Age at arrival in United States: 5
Educational achievement: A's-C's
Vocational aspirations: Social worker

Wilson
Age: 17
Lived with: Father
Parental education: Middle school
Age at arrival in United States: 7
Educational achievement: F's
Vocational aspirations: Skilled trade

CHAPTER 3
Linguistic Resources of Dominican Americans

3.1 Introduction

The variety of linguistic forms used by Dominican American high school students in Providence, and their unmarked juxtaposition in everyday interaction, provide a window into a particular, second-generation social reality. All language, including that of monolinguals, is heteroglot, containing multiple and competing sociohistorical voices and ideologies (Bakhtin 1981). This heteroglossia is particularly salient in the language of Dominican American high school students because they draw forms from grammatical codes that count as distinct languages and from varieties with implications of stark social difference, e.g. AAVE and American English. The explicitly syncretic[13] (Hill and Hill 1986) repertoire of Dominican American language practices symbolizes Dominican American acculturation that does not follow a unitary, discrete trajectory to a monolithic identity. The potential trajectories of acculturation outlined by Portes and Zhou (1993) for the post-1965 second generation--assimilation to a White mainstream, assimilation to native-born minority groups, or maintenance of a Dominican identity defined in reference to the ethic enclave--fail to capture this multiplicity and complexity of social identity formation. Single utterances or short exchanges that include forms drawn, for example, from AAVE, Dominican Spanish, and Providence working class English, index the multiple social forces and processes, e.g. immigration, regional Dominican origins, economic class, and racial/ethnic formation, that form aspects of the identities of Dominican Americans in Providence.

49

In this chapter I review distinctive features of Dominican American high school students' language, describing language varieties that inform it, and giving examples of language contact phenomena, emphasizing code switching, that occur in Dominican American speech.

3.2 The Multi-variety and Hybrid Linguistic Repertoire

The following segment of transcript documents some of the linguistic features of the everyday language used by Dominican American high school students in Providence, Rhode Island (See Appendix A for transcription conventions).

1)
[(JS #2 12:26:40) Isabella and Janelle are sitting on steps outside of the main school building at the end of their lunch period. Isabella has just returned from eating lunch at a diner near the school, and she had previously begun to describe the turkey club sandwich she has just eaten.]

Janelle: Okay, a turkey club is *pan to(s)ta(d)o* ['toasted white bread']
Isabella: *pan to(s)ta(d)o*. Like regular *pan-* ['bread']
Janelle: Yeah
Isabella: *to(s)ta(d)o* ['toasted']. With-- um-- tomatoes and lettuce. And it has mayonnaise.
Janelle: And turkey.
Isabella: Then-- No, that's the=
Janelle: =//the top
Isabella: =//first part. And then it has another *pan* ['slice of bread'] in the middle, and the bottom has more mayonnaise and turkey. Oh it has bacon on it too.
            (.5)
Isabella: Just sla::mming ['great']!
Janelle: How do you eat that?
Isabella: Then they- she cut it in half for me and I ate that, gluk gluk. And I was like, "Yo, let me get a cheeseburger." A cheeseburger has lettuce, tomatoes, whatever you want to put on it, like a Whopper you can make out of a cheeseburger.

Janelle: For real? Look at Mr. Aguiar. ((a teacher, Mr. Aguiar, walks past))

Isabella: And she cut that in half for me, chow, "Oh let me get a lemonade."

Janelle: Da::mn. I can't //eat all that.

Isabella: //Then I drank the lemonade.

Janelle: Only with that turkey thingee //*ya yo estoy llena*. ['I'm already full']

Isabella: //Two dollars and fifty cent.

Janelle: That's good. That's like a meal at //Burger King.

Isabella: //That's better than going to Burger King, you know what I'm saying? And you got a Whopper, french fries, and a drink. And the french fries cost a dollar over there.

Janelle: For real?

Isabella: *Sí, sí cómo no?* ['Yes, really.']

Janelle: *Mírale el ombligo. Míralo. Se le ve, ya se lo tapó.* ((looking at a passerby)) ['Look at her belly button. Look. You can see it, she already covered it.']
(.5)

Isabella: *Seguro porque se lo enseñó.* ['She must have showed it.'] ((laughing))
(1.5)

Isabella: But it's slamming, though, oh my God, mad ['a lot of'] turkey she puts in there.

Janelle: That's one thing I l-, I love the way *como l-* ['how th-'] the American ['White Americans'] be doing sandwich, they be rocking ['are excellent'], them things, yo, they put everything up in there, yo.

Isabella: De pla:ne, de pla:ne. ((an airplane passes overhead))

The above segment of transcript illustrates some aspects of the multi-variety language of Dominican Americans. The exchange is primarily in English, which is typical of the interactions among English-dominant Dominican Americans that I observed and recorded, but it includes many distinctive forms indexing a Dominican American identity. Most salient of these, perhaps, is the alternation between English and Spanish in what is commonly referred to as code switching. Gumperz (1982:59) defines code switching as "the juxtaposition within the same speech exchange of passages of speech belonging to two different grammatical systems or subsystems." Isabella and Janelle use unambiguously Spanish words (*pan, to'ta'o, como*), syntax (adjective *to'ta'o* in post-nominal position), and phrases (*ya yo estoy llena*) in turns that are otherwise in English, and some of their turns are entirely in Spanish (e.g., *Sí, sí cómo no?*).

Based on Gumperz's (1982) definition of code switching as involving speech from different grammatical systems or subsystems, Janelle and Isabella are also using a third code, African American Vernacular English (AAVE). In the stretch of speech "...the American be doing sandwich, they be rocking them things, yo." Janelle uses grammatical structures unique to AAVE as well as one that occurs in both AAVE and various working class vernaculars. She uses the AAVE habitual "be" to capture the recurring way White Americans make sandwiches ("the American be making sandwich") and the ongoing, excellent character of those sandwiches ("they be rocking"). This habitual "be" is one of the most researched features of AAVE (Morgan 1994b), and it is a component of the tense/aspect system of AAVE that sociolinguists use to define AAVE (Labov 1980). A second form characteristic of AAVE that both Janelle and Isabella use is plural nouns without overt plural marking (Baugh 1983:95). Janelle elides the /s/ and /əs/ in "American" and "sandwich," respectively, while Isabella elides the /s/ in "cents". Finally, Janelle's use of the object pronoun "them" in place of the demonstrative adjective "those" in the phrase "them things," is characteristic of both AAVE and other sociolects.

In addition to using syntax associated with Spanish, standard American English, and AAVE, Janelle and Isabella use lexical items that are often defined as AAVE (e.g. Smitherman 1994) and associated with the speech of urban, African American youth. Isabella uses the adjectives "slamming" ['great'] and "mad" ['a lot of'], while Janelle uses the verb "rocking" ['to be great'] and the interjection "yo".

Constellations of linguistic features that are officially authorized as codes or languages, e.g. "English" or "Spanish," are often treated as if they were of monolithic, uniform character in the context of bilingualism. This veils the diversity of linguistic resources available to speakers within codes. The English that Isabella and Janelle use in the exchange above, for example, includes unmarked American English forms, quotation of a television character's non-native speaker English ("De plane, de plane")[14], non-standard vernacular forms, lexical forms associated with AAVE, and grammatical forms that occur only in AAVE, indexing a particular urban American background. Their Spanish similarly indexes particular linguistic histories. Their velarization of /n/ to /ŋ/ in *pan*, and their pronunciation of *tostado* as /totao/ (syllable final /s/ and intervocalic /d/ elided), for example, are characteristic of Caribbean Spanish, particularly Dominican and lower class varieties. Variation among forms within officially authorized codes has social implications--as does code switching--both as a reflection of social identity and as an expanded set of linguistic resources that members can use to enact their identities.

As a result of language contact, Dominican American language also includes novel forms, the result of, e.g. syntactic transference (Clyne 1967) or convergence (Clyne 1987, Gumperz and Wilson 1971), and forms used in novel ways, e.g. calques. Forms used above by Isabella suggest the influence of Spanish discourse patterns on her English. She preposes the direct object of the verb in this segment in what has been called fronting, focal object construction (Silva-Corvalán 1983:135), or focus-movement (Prince 1981) (DO=Direct Object; S=Subject; V=Verb):

2)
mad **turkey she puts** in there
   DO S V

In Spanish such preverbal Objects can serve various discourse functions, depending in part on intonation contour (Silva-Corvalán 1983). Use of this preverbal-Object structure in English allows Isabella to highlight her point--the large amount of turkey put on her sandwich--in a linguistically creative way.

The variety and juxtaposition of linguistic resources by Janelle and Isabella in the above exchange reflect their specific life experiences and aspects of their social world. The mixing of English and Spanish reflects their dual socialization as does Isabella's use of Spanish discourse forms. Their use of forms associated with urban African American youth--particularly Janelle's use of AAVE syntax--suggest extensive contact with African Americans and perhaps identification with inner-city African American experiences. Janelle's use of the term "American" to mean "White people" suggests that she identifies herself with reference to another nation-state and in terms of racial/ethnic

categories in which she doesn't count as White American. The mixing
of these diverse linguistic elements in single utterances, e.g. "I love the
way *como-* the American be doing sandwich" reflects and instantiates a
social reality in which both linguistic practices and social identities fit
poorly into received, unitary categories of language and identity.

3.3 Dominican Spanish

The Spanish spoken by Dominican Americans in Providence is based
on Dominican Spanish, which has been described by Henríquez Ureña
(1940) and Jiménez Sabater (1975), and more narrowly, by Alba
(1990a,b). It can be classified as a Caribbean variety of Spanish,
sharing many features with the Spanish of Puerto Rico, Cuba, and the
Caribbean coasts of Colombia and Venezuela. Caribbean Spanish
varieties are descended from Andalusian dialects, which were spoken
by the sailors and traders who dominated Spanish contact with the
Caribbean in the first centuries of settlement. Many of the differences
between Caribbean Spanish and other Latin American varieties
correspond to historical differences between Andalusian dialects and
the North Central Spanish varieties that were carried to the non-
Caribbean parts of the New World. In addition, a 19th century
Caribbean influx of Canary Islanders, whose Spanish is not unlike
Andalusian varieties, may have also affected Caribbean Spanish. The
use of non-inverted word order in questions with subject pronouns, for
example, is found in varieties of Canary Island Spanish and otherwise
only in areas of the Caribbean with historical concentrations of Canary
Island immigrants (Lipski 1994):

3a) Dominant Variety Spanish:
   Qué quieres (tú)? ['What do you want?']
   What want (you)

3b) Dominican/Caribbean Spanish:
   (FU #1 11:48:30)
   Qué tú quieres? ['What do you want?']
   What you want

Use of non-inverted word order in such questions is just one of a
number of distinctively Caribbean syntactic forms used by Dominican

American teenagers in Providence. Subject pronouns, for example, are regularly used as pre-posed subjects of infinitives in place of subjunctive constructions (See Appendix B for grammatical abbreviations used in these interlinear glosses):

4a) Dominant Variety Spanish:

> *Quita-   te   la **gorra para que yo pueda**   ver*
> take off 2ND-REF ART hat   so   that I can-SUB see
> *la   greña   tuya*
> ART matted hair 2nd-POSS
> ['Take off your hat so that I can see your matted hair'].

4b) Dominican Spanish:

> (FU #1 11:39:15)
> *Quita-   te   la   gorra   **para   yo ver**   la*
> take off 2ND-REF   ART hat   in-order-to I see   ART
> *greña   tuya*
> matted hair   2nd-POSS
> ['Take off your hat so that I can see your matted hair'].

Similarly distinctive in Caribbean varieties is the reduplication of subject pronouns across clauses:

5a) Dominant Variety Spanish:

> *Si tú pones atención, Chocolate, **Ø** puedes hacer tu trabajo.*
> If you pay attention, Chocolate, (you) can do your work.

5b) Dominican Spanish:

> (FU #1 12:03:56)
> *Si tú pones atención, Chocolate, **tú** puedes hacer tu trabajo.*
> if you pay attention, Chocolate, you can do your work.

Some scholars have linked this pattern to the erosion of the second-person singular verbal suffix /s/--a phenomenon more extreme in the Dominican Republic than elsewhere in the Caribbean--which could make utterances without overt subjects ambiguous (Lipski 1994:335). This reduplication of subjects is redundant in varieties of Spanish that retain the person-marking verbal suffix /s/.

A distinctively Dominican structure documented in the speech of one Providence teen-ager is the reduplication of the negative *no*, placed at the end of the clause:

6) Dominican Reduplication of *no*
    (FU #1 11:28:15)
    *Yo **no** quiero quedar* after school ***no***.
    I NEG want stay   after school NEG
    ['I don't want to stay after school.']

Megenney (1990) suggests a possible African origin for this structure, which occurs not only in the Spanish of the Dominican Republic but also in the Portuguese of lower class Brazilians.

In everyday speech, the most immediately distinguishing characteristics of Caribbean Spanish are phonological. Caribbean Spanish aspirates and elides syllable- and word-final /s/, so that, e.g. *tostones* ['fried plantain chips'] is rendered as /totone/ and the phrase *todos los sabados y domingos* ['every Saturday and Sunday'] becomes *todo' lo' sabado' y domingo'*. This elision of /s/ is particularly prominent because of the frequency of syllable- and word-final /s/ in Spanish: it is used to form plural forms of nouns and adjectives, it occurs in many forms of the verb "to be," it occurs in demonstrative pronouns, and it marks some forms of subject-verb agreement.

Another salient phonological features is the weakening or dropping of intervocalic /d/, especially in past participles (formed with the suffix *-ido* or *-ado*), making *mojado*, for example, /moxao/. Many Dominicans in America are discursively aware of these two patterns, and they point out that the phrase *nada más* ['nothing more'] is pronounced very differently by Dominicans, i.e. /na ma/, than other Spanish speakers /naða mas/. As do other Caribbean Spanish speakers, Dominicans in Providence pronounce /y/ as an affricate /dʒ/ (e.g., *yo*→/dʒo/) and /n/ as a velar /ŋ/ in some environments. A final, salient characteristic of Caribbean pronunciation, which tends to vary by social class, region, and context is the weakening or changes in syllable- and word-final /l/ and /r/. Among Dominican Americans in Providence this is most apparent in /r/ being pronounced as /l/, e.g. *puerta* ['door'] becoming /puelta/, a pattern associated with origins near the capital city of Santo Domingo, and /i/ substituting for /r/, e.g. *porque* becoming

/poike/, a pattern associated with the speech of the Cibao, the north central part of the country.

Dominican Spanish diverges further from Latin American and Iberian Spanish standards than other Caribbean varieties. Distinctive Caribbean pronunciations tend to be sociolinguistic markers of education and class in Puerto Rico and Cuba, while in the Dominican Republic they tend to represent the standard pronunciation across regions and class. The weakening or elision of intervocalic /d/ in Puerto Rico, for example, corresponds to social class and region (Lipski 1994:332), while in the Dominican Republic intervocalic /d/ regularly falls in all sociolects and in all regions (Lipski 1994:238). Similarly, word-final /s/ in Puerto Rico is frequently aspirated and sometimes elided. In the Dominican Republic, in contrast, the "rates of loss of word- and phrase-final /s/ are so high as to be nearly categorical" (Lipski 1994:239). When there is sociolinguistic variation in such features in the Dominican Republic, lower status features occur much more frequently in the Dominican Republic and across a wider range of social backgrounds. Alba (1995:42-43) found that the elision of syllable-final /s/ and /r/ within words (as opposed to word-final position) occurred at rates five times higher in the Dominican Republic than in Puerto Rico. Several distinctively Caribbean phonological characteristics of Spanish are thus more pronounced and widespread in Dominican Spanish than in other Caribbean varieties, and features that are associated with lower classes and regional non-standard speech in Puerto Rico and Cuba cross regional and social class boundaries in the Dominican Republic.[15]

Dominican teen-agers in Providence distinguish easily between Dominican Spanish and Puerto Rican Spanish, the local variety which is most similar to theirs and which is most widely spoken in Providence after Dominican Spanish. Dominican Americans report that they recognize Puerto Rican Spanish based on differences in the meaning of certain vocabulary and differences in pronunciation. The most noted difference in pronunciation is the highly salient Puerto Rican pronunciation of word-initial 'r' or medial 'rr' (/rr/) as a velar [x] or as a uvular trill [R]. Dominicans say that Puerto Ricans pronounce /rr/ like Spanish "j", i.e. *carro* is rendered as /kaxo/. Although this velarized "rr" is stigmatized by some in Puerto Rico, it is also regarded by many Puerto Ricans as the "most Puerto Rican" of sounds because it does not occur in other varieties of Spanish. It is thus a marker of Puerto Rican authenticity and pride for some even though it is not used by all speakers (Lipski 1994:334). Dominicans in Providence consider it an improper pronunciation (e.g. Wilson: "I tell them a lot, 'Yo, why yous talk like that?'"), but also a clear marker of Puerto Rican Spanish and identity. When identifying the ethnicity of classmates for the researcher, some Dominican Americans used a playfully rolled or otherwise marked /rr/ sound--despite speaking in English--to describe Puerto Rican students as "Puerrrrto Rican."

Dominicans also report a difference in intonation between Dominican and Puerto Rican Spanish. Their imitations of Puerto Rican intonation include dramatic shifts in pitch and length between syllables, e.g. *mira* becomes *miraaaa* with the second syllable spoken nearly in falsetto and at high volume. Contrary to Zentella's (1990a) (cf. Toribio 2000) findings in New York of Dominican insecurity about their variety of Spanish vis-à-vis Puerto Rican, Cuban, and non-Caribbean varieties, my principal subjects did not see their variety of Spanish as less appropriate than other varieties.[16]

Many consultants pointed out that they could distinguish between Dominican and Puerto Rican speakers when they were speaking Spanish but not when they were speaking English. While Dominicans and Puerto Ricans brought up in Providence share very similar varieties of Spanish, they share virtually identical varieties of English. Intra-Hispanic language differences are even more prominent in contact with Guatemalan Spanish, the third most widely spoken variety in Providence. Several students reported misunderstandings with Guatemalan students because of divergent uses of *ahorita,* which means 'right now, this very minute' in Guatemala, but 'later' in Dominican Spanish. One graduate of Central High School explained that he was generally more comfortable with African American peers than with non-Caribbean Hispanics partly *because* of language:

> We might have more contact with them [Blacks] than with Mexicans and Guatemalans, even though we might speak the same language, I don't really see Mexicans over here or Guatemalans, I rarely hang with Guatemalans or Mexicans. Speaking with Guatemalans I feel like I'm speaking a whole different language because their Spanish, they have a different dialect, like if they talk among themselves, I wouldn't be able

to understand what they're saying. They could speak so fast and use different words.

Paradoxically, Spanish is not always a "language of solidarity" among Hispanic American youth, because it marks intra-Hispanic differences more clearly than English.

3.4. Use of Forms Associated with AAVE

The English spoken by Dominican American high school students in Providence includes features associated with a variety of sociolects: prestige Standard English, local working-class vernacular, AAVE, and forms resulting from Spanish-English contact.

Use of features of AAVE is central to the current study because of the confluence of several social and historical factors: AAVE is strongly associated with African American identities, the Black-White racial dichotomy is a primary social organizing principle in America, and most Dominicans have African ancestry, thus meeting the criterion for classification as Black.

Notions of what constitutes African American Vernacular English vary, and even working definitions are conspicuously absent from some works on the topic (e.g. Mufwene, Rickford, Bailey and Baugh 1998). Morgan (1994a:327; see also 1996:428) defines African American English as "the language varieties used by people in the United States whose major socialization has been with United States residents of African descent." This definition is clearly problematic given the many hundreds of thousands of African-descent residents of the U.S. whose languages include Spanish, Haitian Creole, African languages, etc. A central point of this monograph is that African descent in the United States does not imply homogeneity of language, culture, or identity.

Labov (1980:379) explicitly distinguishes between the popular social construction "speaks Black English" and a much narrower "linguistic definition." In Labov's linguistic definition of BEV (Black English Vernacular), only those speakers who regularly use a prescribed set of tense/aspect forms count as actual speakers. Labov (1980) makes this distinction in analyzing the forms used by an Italian American girl who had adopted many lexical and phonological features of her African American peers, and whose speech--and consequently social identity--was consistently judged to be African American by consultants hearing audiotapes (Hatala 1976). His definition excludes the many individuals, including many African Americans, who make use of some prosodic, phonological, lexical, and/or syntactic phenomena popularly associated with the speech of African Americans. In contrast to other researchers, e.g. Morgan (1994a, 1996), who see AAVE partly in terms of its sociopolitical/ideological meanings, Labov emphasizes that linguistic variation is "almost independent" of individual ideology (Labov 1979:328). Labov's notion of BEV is particularly narrow because he defines it in terms of the forms common among "the speech of black [male] youth from 8 to 19 years old who participate fully in the street culture of the inner cities" (Labov 1972a:xiii). The speech of this group diverges more from that of dominant American groups than does the speech of other African American groups.

The popular construction "speaks Black English" is much broader and more subjective: individuals who use at least some forms popularly associated with stereotypes of African American speech can thus be said to be "speaking Black English." Use of such English is strongly associated with Black social identities, and individuals who are perceived to be "speaking Black English" on audiotape are generally presumed to *be* Black (Hatala 1976, Jacobs-Huey 1997).

Both popular and more formal definitions of AAVE are relevant to understanding the language and identities of Dominican Americans. Categorization and analysis of features they use helps to differentiate between Dominican American use of AAVE features and the fashionable adoption of hip hop terms and expressions by teens who have little contact with African Americans. While hip hop vocabulary have crossed over to teens of many social categories, distinctively AAVE syntax has crossed over much less. The syntactic rules regarding distribution of tense/aspect forms are much less accessible to individual awareness than vocabulary or pronunciation (Silverstein 1981)[17], for example, so it is more difficult to adopt these forms as a matter of conscious choice or fashion. The extent to which AAVE syntax and Dominican American syntax overlap thus reflects the longer-term extent of Dominican American contact with African Americans and the prestige of these ways of speaking among low-income, urban, non-White youth.

Dominican American high school students in Providence regularly employ vocabulary, expressions, and grammar associated with AAVE, and the speech of many--in combination with phenotype--leads them to be perceived as African American, even by African American and Dominican American peers. Newly arriving Dominican teen-agers with limited proficiency in English quickly adopt stock phrases with grammatical forms and vocabulary that are associated with AAVE, e.g. "You wack" ['You are not cool/with it'].

A frequent and salient feature of AAVE in the speech of Dominican American high school students is the use of the habitual "be". This form, which expresses a habitual or recurring activity or state, does not occur in other varieties of English. In AAVE it contrasts with simple present tense. Thus "He (is) sick" in AAVE suggests that the subject is currently sick, while "He be sick" suggests that the subject is frequently and/or recurrently sick (Labov 1972a). Dominican Americans use the habitual "be" for both activities ("I be benching everyday") and states ("I just wear something comfortable, because it's--cause it be hot in there."), and they use it to contrast habitual and non-habitual activities and states. Many use habitual "be" across contexts, e.g. both in peer interactions and in more formal settings that include White American adults such as teachers. One student, Maria, extended the habitual "be" form to situations that were not recurring or habitual. She asked a student who was leaving gym class early, for example, *"Where you be going?" even though she was asking about a one-time event of short duration. In this hypercorrection (Labov 1972b) to a locally prestigious variety, AAVE, "be" remains a distinctive social marker even as it loses the tense/aspect meaning that it has in AAVE.

Dominican Americans use other distinctive tense/aspect features of AAVE, including deletion of the copula. Although copula deletion occurs less frequently and obtrusively than the "habitual be", it occurs in a variety of grammatical environments, e.g. as an auxiliary ("Oh, you slipping on me," "We studying") and before predicate adjectives ("She crazy," "You stupid."). The third person singular subject-verb agreement marker /s/, which can be elided in AAVE, is sometimes elided by Dominican Americans ("She look like a witch"). A final feature of Dominican American speech that is incontrovertibly African American in origin is the stressed "bin," which was used by one student ("He's lying! He bin had it on."). The stressed "bin" emphasizes the validity of an assertion or the irrefutable nature of a stated fact (Smitherman 1977:23). These forms--the use of "habitual be", deletion of copula, elision of subject-verb agreement /s/, and use of stressed "bin"--are defining characteristics of AAVE from a sociolinguistic point of view (e.g. Labov 1980), and they occur, some regularly, in the speech of Dominican American high school students in Providence.

Dominican Americans also use forms associated with AAVE that can be considered either syntactic or phonological. Plurals, for example, are not always explicitly marked with "-s", ("These are all the recipe and all the market order", "I love the way...the American be doing sandwich"). Although Baugh (1983:95) reports that elision of plural "-s" occurs less frequently than the elision of possessive "-s", I found no instances of zero possessives, perhaps because of the small number of possessives in my corpus.

Dominican American speech can variably include a number of phonological features that have traditionally been associated with AAVE, but which also occur in other American sociolects (Morgan 1994b). Perhaps the most categorical such feature of Dominican American phonology in Providence is the absence of /r/ in syllable- and word-final position. While this is considered by some to be a characteristic of AAVE, it is also a characteristic of urban, working-class varieties of English in the Northeastern United States (e.g. Labov 1966). In Providence it is the standard pronunciation even among many in the middle class. Many teachers in the public school system, for example, weaken or lose /r/ in word- and syllable-final position. Regardless of the source(s) of this feature of Dominican American speech, whether from AAVE or local sociolects, the effect of it is a pronunciation that is indistinguishable in its r-lessness from local African American speech.

There is some degree of weakening or occasional replacement of word-initial /ð/ with /d/, but not necessarily more than in other working-class communities, especially in immigrant enclaves. The replacement of word-final /θ/ with /f/ or /t/ can occur as attested by Wolfram (1974) and Zentella (1997) for Puerto Ricans in New York City, although this too occurs in working-class speech among White Americans. Some speakers pronounce the diphthong /ay/ in ways that approached /a/, as in "Ah" for "I", which is characteristic of AAVE and Southern White speech but not White Providence sociolects. I found some simplification of consonant clusters, e.g. "tha's" for "that's". I found no evidence of shift from /I/ to /æ/ before velars, i.e. from "thing" /θɪŋ/ to "thang" /θæŋ/, and no evidence of non-standard plurals

in words that had simplified consonant clusters, e.g. "tesses" for "tests" (cf. Zentella 1997:46).
There is considerable individual and situational variation in the use of these features. Speakers, for example, produce /d/ for "th-" (/ð/) in the same sentence as they produce /ð/. Speakers who delete the copula in one utterance do not necessarily delete it in the next utterance even though it occurs in the same syntactic environment. No speaker who deletes the copula or replaces word-final /θ/ with /t/ does so categorically, and all speakers vary in their use of non-standard forms, including those associated with AAVE. Not surprisingly, those Dominicans who were born in the United States and have had more intimate relationships with African American peers display more evidence of AAVE phonological features than others. Although pronunciation alone would not define many Dominican American high school students in Providence as speakers of AAVE, in combination with AAVE syntactic features and lexical items and expressions, it leads others to identify their speech as African American.

3.5 Spanish-English Language Contact Phenomena

The bilingual background of Dominican Americans in this study is evident not only in code switching, which will be addressed below in Chapter 3.7 and Chapter 4, but in the forms and meanings of both their English and Spanish. The influence of Spanish on English can result from bilingualism of the individual speaker and/or from acquisition of a variety of English that was historically affected by such bilingualism and then passed on (Wolfram 1974, Zentella 1997). The Dominicans in the present study all spoke Spanish as a first language, and all were raised in contact with Hispanic Americans who had been in the country for generations, so both types of effect may be relevant.

3.5.1 Phonology

The most salient effect of Spanish language background on Dominican American English in Providence is in pronunciation. This is particularly evident in the pronunciation of individuals who spent more of their early years in the Dominican Republic and who participate more actively in social networks with monolingual adults and recently arrived immigrants. Even those who were born in America, however, display evidence of contact between English and Spanish in their pronunciation. This effect on English phonology is most widespread at the level of syllable stress. Distinctive stress patterns are evident in the speech even of those individuals who judge themselves--and are judged by their peers--as having little or no "Spanish accent."

American English is a stress-timed language in which the pronunciation of stressed syllables diverges dramatically from that of unstressed syllables. Stressed syllables are spoken at relatively high pitch, are held longer, and are pronounced more clearly than unstressed syllables (Gilbert 1993). In discourse, the stress of a syllable depends not just on word-stress patterns but also on the grammatical function of the word of which it forms a part. Thus, "content words" such as nouns, adjectives, adverbs and main verbs are stressed while such words as articles, pronouns, conjunctions, helping verbs, and prepositions are unstressed. What sets American English apart from Spanish is not the intensity of stressed syllables, but rather the brevity, lower pitch, and lack of clarity (e.g. vowels become schwas) of *unstressed* syllables. In spoken American English, utterances are dominated by the stressed syllables and remaining syllables are pronounced relatively quickly and indistinctly.

Spanish, in contrast, is a syllable-timed language, in which all syllables tend toward equal length (Anisman 1975). Differences between stressed and unstressed syllables (i.e. differences in pitch, length, and vowel clarity) are not so great as in English. When this stress-pattern is applied to English, syllables that would be spoken quickly and indistinctly by most native speakers of American English receive a relatively long, high pitched, and clear pronunciation. Vowels in such syllables are not reduced to identical schwas, but rather are fully articulated.

3.5.2 Lexical Transference, Modeling, and Syntactic Transference

In addition to code switching and using unassimilated loanwords, Dominican Americans assimilate vocabulary from English to Spanish phonology and morphology. In the following example, Alejandro adds the Spanish verbal affix "-ear" to the local English word for skipping class--to "bunk"--and assimilates the /ʌ/ of the English /bʌnk/ to the /o/ of the Spanish /bonk-/.

7)
[(LD #3 8:45) Several students, including "G", with whom Alejandro
has been speaking in Spanish are preparing to leave the building where
their class is about to begin.]
Alej.:   *Para donde Ustedes van?* ['Where are you guys going?']
?:   ( )
Alej.:   *Yo no puedo bunkear hoy.* ['I can't bunk today.']
G: *El tipo lo está grabando.* ['The guy is recording him.']

Sometimes the assimilation is only partial, as in the following use of
tickets:

8)
[(LD #1 11:47) Alejandro and his friend Jonathan are trying to sell
tickets in the hallway to a school sponsored roller skating party that
evening.]
Alej.:   I'm selling the tickets, four dollars.
Jonath.:   You gonna come here for the bus?
G: How? *Y no los podemos comprar ahorita los tickets?* ['And
           can't we buy the tickets later?']
Alejan.:   *Son cincuente gente, cogen la guagua.* ['There are 50 people,
           they're taking a bus.']
Jonath.:   You gotta get here first.
G: *Alejandro, Alejandro, ven acá. Dame los tickets, yo te los
           pago cuando venga.*
           ['Alejandro, Alejandro, come here. Give me the tickets, I'll
           pay you for them when I come']

The use of *tickets* is phonologically assimilated except for its plural
formation: nouns ending in consonants add "-es" for plurals in Spanish
rather than just "-s." This irregular plural ending can occur in words
that have entered Spanish from other languages, e.g. *complots* ['plots'],
although these words may also exist in a more assimilated form, e.g.
complós.

The single recorded instance of a Spanish word being assimilated
to English morphology and phonology was "platanation" /plætəneʃʌn/.

9)
[(GR #1 10:31:29) Maria encounters two friends, R and G, between classes and decides to accompany one to class.]
Maria: Yeah, I'll go with you. He's gonna come with me. ((indicating researcher))
R: (Oh   )
Maria: *(Porque) me está grabando.*
R: Why?
G: For what?
Maria: *Una cosa que está- está-* he's like- um- (→BB) How you say that? *He's- está- estudiando todos los dominicanos* ['A thing that he's- he's....he's studying all the Dominicans.']
G: Oh, Dominica:ns! We know (   ) ((indicating herself, G., and R. with her hand))
Maria: Platana:tion! ((laughter))
(1.0)
Maria: (→gym teacher) Bye Mr. Goldman.

Platanos ['plantains'] are used by many Dominican Americans as a metonym for Dominicans, and "platanation" is used here by Maria to refer to "Dominican-ness" or Dominican phenomena. Maria and her interlocutors treat this usage as humorous, a one-word joke that closes immediate discussion of the researcher's presence. This suggests that "platanation" is a nonce borrowing, without the level of social and discourse integration typical of established loanwords (Poplack 1988; Poplack, Sankoff, and Miller 1988).

In these examples of lexical transference, forms from English or Spanish are transferred and assimilated to the other code. In *modeling* (Weinreich 1953), in contrast, it is not linguistic forms that are transferred from one language to the other, but rather *meanings*. Otheguy, García, and Fernandez (1989) use the term *calque* to describe words that fit the morphological, syntactic, and phonological rules of one code, but derive their meaning from a form that bears some similarity in a distinct code.[18] Thus the Spanish word   *parientes* ['relatives'] may be used by bilinguals in the U.S. to refer to parents, which is similar in form (and also meaning) to the Spanish *parientes*.

Otheguy et al. (1989) and Silva-Corvalán (1994, Ch. 6) provide taxonomies of various kinds of calques. The meanings of some calques, for example, migrate between words that are similar both semantically and phonologically, as in the following use of the word "gain" by Wilson modeled on Spanish *ganar*:

10)
[(WR #2 ca. 11:50) The teacher ("Teach.") and students have been discussing fund raising activities and the value of prizes they could award in a basketball shooting competition.]
Teach.: I would like to talk to him also about the cash prize. And keep in mind that the whole- the whole thrust of this thing is to uh- to-
Wilson: gain money
Teach.: to make money. Is to- you know, make a few dollars...

While "gain money" is very similar in meaning to "make money" it is a marked form. The teacher had previously used the words "make money" at least two times in emphasizing that the value of the prizes awarded could not exceed the income from the event, and he uses the word "make" two more times immediately after Wilson says "gain." In Spanish, in contrast, the unmarked translation for "make money" is *ganar dinero*.

Otheguy et al. (1989:45-6) differentiate between "duplicating-message" and "innovating-message" calque words. In the above example, Wilson's use of "gain money" duplicates an existing form without any novel reference. In the following examples of the calque-word "indian", the referent of the English term is novel, drawing on a Dominican frame of reference:

11)
[(JS #2 12:05:08) Janelle is describing the student with whom she has been assigned a summer job.]
Janelle: I'm gonna work with that girl Monique, I don't know, she looks black or indian or something, she has like light (touching arm)
Isabella: I'm by myself again.....

Janelle subsequently describes Monique as having "nice hair" (i.e. not too kinky), "light-skin" (i.e. not white but lighter than other African-descent individuals) and added "but she's not Spanish." Janelle is using the term "indian" to describe a phenotype. It is not that Monique is a

Native American or from India, but rather she appears *indio* ['indian-colored']. *Indio* is used in the Dominican Republic to describe the phenotypes of individuals who are of African and European descent, and it is the category into which at least three-quarters of Dominicans classify themselves[19] (See Chapter 5 for a description of Dominican phenotype categories). In this case, an innovative calque-word is used to characterize a phenotype for which English lacks terms.

Modeling can extend beyond individuals words to idiomatic phrases, which Otheguy and García (1988) call phrasal calques and Silva-Corvalán (1994:174) calls "lexico-syntactic calques." While individual calque words generally involve the migration of meaning from one language into a pre-existing form in another, phrasal calques can involve the transfer of the shape of an utterance. In the following example, Dominican American Ana twice uses the expression *qué hora tú tienes?* [lit. 'what time you have'] modeled on the English expression ("What time do you have?"), rather than the dominant Spanish *qué hora es?* ['What time is it?']:

12)
[(IN #1 9:30) Isabella and Dominican American Ana are seated next to each other in class.]
Ana: *Mira, qué hora tú tienes?* ['Hey, what time do you have?']
Isabella: *Eh?*   ['Huh?']
Ana: *Qué hora tú tienes?*   [What time do you have?']
Isabella: I'll have to check my beeper

In the next segment, this same Dominican American student Ana models an initial request for information on an English expression although she is using Spanish code. She says *"como tú haces-"*--modeled on 'how do you do-'--rather than using the dominant Spanish impersonal *se* in a structure such as *"como se hace-."*

13)
[(IN#1 9:00:39) Ana asks Isabella's help with keyboard commands in her word-processing class.]
Ana: *Isabella, cómo tú haces* outline, I mean to underline stuff.
            ['Isabella, how do you do...']
Isabella: Control 'u'.

The widespread loss of impersonal *se* among mainland-raised Puerto Ricans has been documented by Morales (1995).

Dominican Americans also model expressions in English on Spanish ones. In the following segment, Maria repeatedly proclaims "I got you" to Alejandro when he fails to buy her a soda when she requests that he get her one.

14)
(GR #1 10:47:24)
Maria: *Alejandro, cómprame a mí una soda.* ['Alejandro, buy me a soda.']
Alejan.:   Huh?
Maria: *Cómprame una soda.* ['Buy me a soda.']
Alejan: (bus)=
Maria: =No, okay, I got you, I got you. I got you.

In Dominican Spanish *Te agarro*, ['I got you'] is used to communicate the idea "You've let me down and now you owe me one." This meaning is supported in this case by the manner of Maria's response to Alejandro. She appears prepared for Alejandro to turn her down: she latches her "no" as if she had expected it and then suggests that she is accepting the state of affairs ("okay"). However, she then immediately declares Alejandro's obligation to her ("I got you."). In this case, an utterance that is in English--phonologically, syntactically, and lexically--is invoking a Dominican interpretive framework and a Dominican cultural meaning that is distinct from the meanings commonly attributed to the English "I got you" (cf. Duranti and Ochs 1997 on relationships between codes and cultural frameworks).

Other calques, in contrast, result in novel, non-standard forms but carry meanings that are transparent. In the following example, Isabella asks an African American classmate "You like, you like?" ['Do you like it, do you like it?'] as she holds out her hand for her classmate to smell her scented hand lotion.

15)
(IN #1 11:09:09)
Aisha: What's that smell?
Isabella: It's my lotion, pear. **You like, you like?**

This novel structure is a result of opposing syntactic-semantic relationships between *gustar* ['to please'] and "like". In Spanish, the subject of *gustar* has the semantic role of "theme" or "patient" while the indirect object has the semantic role of "experiencer." In English, in contrast, the subject of the verb "like" is the "experiencer" (marked with an "i") while the "theme" or "patient" (marked with a "q") is a direct object (Silva-Corvalán 1994:180)[20]:

Te$_i$ gusta (el$_q$)?   ['Do you like it?']
IO$_i$ S$_q$

You$_i$ like it$_q$?
S$_i$ DOq

The syntactic constituents in these English and Spanish constructions are often thus the reverse of each other, while the ordering of semantic elements is often identical. Isabella maintains the word order and semantic content and roles of the two Spanish words, but the syntax is partially accommodated to English. In the Spanish *Te gusta?*, the subject/patient is understood as "it", as in "(It) pleases you, whereas in Isabella's English version, the object is understood as "it", as in "You like (it)." This transformation results in an expression that has a marked form but a clear meaning. Isabella's use of a novel form is evidence not of an inability to use dominant standard forms--Isabella uses the constructions "You like it?" and "Do you like it?" during the previous hour on this tape--but of an expanded repertoire of linguistic resources including Spanish-English syncretic forms.

3.5.3 Syntactic Transference

Although Spanish and English are very similar syntactically, the effects of Spanish syntax on English usage are evident in some constructions. In the following sentence, for example, the subject of the relative clause, "that", is duplicated by the immediately following pronoun "he", a construction that regularly occurs in Spanish but not English:

16)

[(LD #1 11:13:50) Alejandro and JC are discussing the fact that Alejandro had passed a ball to JC, a close friend, during a gym class game, but JC had then turned and struck an unsuspecting Alejandro with it.]
JC: (→Alejandro) Last time I wanted to fuck you up, this time I slipped.
Alejan: Naa, that's fucked up, yo. (→classmates) I passed him$_i$ the ball so he$_i$ could hit some kid$_j$ that$_j$ he$_j$ was bugging all the time, and he$_i$ threw it at me

"Bugging" in this case is an intransitive verb meaning to "act crazy." The student (marked with a 'j') who has been acting crazy is the one that Alejandro wanted JC (marked with an 'i') to hit with a ball. Because most varieties of English do not duplicate the subject of the relative clause with an immediately following pronoun, the sentence as spoken could suggest that the "he" in the phrase "some kid that he" referred to an individual distinct from the one referred to by "kid" and "that", changing the meaning of the sentence. The dominant American English version of this utterance would not contain the "he" following the "that".

Tense forms in Dominican American English that diverge from dominant American varieties of English can also match Dominican Spanish tense forms, especially in contexts in which English uses present perfect tense to describe activities/states that began in the past and have continued to the present. Thus, Dominican American utterances such as "I have a long time I don't write letters" (Alejandro), and "I have fever since yesterday" (Janelle) transfer Dominican tense patterns to utterances that otherwise follow English syntactic rules, e.g.:

17)
Tengo   mucho tiempo que   no   escribo   cartas.
Have-1ST   much time   that NEG   write-1ST   letters.
['I haven't written letters for a long time.']

The influence of Spanish on English syntax extends to speakers who were born in America, never lived in the Dominican Republic, and view themselves as weak Spanish speakers. Janelle, for example, uses

the following utterance to comment on the barking dogs around her
friend's backyard:

18) (JS #DV 39:16)
"Here are mad dogs" ['There are a lot of dogs here']

This form does not occur in most varieties of English, but it maps
word-for-word with the standard form of the corresponding Spanish
utterance *Aquí hay/están muchos perros*. Janelle exploits the flexibility
of word order inherent in Spanish--while speaking English--to highlight
a characteristic of the particular location that her "here" indexes. In this
case it was not the sheer number of dogs that was so noteworthy, but
the way in which her vantage point was surrounded by yards with
barking dogs.

3.6 Multiply Determined/Convergent Features

A number of syntactic and phonological features of Dominican
American English in Providence may be multiply determined, or
convergent. By convergent I mean that certain forms are selected by
Dominican American speakers over others because they represent areas
of structural/formal overlap between language varieties (Beniak,
Mougeon, and Valois 1984-5). The non-inverted word order in
questions with subject pronouns--"What you want, the sports page?" or
"Where you bought that?"--occurs in both Caribbean Spanish and in
AAVE, for example. Dominican American use of this pattern in
English may be a function of transferring the Spanish pattern, following
local AAVE patterns, or both. Multiple negations, which are very
common in Dominican American speech, may also be multiply
determined: they are common to Spanish, AAVE, and various other
sociolects of American English. I documented double negatives ("I
don't have that class no more") and triple negatives ("We wasn't doing
nothing to nobody") but none of the negative inversions (Labov
1972a:60) attributed to AAVE (e.g. "Ain't nobody going to win.").
     The Dominican American use of "yous" as a second-person plural
form (Isabella: "Where's yous guys going to be at, so I can meet yous
guys", "What's up with yous today?") also corresponds to an overlap
between local working class sociolects and Spanish. "Yous" is used by

working class African Americans and Whites in Providence, but its form and function also correspond to the Dominican second-person plural *Ustedes*.

Several notable phonological features of Dominican American English may also be multiply determined. The r-less pronunciation of Dominican Americans in Providence is shared with AAVE, but also many sociolects in Providence. The variable absence or replacement of voiced and unvoiced interdental fricatives (the "th-" in "this" /ð/ and "thing" /θ/, respectively) can occur in AAVE but also in other sociolects, especially in speech communities that include non-native speakers. Word-final consonant-cluster simplification, which occurs in AAVE (Labov 1972a), is also characteristic of Spanish-influenced English, as Spanish has few such clusters (Zentella 1997:47).

3.7 Dominican American Code Switching

Code switching, like any form of language use, is meaningful at many levels and can be analyzed from a variety of perspectives.[21] Approaches to code switching have generally focused on its: 1) syntax, 2) discourse/conversation management functions, and/or 3) more global social functions. Although syntactic analysis of code switching is typically presented discretely from more social analyses, conversational/discourse management functions are not always differentiated from more metaphorical socio-political functions.[22]

In the remainder of this chapter, I first review and critique syntactic and discourse approaches to code switching, and then examine code switching in several segments of Dominican American interaction from a conversation analytic perspective. In the next chapter, I examine examples of Dominican American code switching from a more global social perspective, after first sketching aspects of Dominican Americans' socio-political position. The broader metaphorical meanings of code switching that I present in Chapter 4 cannot be explained without first describing Dominican Americans' local linguistic ideologies, intergroup relations, and historical and political economic position (e.g. Gal 1988).

3.7.1 Syntax of Code Switching

Many studies on the syntax of Spanish-English code switching have focused on the grammaticality of such speech (e.g. McClure 1977; Poplack 1982; Sankoff and Poplack 1981; Lipski 1985), countering the notion that code switching represents an unsystematic, degenerate form of language. Classification of switches in such studies are based on syntactic criteria, yielding such categories as "tag-switching," "intersentential switching," and "intra-sentential switching" (Poplack 1982). Such studies also address linguistic/grammatical constraints on code switching (e.g. Pfaff 1979, Clyne 1987). Sankoff and Poplack (1981), for example, postulate two rules to account for the position of code switches between Spanish and English: 1) the "equivalence constraint" and 2) the "free-morpheme" constraint. The equivalence constraint posits that the syntax on either side of a code switch must be grammatical for the language used, i.e. that switches can only occur where surface structures of the two languages map onto each other. Where Spanish and English differ syntactically, e.g. in the position of most adjectives with respect to the nouns they modify, there are inappropriate sites for code switching, e.g. "*la casa* red" or "*the house *rojo*." The "free-morpheme constraint" predicts that a switch will not occur between a bound morpheme and a lexical form unless the lexical form has been phonologically assimilated to the language of the morpheme. Thus *flipeando* ['flipping'] can occur but not *catcheando*. A common thread of syntactic approaches to code switching is that they address the syntactic sites where code switching *can* occur, but they generally do not address *why* a code switch might occur to begin with, or the discursive and social functions that such code switching may serve.

3.7.2 Pragmatic Approaches to Code Switching

What have been referred to as pragmatic (e.g. Romaine 1995) approaches to code switching, in contrast, have focused on overlapping social and discursive functions of code switching. A widely discussed bipartite social categorization of code switches is Blom and Gumperz's (1972) *situational* code switching vs. *metaphorical* code switching. *Situational* switching involves a direct relationship between code use and observable factors of the situation:

Distinct varieties are employed in certain settings (such as home, school, work) that are associated with separate, bounded kinds of activities (public speaking, formal negotiation, special ceremonials, verbal games, etc.) or spoken with different categories of speakers (friends, family members, strangers, social inferiors, government officials, etc.). (Gumperz 1982:60)

Such situational code switches occur in response to changes in the situation--what Zentella (1997:82) refers to as "on the spot observables"--such as the approach of an individual who does not understand the language being spoken, This pattern of code switching is characteristic of diglossia (Ferguson 1959) and the compartmentalization of codes by social domains (Fishman et al. 1971).

Blom and Gumperz's (1972:425) *metaphorical* code switching is defined precisely by the violation of expected code-situation relationships, i.e. code switches that occur without any observable change in the physical situation:

The context in which one of a set of alternates [codes] is regularly used becomes part of its meaning, so that when this form is then employed in a context where it is not normal, it brings in some of the flavor of this original setting.

Thus, switching from a variety that is associated with formal relationships and roles to one that is associated with more intimate and informal relationships, for example, "may, depending on the circumstances, add a special social meaning of confidentiality or privateness to the conversation" (1972:425). Blom and Gumperz (1972:425-6) give the example of a customer and clerk switching from a more formal language variety used in their business transaction to a less formal variety for subsequent, more personal talk. In such metaphorical switching, then, changes in language effect changes in context and social roles, without apparent changes in the physical context.

3.7.3 Conversational Strategies in Code Switching

In later work, Gumperz (1982) uses the term "conversational switching" in place of the term "metaphorical" switching. The assumption that non-situational switching is metaphorical relies on a diglossic notion of 'we' vs. 'they' codes which is only present in situations where codes are compartmentalized (e.g. Kroskrity 1993), and it fails to explicitly define the link(s) between code choice and social meaning. Blom and Gumperz (1972:425), for example, rely on a vague metaphor to describe this code-meaning link: a switch to a variety associated with informal interactions "brings in some of the flavor of this original setting."

In Gumperz's (1982) conversational switching, in contrast, the emphasis is on the role of code switches in managing discourse. Thus in addition to whatever social/metaphorical meanings such switches may carry, they are used as contextualization cues (Gumperz 1982, 1992) to mark, for example, a particular sequence of speech as a quotation or to emphasize or qualify a message.[23]

According to Gumperz (1982:98), code switching is a metadiscursive activity that "signals contextual information equivalent to what in monolingual settings is conveyed through prosody or other syntactic or lexical processes." This approach locates the study of code switching among studies which examine the multiple means and activities through which talk continuously comments on itself and itself provides context for its interpretation (Duranti and Goodwin 1992). Approaches to such metadiscursive behavior have included work by Bateson (1972), Goffman (1974), and Hymes (1974) on frames and keys, Goffman (1981) on footing, and work in ethnomethodology (Garfinkel 1967, Heritage 1984b) and conversation analysis (e.g. Schenkein 1978, Psathas 1979) that emphasize what Heritage (1984b:242) calls the "doubly contextual" nature of talk.

Gumperz (1982) enumerates six specific functions of conversational code switching: 1) quotation, 2) addressee specification, 3) interjection, 4) reiteration, 5) message qualification, and 6) personalization vs. objectivization. Some of these categories/functions, e.g. quotations and reiterations, are relatively directly derived from surface features of language, while others, e.g. "personalization vs. objectivization", are more metaphorical. Zentella (1997) describes 21 categories[24] for conversational code switches in her data, closely linking categories to surface constituents and conversational management activities, and avoiding more metaphorical categories. A number of Zentella's subtypes could fit under Gumperz's more general categories, e.g. her "aggravating requests," "mitigating requests," "appositions/apposition brackets," and "accounting for requests" could all be classified under Gumperz's "message qualification." The five types of switches that occur most frequently, accounting for the majority of Zentella's assigned switches, overlap significantly with those of Gumperz: 1) topic shift, 2) quotation (both direct and indirect) (Gumperz's "quotation"), 3) translation (Gumperz's "reiteration"), 4) apposition/apposition bracket (Gumperz's "message qualification"), and 5) accounting for requests (Gumperz's "message qualification" and/or "personalization vs. objectivization").

What nearly all of these categories have in common is that they describe shifts in topic, activity, and/or perspective. Implicit in many of these categories is a notion of speech as action (Austin 1962, Searle 1969), i.e. that language is not just a system of reference but also simultaneously a mode of action at various levels. The shift in codes is a signal that there may be a concurrent shift in speech activity. The direction of the shift is not necessarily the important dimension, but rather the change itself.

3.7.4 Problems with Functional Taxonomies of Conversational Code Switching

The code switches that I recorded among Dominican Americans in Providence could easily be classified under the functional strategies described by Gumperz (1982), Appel and Muysken (1987)[25], Zentella (1997), or other researchers. The ease with which such categories can be created--and discrepancies between the code switching taxonomies at which researchers have arrived--hint at the epistemological problems of such taxonomies. Classificatory schemes for types of code switches are problematic because there are *innumerable* functions that code switching can serve, many of them simultaneously, and any closed classificatory system of switches is inherently arbitrary to some degree in the number and kinds of categories that can be made. Functions of code switching can range from micro-interactional exigencies, e.g. attracting someone's attention, to more metaphorical issues, e.g. displaying to an interlocutor that one is not Haitian (see Chapter 6).

Even short stretches of speech by one interlocutor with one switch can suggest the multiple and simultaneous functions of code switches:

19)

[(IN #2 11:56:35) A Dominican American male, Woody, is walking toward the exit of a classroom when Isabella addresses him. (I present each of Isabella's utterances as a turn. Periods of silence between utterances are not long gaps but the brief absence of speech typical of inter-turn intervals.)]

Isabella: Where you going?
Isabella: Huh?
Isabella: *Eh /ˉe/?*   ['Huh?']
Isabella: Woody!

The nasal vowel and rising high pitch of *Eh?* mark this interjection as Dominican Spanish, which represents a code switch from the prior English. What is/are the function(s) of this code switch? Isabella appears to be trying to attract Woody's attention before he exits the classroom. In this case, the use of a Spanish paralinguistic utterance may function to attract Woody's attention after he does not respond to a Dominican English question ("Where you going?") and English interjection ("Huh?"). The *Eh?* more clearly identifies the intended recipient of the utterance than the prior English question and interjection, by singling out the Spanish speakers within earshot, particularly those who might respond to the characteristically Dominican *Eh?*. Isabella subsequently identifies the intended audience of her utterance even more narrowly by using the intended recipient's name, "Woody." This code switch involving just one word, *Eh?*, easily fits under multiple categories of Gumperz (1982) (e.g. "reiteration," "interjection," and "addressee specification").

In addition to being arbitrary in number and kind, decontextualized functional categories fail to attend to the interactional. nature of language and the constant, ongoing work that social actors do to achieve a degree of intersubjectivity. In the above example, it is Woody's lack of response to Isabella's initial question ('Where you going?') and interjection ('Huh?') that, in one sense, explains the code switch. It is not a pre-existing conversational strategy in Isabella's head that results in this switch, but the exigency of the local situation, i.e. that no second pair part "answer" has resulted from Isabella's first pair part "summons" (Schegloff 1972). Talk is locally and interactionally managed (e.g. Sacks, Schegloff, and Jefferson 1974), and even the contours of individual clauses are shaped by speaker-hearer interaction (Goodwin 1981) rather than just productive abilities of an individual speaker.

Two factors have worked against researcher's foregrounding the *interactive* nature of code switching: a) the sentence-based approach of much linguistic analysis (e.g. Bloomfield 1933, Chomsky 1965) with its assumption of an individual speaker-hearer, and b) the fact that most code switching data has been limited until recently to audio, rather than audio-*video* recordings. As shown by Goodwin (Goodwin 1981, Goodwin and Goodwin 1992), the interactive shaping of individual turns, for example, is frequently only evident with documentation of participants' gaze, head nods, bodily orientation, etc.

Many of Zentella's (1997) examples of code switches implicitly invoke the work of interlocutors, but this interactional work is not the basis of categorization. The following switch is categorized under the rubric "Future Referent Check and/or Bracket":

Le dió con irse para--you know Lucy?--*para la casa del papá de Lucy.*
['She up and decided to go to-...-to Lucy's father's house.'] (Zentella 1997:94)

In this example, the end of the bracketed activity--and subsequent switch back into Spanish--is likely coordinated with an activity from the interlocutor suggesting that he/she does, in fact, know Lucy. In many examples, the interactive nature of the initial switch is explicit but not the basis of categorization, e.g.:

(Categorized as "Aggravating Requests")
Ella tiene--Shut up. Lemme tell you. ['She has--...']
(Categorized as "Attention Attraction")
Este se está llenando, lookit, Ana.   ['This one is filling up,....']
(Zentella 1997:95)

In both of these cases, speaker's switches co-occur with explicit reference to another's behavior: the failure to listen appropriately in the first case and the failure to orient one's gaze/attention properly in the second case.

Bias toward the sentence as the unit of analysis masks the interactional nature of utterances. In analyzing the grammar of code switching, Zentella (1997:118) treats the following utterance, for example, as a "sentence" with a code switch at an adverbial phrase:

Ráscame allí, allí mismo, a little bit down. [('Scratch me there, right there...']

The itchy speaker, however, is clearly saying *allí mismo* and "a little bit down"--and thereby code switching--in response to the scratcher's behavior. From an interactional or conversation analytical perspective this utterance consists of at least five interactional moves, two of them by a participant who is made invisible in sentence-based accounts:

1) First Pair Part: Request: *Ráscame allí*   ['Scratch me there']
2) Second Pair Part: Acceptance and Enactment: Interlocutor scratches speaker on a spot, displaying candidate understanding of *allí* ['there'].
3) Speaker confirms candidate understanding of *allí* as the correct one: *allí mismo* ['right there']
4) Scratcher changes scratch site (and/or itch migrates).
5) Speaker other-initiates repair of scratching behavior: "a little bit down"

The linguistic orientation toward sentence-based syntax leads to a categorization of this switch based on syntactic constituents as if the three utterances were produced by a speaker in a vacuum. While these three successive utterances can be juxtaposed and presented as a single awkward "sentence", they are better understood as *turns* or *turn constructional units* in an interactional, sequential, locally managed context (Sacks, Schegloff, and Jefferson 1974), in which the code switch is an interactional phenomenon.

The lack of attention to code switching as an interactional phenomenon and the epistemological problems with analysts' functional categories of code switches lead Auer (1984a:11) to argue for a more ethnomethodological approach to code switching:

Participants apparently do not interpret code-switching or transfer by subsuming a given instance under one of a preestablished set of types; instead, they dispose of certain procedures for coming to a local (situated) interpretation where the exact meaning or function of language alternation is a result of both contextual information and these more general procedures.

Participants' interpretation of switches depends in part on understandings of discourse strategies that commonly occur in talk (similar in scope, perhaps, to analysts' functional taxonomies), but also on a variety of other contextual information and *local* co-occurrence expectations (Ervin-Tripp 1972).

3.7.5 Interactional Strategies in Dominican American Code Switching: Example 1

In the segments of Dominican American code switched interaction transcribed below, I attempt to highlight the locally negotiated and interactional nature of such switching. Presentation and analysis of switches in their sequential, interactional context serves as an antidote to the sentence-based syntax bias in listing decontextualized switches under category headings. Presenting actual segments of discourse also captures contact phenomena beyond code switching, e.g. loanwords and phonological transference, that characterize the language of Dominican Americans.

In my analyses of these segments, I emphasize the conversational management techniques, e.g. repair (Schegloff, Jefferson, and Sacks 1977), that occupy significant parts of the talk and have been backgrounded in many accounts of the discourse functions of code switching. Participants' noticeably attend to such conversational management activities, and many switches occur at the initiation and conclusion of such activities, suggesting that such analysis can contribute to our understandings of the "when" and "why" of Dominican American switching. In the following example, a switch into English occurs with the initiation of a repair sequence, and English is maintained until the end of the repair sequence, after which speakers switch back to Spanish.

20)

[(FU #1 12:06:13) Frangelica and Annie are sitting in physics class where they have been discussing in Spanish (without switches for many turns) the details of their respective eating habits. Translation is below the transcribed segment.]

Frang: *Yo como mucho.*
Ana: *Yo no quiero. Yo quiero estar bien para mi* prom.
Frang: *Ah, yo tambien. Las uñas- tengo que* //*tratarlas bien.*
Ana: //*Tú no tienes que ir con*
        senior, right, *no (es)*?
        (.5) ((Frangelica does lateral headshakes))
Ana: //(   )
Frang: //*Yo soy un* junior.
Ana: No-
Frang: <If you're a junior or a //senior- >= ((depresses fingers as she
        enumerates))
Ana: //Oh, okay
Frang: =you could go with anybody.
Ana: Alright
Frang: But if you're not- a sophomore or a freshman, you have to get
        yourself a junior or a senior.
Ana: I see.
        (4.0)
Ana: (   ) *te vas a ir* ?
Frang: Mm hmm.
Ana: *Para donde? Para comer? No, yo digo para comer- no yo digo
        para fuera* chillin'?
Frang: *Ah- para fuera*?

[Translation of segment 19]:
Frang: I eat a lot.
Ana: I don't want to. I want to look good for my prom.
Frang: Oh my, me too. My nails- I have to //take care of them]
Ana: //You have to go with a
        senior, right, don't you?
(.5) ((Frangelica does lateral headshakes))
Ana: //(   )
Frang: //I am a junior.

Ana: No-

....

(Translation of final five lines)
(4.0)
Ana: (   ) are you going?
Frang: Mm hmm.
Ana: Where to? To eat? No, I mean to eat- no, I mean outside
          chillin'?
Frang: Oh my- outside?

The first two contact phenomena in this segment are Annie's "prom" and "senior," both loanwords with a source in Annie and Frangelica's United States school experience. Annie then uses a tag switch (Poplack 1982) "right." Zentella (1997:94) terms such switches "checking," in which "the shift seeks the listeners' opinion or approval." In this case, Annie is doing something more interactionally concrete and specific than seeking an opinion or approval: she has offered a candidate understanding that she would like confirmed or rejected. Intersubjectivity in talk cannot be assumed by analysts because participants themselves do not assume it: they regularly display and continuously update intersubjective understandings (Heritage and Atkinson 1984), e.g. through displaying candidate understandings, self- or other-initiated repair (Schegloff, Jefferson, and Sacks 1977), displays of agreement or disagreement with assessments (Goodwin and Goodwin 1992), etc. Annie's code switch serves to bracket prior discourse from the activity of requesting confirmation of a candidate understanding. Annie then switches back to Spanish *no (es)?*, reiterating her request, in translation, for confirmation of her candidate understanding. Such reiterations can serve to emphasize or clarify a message (Gumperz 1982; Zentella 1997). In this case it is not propositional content that is the "message" that is emphasized, but a conversational activity: the request for confirmation of a displayed understanding.

As the first pair part of an adjacency pair, Annie's request makes an answer--specifically a confirmation or rejection of her candidate understanding--conditionally relevant (Schegloff 1972). Both Annie and Frangelica treat a response as conditionally relevant, although it is not obvious from Frangelica's initial response to the request ("*Yo soy un* junior") that she is oriented toward this conditional relevance.

Annie's *No-* is an other-initiation of repair (Schegloff, Jefferson, and Sacks 1977) directed at Frangelica's *"Yo soy un* junior." It is not directed at the truth value of Frangelica's statement but rather at its apparent failure to address the issue made relevant by Annie's code switched tag question(s).

Frangelica then switches into English, in a form of self-repair, to describe the rules for prom attendance. This switch coincides with the onset of slower tempo speech and gestures in which Frangelica uses the index finger of one hand to depress successive fingers on her other hand as she says "junior" and "senior," as if enumerating points in a logical argument. The switch into English, along with these prosodic and gestural features, coincides with initiation of a different discourse activity, a formal account of institutional rules. Discussion of school rules in the abstract (versus the more personal implications of such rules: *Tú no tienes que ir con* senior?) may favor English, but the switch itself may be the important issue, and the fact that it was to English simply a function of the prior speech being in Spanish.

Annie's overlapping backchannel response "Oh, okay" displays her changed understanding (Heritage 1984c) of the relevance of Frangelica's talk to the original tag-question. She displays this changed understanding after Frangelica begins "If you're a junior or", even before Frangelica is able to state the rules for who can go to the prom with whom. Frangelica's switch to English, in conjunction with co-occurring contextualization cues, may function as a particularly powerful framing device to repair a misunderstanding, even before the relevant referential content is uttered. Annie's subsequent questions about lunch-time plans, following a long gap, are in Spanish. The use of Spanish coincides both with a change in topic and a change in conversational activity. English had been used by Frangelica to repair difficulties resulting from her initial response to Annie's tag-request, and those problems have now been resolved. Even when speaking Spanish, however, Annie and Frangelica use lexical transfers, as in the first part of this segment, and Annie suggests that they go *"para fuera* chillin'" ['hanging out']. Frangelica does not treat the inflection of "chillin'" as unusual or marked, and consultants did not flag this form, although they agreed, when specifically questioned, that they would probably say *para chilear* ['in order to chill'] or "to/and chill."

3.7.6 Interactional Strategies in Dominican American Code Switching:
Example 2

In the following segment of transcript, switches again coincide with
conversational management activities, and code choice can be predicted
in part by the code used in prior sequence initiating activities.

21)
[(FU #1 12:08:39 This segment occurs two minutes after the one
transcribed above. Annie and Frangelica have been taking part in
various conversations in Spanish and English with Hispanic, Haitian,
and Asian American classmates. Both are gazing at another classmate
when Frangelica suddenly turns to Annie:]
Frang.: Oh *cómo está yendo tu trabajo?* ['Oh, how is your work
         going?']
Ana: ([Spanish language?]   )
Frang.: *Ay dios mío! Todavía?*   ['Oh my God! Still?']
Ana: <*Todavía.*> I want money for (the) prom. ((mock anguish))
Frang.: *Ay, el* prom *es (en/in)* May. ['Oh my, the prom is in May.']
Ana: I want <money.> >°Yeah.< *Yo creo que empezamos al final de
         este mes* ['I think we're going to start at the end of this
         month.']
Frang.: Mm hmm
Ana: I think I'm gonna save like three checks, to buy my- to buy
         //my shit.
Frang.: //*Ay, pero* three checks, *si tú trabajas bien, son* //(   ) ['Oh
         my, but...if you work properly, that's..']
Ana: //*Ciento pico.*
         ['One hundred something']
Frang.: ((nods))
Ana: *Por eso,* yeah. ['That's why,...']
Ana: I think I'm gonna- I'm gonna save like three checks to buy my
         shit for the prom.
Frang.: Mm.
Frang.: *Bueno.* ['okay']
Ana: I don't know if I'm going anyway, you know what I'm
         saying?
Frang.: Mm.

Ana: Cause like I want to go with somebody, like a date, (like) I
         don't want to go alone and stuff, so I don't know.
         (6.0)
Frang.: *Si tú vas con Victor, te paga la entrada* ['If you go with
         Victor, he'll pay for your ticket']
Ana: I need a date ((laughing))
         (3.0)
Frang.: *Él tiene un raid.* ['He has access to transportation.']
         (10.0) ((Annie next addresses another classmate in English.)

         Accounts of code switching generally focus on the *occurrence* of
switches, rather than on the *absence* of switches. A focus on the
occurrence of switches makes sense in bilingual contexts in which
codes are compartmentalized and switching is an infrequent, marked
activity with obvious sociopolitical implications. In situations in which
switching is argued to be an unmarked discourse mode in its own right
(e.g. Poplack 1982, Zentella 1997; see Chapter 4), the absence of
switches can serve as a resource for analysis just as their occurrence
can.
         In this sequence the location of Annie's switch in her second turn
("*Todavía.* I want money...") is analytically meaningful in part because
of where it does *not* occur. Frangelica completed her prior turn by
proffering a candidate understanding of Annie's work situation in
Spanish (*Todavía?*). In this instance Annie's *not* switching to confirm
Frangelica's candidate understanding *Todavía?*--a second pair part--
helps to both display her precise understanding of Frangelica's
confirmation request and unambiguously confirm it. Her subsequent
utterance in the same turn is in English ("I want money for the prom").
This code switched utterance initiates a new sequence and does not
need to be so exquisitely tailored to display understanding of the prior
turn and relevance to it. Auer (1995, 1998b) finds that not all sequential
junctures are equally likely to contain a switch, e.g. second parts of
adjacency pairs (Schegloff and Sacks 1973) are less likely to be
switched than turns that initiate sequences, suggesting a distribution of
switching that can be described in relationship to specific
conversational sequences. Code switching may have a sequential
preference organization, as do other conversational activities (Levinson
1983:307).

Frangelica responds to Annie's mention of the prom in a base, or matrix, language (based on the determiner, verb, and, consequently, verb inflection (Romaine 1995:145)) of Spanish with two English lexical transfers. Although this utterance occurs in a sequence that was initiated in English, it is not directly made relevant by Annie's statement in the way that first pair parts (e.g. requests) make second pair parts (e.g. acceptance/rejection) conditionally relevant, so the switch is not occurring as a direct and obligatory response to the prior turn.

Annie continues speaking in English, repeating her plaint "I want money." Such reiteration suggests that Frangelica's turn did not address Annie's original "I want money for the prom" in a way that would encourage further development of a specific "talking about needing money for the prom" sequence. This reiteration serves as a form of repair to re-establish such a sequence. This repetition, however, does not address the surprise/distress that Frangelica displays in her turn at the rapid approach the upcoming prom. Annie subsequently acknowledges Frangelica's turn with "Yeah," bracketing it as a distinct discursive activity with prosodic marking, i.e. a lower volume and accelerated tempo.

Annie switches to Spanish, in the same turn, to say when she thinks she will start working. This utterance links topically to her need for money, but it also serves as a response to Frangelica's exclamation regarding the rapidly approaching prom date. The use of Spanish may be favored as a response to Frangelica's Spanish utterance, and it may more effectively link her utterance to the initial two turns of this segment which were in Spanish and about Annie's work.

Annie switches back to English to discuss her specific plans for allocation of paychecks for the prom. Although this is a "switch" of code from the last words of her prior turn, it is arguably the maintenance of the code in which she chose to initiate talk--and will maintain throughout this segment--about money for the prom. Annie has twice stated that she wants money for the prom, but Frangelica has not asked her specifics about her money needs that would enable to discuss the allocation of checks as a response to a question. Frangelica interrupts her in Spanish to suggest that three checks might not be the appropriate number to save. Because this turn represents the initiation of a new sequence--an other-initiated repair--the switch is unmarked by Auer's preference organization for code switching. In terms of the preference organization of repair more generally, however, any form of other-initiation is less preferred than self-initiation (Schegloff, Jefferson, and Sacks 1977), and the switch to Spanish may draw attention to the point of contention that Frangelica is making in questioning the number of checks needed to cover prom costs.

Despite speaking Spanish, Frangelica uses the English lexical transfers "three checks," duplicating the phrase from Annie's prior turn. Approaches to code switching and transfer that rely on isolated utterances and treat switches as a function of a) speaker language fluency, b) domains of language usage, and/or c) conversational strategies that are "in the speaker's head" account for this type of switch/transfer poorly. Such taxonomies suffer from their failure to consider adequately the sequential implicativeness of language choice in conversation. Whatever language a participant chooses for the organization of his/her turn, or for an utterance which is part of the turn, exerts an influence on subsequent language choices by the same or other speakers. (Auer 1984a:5)

Zentella (1997) takes into account sequential implicativeness of language use in classifying one particular type of switch, "parallelism," in which a speaker copies a prior speaker's switch:

A: You sleep with *los ojos abiertos*? ['your eyes open?']
B: So, people die with *ojos abiertos*! ['eyes open'] (Zentella 1997:97)

Although Zentella recognizes the significance of sequential context in isolating and labeling this type of switch, she classifies it as a form of "Crutch-like Code Switching," grouping it with switches in which a speaker does not know or momentarily can't remember a particular word. Such switches that produce parallel forms are not necessarily evidence of compensating for a weakness, as might be understood from the term "crutching," but rather can represent a sophisticated means of maintaining conversational coherence and intersubjectivity. Building one's response to another's turn around identical forms (not just the same referents) displays unequivocally that one has heard the prior turn and helps display that one is talking about the same thing(s) as the other.

Such parallelism occurs in several interactions in my data:

22)
(JS #2 11:12:40)
Jose: *Es que a tí te duele todo,* man. ['It's just that everything hurts you...']
Janelle: *Es que* I'm telling you I'm fragile. ['It's just that I'm telling you....']

In this case Janelle uses *Es que* to introduce her claim that she is fragile. This *Es que* has little propositional content, but it displays her attendance to Jose's turn and allows her to use his precise words to counter his criticism of her.

In the following example, parallelism helps Jose to display his understanding of Janelle's turn and the coherence of his turn with hers.

23)
(JS #2 10:55:23)
Janelle: *Tengo sueño.* ['I'm sleepy.']
Jose: You always got *sueño.* ['You're always sleepy.']

Jose switches or transfers for *sueño*. In this case, the use of *sueño* not only displays understanding of the prior utterance, it saves Jose from a problematic English structure. Jose begins an English phrasal calque of *Tienes siempre sueño*, which parallels the structure used by Janelle, but which can only be completed awkwardly in English: *"You always got sleepiness." Intrasentential switching is frequent in talk between Janelle and Jose, so this code switch may be less marked than, and therefore preferable to, an utterance awkwardly completed in English.

In the above transcript, Frangelica's use of the English "three checks" in a turn that is otherwise in Spanish serves to connect her initiation of repair to Annie's prior English turn. Annie switches (from her prior English turn) to Spanish to complete the repair that Frangelica has initiated in Spanish. Frangelica's repair initiation turn employs a *compound turn constructional unit* (Lerner 1991, 1996) with an "if" component (*si tú trabajas...*) that projects the final shape of her turn. Spanish is the code that Frangelica has used to initiate this conversational activity, and Annie maintains its use to complete Frangelica's utterance semantically, syntactically and in the same code, displaying precise understanding of Frangelica's turn even as it develops. Among bilinguals, there may be a preference for same code use in collaborative turn completion, just as there is a preference for second pair parts to match the code of first pair parts.

Frangelica displays agreement with the monetary figure given by Annie by nodding. Annie continues in Spanish, *Por eso*, treating her prior turn as an explanation as to why "three checks" were an appropriate number to save for the prom. Her subsequent "yeah" displays Annie's acknowledgement of Frangelica's nod of agreement with Annie's explanation, suggesting that they now share a common understanding. Annie then continues in English, repeating virtually word-for-word her pre-repair sequence utterance, that she thinks she's going to save three checks to buy her things for the prom. Use of English serves to set this utterance off from the repair sequence, and it may more effectively orient Frangelica back to the activity that Annie previously initiated in English but to which Frangelica responded only by initiating repair. Frangelica gives only noncommittal responses ("Mm" and *Bueno*) to Annie's subsequent talk in English of the problems she faces in going to the prom: money and the need for a date.

After the repair sequence (effected in Spanish following Frangelica's initiation of it in Spanish), this interaction develops a pattern of non-reciprocal language use (Gal 1979), Annie speaking in English and Frangelica in Spanish. Zentella (1997) suggests that such non-reciprocal conversation can index more formal or distancing discourse in some situations among bilinguals. In this case, non-reciprocal talk coincides with Frangelica displaying little enthusiasm for Annie's concerns about the upcoming prom (whether she's going, whom she's going with), and Annie treating Frangelica's suggestion of Victor as inappropriate. After a six second gap, Frangelica suggests in Spanish that Annie could go to the prom with Victor. She does not define him as a "date," which is what Annie has been talking about, but rather as someone who would pay for her ticket. Annie responds in English that she needs "a date" and laughs, implicitly treating Victor as an inappropriate partner for the prom, whether date or not. After a gap of three seconds, Frangelica volunteers in Spanish that Victor has access to transportation (of some significance on prom night), but Annie does not respond. Frangelica takes the stance that Victor is someone who can minimally pay for Annie's ticket and give her a ride, providing an opportunity for Annie to display a congruent stance and alignment with Frangelica, but she does not do so, highlighting this lack of alignment through a non-reciprocal code switch.

3.7.7 Interactional Strategies in Dominican American Code Switching: Example 3

This segment illustrates the use of code maintenance and switching to organize specific sequences and to achieve a common understanding of a third-party referent. This third-party, Diana/*Diana*, is variously referred to as /dayænʌ/, /dayana/, and /diana/, reflecting American English, hybrid English/Spanish, and Spanish pronunciations of her name. Paradoxically, code switching in this instance is used in repairing difficulties that are a result of the very bilingualism of the interlocutors to begin with. While Alejandro uses pronunciations of Diana's name that are assimilated to English, Pamela recognizes the referent only in an unassimilated pronunciation.

24)
(LD #1 11:47:25) [Alejandro and his Dominican American friend Jonathan are trying to sell tickets between classes to a school sponsored roller skating party. Alejandro calls out to Pamela in the hallway between classes.]

Alej.:   You gonna go?
Pam.:   *Y tú?* ['And you?']
Alej.:   You gonna go?
Pam.:   I wanna go, but I don't wanna go by myself.
Alej.:   What do you mean you don't want (   )
Pam.:   (   )
Alej.:   I'm gonna be there!
Pam.:   Yeah, but you're gonna be with your friends
Alej.:   No I'm not.
Pam.:   Yes.
Jon.:   Nuh uh.
Alej.:   Jonathan's going
Jon.:   (He's) going. ((indicating Alejandro))
Alej.:   Jo- Diana's /dayænʌz/ going.
         (.8)
Alej.:   *Oístes?* ['Did you hear?']

```
        (.5)
Alej.:  Diana /dayana/ va.    ['Diana is going.']
Pam.:   Qué Diana /dayana/?    ['What/Which Diana?']
Alej.:  Diana /dayana/
Pam.:   Qué Diana /dayana/?    ['What/Which Diana?']
Alej.:  Yeah, Diana /dayana/ (   ) la Claudia,
Pam.:   Diana! /diana/
Alej.:  Diana /diana/, Diana, Diana
Pam.:   Y ella va para allá?          ['And she is going there?']
Alej.:  Yeah
Pam.:   O::h. Y que nos juntamos aquí?  ['And we're supposed to meet
        here?']
Alej.:  I'm selling the tickets, four dollars.
```

This segment is organized around getting from a pre-offer/announcement, made in the first line ("You going?"), to the actual offer/announcement, in the last line ("I'm selling the tickets, four dollars."). While such pre-sequences can take as few as two turns (e.g. A: You going? B: Yes.), various nested insertion sequences (Schegloff 1972) here--regarding who is going to be on the rollerskating trip--separate the initiation of the sequence from the actual offer/announcement.

Alejandro initiates the pre-sequence with a request in English, but Pamela counters with her own request, in Spanish, initiating an insertion sequence. While there many be a preference among bilinguals for second pair parts of adjacency pairs to match the language of first pair parts, Pamela is not giving a second pair part, but rather initiating her own sequence. Alejandro treats the insertion sequence as closed by reiterating his pre-offer, and both Alejandro and Pamela subsequently treat Alejandro's attendance as given information, suggesting that Alejandro gave an affirmative visual signal, e.g. vertical head nod to answer Pamela's first pair part request Y tú? (the camera was not directed at Alejandro at that moment).

After debating whether Alejandro would spend time with Pamela at the skating event and noting that Jonathan was going, Alejandro states that "Diana's going." This statement refers back to Pamela's initial utterance of the insertion sequence, "I wanna go, but I don't wanna go by myself." Alejandro's "Diana's going," however, leads to a new kind of trouble and new insertion sequences, concerned with repair and achieving a common understanding of the referent of "Diana."

Following Alejandro's mention of Diana going, there is a gap of .8 seconds, suggesting some sort of interactional trouble, e.g. misunderstanding or impending dispreferred sequences. Alejandro treats Pamela's lack of response to his announcement as meaningful, as if his mention that Diana was going should have led to a response from her. He switches to Spanish, initiating a repair (*Oístes?* ['Did you hear?']). He then repeats the same phrase in Spanish "Diana *va.*" Such translation code switches are one of the six types listed by Gumperz (1982) and the single most frequent type of switch in Zentella's (1997) data.

Alejandro's reiteration in Spanish (Diana /dayana/ *va*) does not lead to a shared understanding, however, and Pamela other-initiates another repair sequence with the first pair part, *Qué* Diana? Alejandro's second pair part is a reiteration of "Diana." While Alejandro used an American English pronunciation of Diana in his first turn, he then shifts to a hybrid English-Spanish pronunciation for his next three utterances. He maintains the English /ay/ as the initial diphthong but uses a Spanish /a/ for the second two vowel sounds (/dayana/), a pronunciation that Pamela duplicates as she tries to identify its referent in repair initiations. Pamela once again initiates repair *Qué* Diana? Alejandro treats Pamela as referring to the individual he is invoking, by saying "Yeah" and reiterating "Diana."

Only when Alejandro names another student with intonation and prosody that suggests that he is enumerating a list (possibly friends of Diana) does Pamela identify the referent of Diana, a student she calls *Diana* /diana/. Alejandro verifies this candidate understanding by repeating her name with Spanish phonology three times. Pamela then proffers another candidate understanding *Y ella va para allá?*. Alejandro again confirms this candidate understanding, this time in English. Pamela displays her changed state of understanding with the English token "Oh" then initiates another insertion sequence in Spanish regarding further details of the trip: *Y que nos juntamos aquí?*

Alejandro does not respond to her Spanish initiation of another insertion sequence. Instead he treats Pamela's expressed change of state ("Oh") as satisfying the original conditions that prevented her from agreeing to go ("I wanna go, but I don't wanna go by myself"). Thus freed from the conditions/hesitations set up in Pamela's initial insertion sequences, Alejandro makes the offer/announcement ("I'm selling the tickets, four dollars."), which was the basis of the pre-offer ("You gonna go?") that launched the interaction. Although various insertion sequences were executed in Spanish, or Spanish and English, the announcement/offer of the last line is made in the code of the pre-offer.

3.7.8 Sequential Preferences in Dominican American Code Switching

Data presented here suggest patterns of code switching to be further explored among groups such as Dominican Americans among whom switching is generally unmarked, namely:

A) The tendency for other-initiation of repair to coincide with code switching:

(From example 21)
Frang.:   *Yo soy un* junior.
Ana: No-
Frang.:   <If you're a junior or a //senior- >=   ((depresses fingers as she
          enumerates))
Ana: //Oh, okay
Frang.:   =you could go with anybody.

(from example 20)
Ana: I think I'm gonna save like three checks, to buy my- to buy
          //my shit.
Frang.:   //*Ay,   pero* three checks, *si tú trabajas bien, son* //(   ) ['Oh
          my, but ...if you work properly, that's..']
Ana: //*Ciento pico.*
          ['One hundred something']
Frang.:   ((nods))
Ana: *Por eso*, yeah.   ['That's why,...']
Ana: I think I'm gonna- I'm gonna save like three checks to buy my
          shit for the prom.

(From example 24)
Alej.:   Jo- Diana's /daiænʌz/ going.
      (.8)

Alej.:   *Oístes?* ['Did you hear?']
(.5)
Alej.:   Diana /dayana/ *va*.

B) A tendency more generally for specific communicative *sequences* (as opposed to the overall interaction) to have a "base language" and for switches to coincide with a) the beginning of insertion sequences and b) the resumption of sequences that had been temporarily suspended for insertion sequences. This is commensurate with Auer's (1998b) finding that responsive turns or turn-components are less likely to be switched than initiative ones. This pattern is particularly evident in example 19) in which Annie not only uses the same code, but almost the identical words after insertion sequences: "I'm gonna save like three checks to buy my shit for the prom." It is also suggested by Alejandro's code use in example 24) in maintaining his pre-sequence and eventual offer/announcement in one code despite their separation by multiple insertion sequences:

A: You gonna go? [Pre-Offer/Announcement sequence initiation]
P: *Y tú?*   [Insertion with code switch]
A: You gonna go? [Pre-sequence]
[Multiple insertion/repair sequences, many of them in Spanish.]
A: I'm selling the tickets, four dollars. [Offer/Announcement]

In this analysis, code switching has been approached as an interactional phenomenon among bilinguals in which switching is part of the nuts-and-bolts work, e.g. achieving repairs, done by interlocutors to maintain a degree of intersubjectivity, a task of all conversation. Interlocutors visibly attend to this local management of conversation, but these interactive exigencies are seldom a focus in studies of code switching (though see Auer and collaborators 1984a, 1984b, 1988, 1998a; Bailey 2000c).

3.8 Conclusions

Dominican Americans use and juxtapose linguistic resources that are commonly associated with disparate social identities in ways that are unmarked for participants. These resources include forms associated with local low-income and working-class sociolects, forms representing convergence of Spanish and English patterns, forms that are frequent, or unique, in African American Vernacular English (AAVE), and Dominican Spanish forms. This variety and alternation of forms reflect the hybrid acculturation Dominican Americans experience in a low-income, multi-ethnic urban environment in the larger context of a racially organized society. The varied linguistic forms used by the Dominican second generation show that their acculturation is not to any one group, but to a newly instantiated Dominican American identity.

Prominent among the language contact phenomena in Dominican American speech is code switching. In this chapter I have addressed social functions of code switching in a narrow sense, focusing on local management of conversation and the achievement of common understandings. On a more global level, the meanings and forms of code switching are part-and-parcel of a larger sociopolitical context in which codes, communicative behavior, and identities are imbued with competing value and meanings. In the next chapter I will address the sociopolitical context of Dominican American identities in Providence, and describe some of the multiple and conflicting metaphorical meanings of particular codes or varieties. Examples of code switching from this perspective will help illuminate the specific interplay of linguistic and social processes in Dominican American interpretation of experience and construction of social reality and identity.

CHAPTER 4
Second Generation Identities and Language in a Racialized America

> In America, there's only White and Black, that's the only
> colors we have. Spanish people are considered Black, that's
> the way they consider us, Black. (Maria)

4.1 Introduction

The language and identities of the Dominican second generation in
Providence, Rhode Island reflect a dual social reality of being raised in
Dominican families with Dominican social networks, but residing and
going to school in an American inner-city. Growing up in a low-
income, multi-ethnic, urban American context, Dominican Americans
in Providence come to see themselves as ethnic/racial minorities in a
hierarchical, White-dominated society, and they experience significant
solidarity with African Americans and other non-Whites with whom
they share a structural position in the United States. At the same time,
their Dominican socialization gives them linguistic resources and
cultural frameworks through which to see their identities in Dominican
terms and, in many ways, as outside of historical United States Black-
White social categorization frameworks.

The language of Dominican Americans is intertwined with their
sociopolitical position and the competing racial, ethnic, and national
identities variously and situationally available to them. Dominican
Americans in Providence find themselves in a multiply marginalized
(Vigil 1988:9) position in both local and global contexts. They are the
children of international labor migrants moving from periphery to core

(Wallerstein 1974); many live in poverty as defined by federal guidelines; this poverty leads to residence in neglected neighborhoods and attendance of substandard schools; the majority are of African descent, which subjects them to United States categorization as Black and attendant disparagement; the immigrant and permanent-resident status of many denies them due process extended to citizens; and their Latin American/Spanish ethnolinguistic heritage is denigrated and periodically assaulted through English-only movements that would criminalize their speech.

Although the Dominican second generation in Providence display agency in successfully rejecting categorization as Black or White, their language and identities are fundamentally channeled by the stratification of American society by phenotype/race, language, and class. Dominican Americans learn to think of themselves as expressly *non-White*, regardless of phenotype, based on the repeated ascriptions of identity they experience from various groups in America and daily confrontation with racial/ethnic hierarchy. Dominican American high school students' language and language attitudes--including explicit avoidance of White English and extensive adoption of AAVE forms-- reflect aspects of their sociohistorical position as they interpret and construct their social reality. The intertwining of language and social processes is evident, for example, in the ways that low-income Dominican American youth use AAVE to resist dominant, disparaging discourses, just as African American youth do (Morgan 1994b, 1998).

Paradoxically, while use of AAVE helps many in the Dominican second generation to resist one set of disparaging discourses, it makes them more subject to a more totalizing set of social assumptions--that they are Black. A different language of resistance--Spanish--is a key to resisting ascription to the category Black and a means of identifying oneself outside of the Black-White dichotomy. Spanish language serves both as a non-phenotype metonym for Dominican American identities and a code that embodies an alternate cultural framework and system of social categorization.

In relating the use of codes and language varieties to social meanings in both local and larger-scale sociopolitical contexts, I hope to decenter dichotomous assumptions about language and social identity that are implied by the term bilingualism and associated static, metaphorical notions of "us" vs. "them." Identities are not reified dichotomies but rather involve multiple alignments and oppositions that are situationally activated or backgrounded vis-à-vis other individuals or groups. As described in Chapter 3, Dominican American linguistic resources include forms drawn from multiple varieties of Spanish and English as well as convergent forms. These linguistic forms and varieties have ranges of metaphorical social associations that individuals exploit in particular contexts for particular ends in highlighting various aspects of their identities.

4.2 Becoming Non-White "Minorities"

For the Dominican second generation, American social and cultural frameworks--including ethnic, racial, and linguistic hierarchies--are central to identity formation. Unlike their parents, whose social networks are frequently limited to Dominicans and other Spanish-speaking immigrants, members of the second generation have extensive and intimate contact with native-born Americans and non-Hispanic immigrants. Although the second generation are socialized in Dominican families and social networks, they go to American schools, watch American TV, shop outside the enclave, and work with non-Hispanics in jobs requiring English. Even the Dominican Americans who lived in the Dominican Republic long enough to start elementary school there have typically become English dominant by their high school years. The second-generation frame of reference in Providence is not a Dominican one, but an urban, low-income, multi-ethnic Dominican American one.

Being "Dominican" thus has a very different meaning for the second generation than it does for the first. For those who grow up on the island, being Dominican, speaking Spanish, and having both African and European ancestry are unmarked, for example. In America, such characteristics define Dominican Americans as non-White, minority ethnics. White, monolingual English, middle-class Americans are the unmarked, ideological default group against which difference is constructed in the United States (Urciuoli 1996:16). Claiming a Dominican identity in America means being defined by dominant groups as something other than "just American," and being assigned to stigmatized social categories and a subordinate position in the American social hierarchy.

Dominican Americans who spend their early childhood on the island experience this shift from an unmarked identity to an ethnically/racially/linguistically marked one especially clearly. A Dominican American consultant who had come to America in the 1960's during his elementary school years, for example, contrasted the social prestige he enjoyed in the Dominican Republic with the stigmatized identity he was assigned in New York City. In the Dominican Republic, his parents' education and income made him a member of the upper middle-class, and his status as first-born son in a patriarchal society was particularly privileged. In New York he realized that decisive characteristics for social classification, e.g. skin color and hair texture, were different than in the Dominican Republic, and that attributes that had not been meaningful to him on the island received a negative valuation in the United States:

> Also for the first time, we were confronted with our ethnic background--and I was confronted with my ethnic background--as a negative thing. I never thought that being black or being dark-skinned or having curly hair meant that you were less than or different than. I was the first-born in my family, I was always the privileged child, I was supposed to be-- you know, everyone loved me. I never felt rejection in my life. I went to private school when I was there, I never went to anyplace where I heard that people were turned away because of the color of their skin. When I came to New York, it was the first time that I heard that people belong in certain areas, in certain places, that there were certain areas that were reserved for Whites, and that there was a distance, and then I noticed that White people would kind of look at you differently and treat you as a certain type and then I learned when I went to school there were certain positions, and that the teachers were White and maybe the janitors were Hispanic and Black and that they were a majority and then you see Harlem and it was horrible and then you go to the Westside and it was really nice and clean. For a while it doesn't make sense, and after a while you start looking at your skin [looking down at the skin on the back of his hand and wrist, comparing it in turn to the color of his charcoal-colored suit and the color of his dark brown

desk], say "Wait a minute--Uh oh! Wrong color!" But you never thought of that.

As a result of this exclusion and discrimination, Dominican Americans grow up thinking of themselves as something other than "American." This markedness of Dominican American identities is reflected and reproduced in the ways in which members of the second generation label themselves and others. In everyday Dominican American usage, the term "American" (or *americano*) refers to "White American." United States-born Dominican Americans identify themselves as "American" in some contexts, e.g. in referring to citizenship or the passport they have, but they identify "what they are" as Dominican/Spanish/Hispanic. These categories are mutually exclusive from the category White/American in local terms. Dominican Americans refer to other non-White groups in similarly marked terms: African Americans are not "Americans" (or *americanos*) but "Blacks" (or *negros/prietos/morenos*); Asian Americans are not Americans but rather "Asians" (or *chinos*). Dominican Americans label themselves as Americans in certain narrow contexts, but they define themselves as Dominican or Spanish in their everyday lives in multi-ethnic schools and neighborhoods.

The following excerpt from an interview illustrates some of the conflicting ways that Dominican Americans think about their Dominican and American identities, and it suggests the social pressures they experience to identify in particular ways. Janelle, who was born in America of Dominican parents, discusses how she should refer to herself with her friend Jose, who was born in the Dominican Republic and came to America as a child. Although they agree that she is "American" in one sense, and "Dominican" in another, Janelle points out that when people ask her "What are you?", they do not want her to answer that she is "American":

BB: If someone asks "What's your race?", what would you say?
Janelle: I would say Hispanic.
BB: If a person says, "I'm American", what group do you think they belong to?
Janelle: "American" to me would be White, but I consider myself American even though I would say Spanish.

BB: If a person has Dominican parents but was born here and grew up here, should they say they're American or should they say they're Dominican?

Janelle: See that's what I think is American, you born here, the fact that you was born here, no matter what your parents are.

BB: So what should those kids say?

Janelle: What should they say? I say Dominican, but ...I know I'm not really Dominican, my parents are....

Jose: How about you [addressed to BB], if you was born in the Dominican Republic, you would say you're Dominican. You're Dominican cause you was born in that land, that's why.

Janelle: But then they ask you what's your blood, your parents, and then they figure that's what you are.

Jose: If they ask you what's your race, like where are your parents from and stuff like that, then you would tell them, my parents, they come from the Dominican Republic, before I was born here, so my blood is from Dominican Republic, my blood is Hispanic, or whatever you want to say, but I was just born here, that's why they call me American.

Janelle: That's why they call me bootleg (laughing). Cause I live here....So what am I supposed to say, I'm American?

Jose: You're American.

Janelle: I know I'm American but--

Jose: You're American but you got the blood of Dominican.

Janelle: But when people say, "What are you?" they usually want like "Dominican." I'm saying that's what they want, or "Puerto Rican", not "I was born here."

Jose: Cause if it was like that everybody over here would be American.

Janelle: Yeah most people would be "I'm American, I'm American."

Even those individuals like Janelle who are United States-born, thus fulfilling a defining and sufficient criterion for citizenship, exclude themselves--and are excluded by others--from the unmarked category of "American." The notion that they are something other than simply American--implied in the very question "What are you?"--is central to the way Dominican Americans think of themselves.

Being defined as different from--and less than--White Americans intensifies self-identification as "Dominican" in the second generation. Dominican Americans contest the dominant discourses that disparage them in part through pronounced, proud affirmation of the very characteristics that are disparaged. Spanish speaking, for example, becomes a point of pride and solidarity among many in the second generation. Stigmatization and consequent contestation of dominant discourses frequently produces intense collective consciousness and a high degree of internal solidarity in social groups (Spicer 1971:797). Those who downplay or deny their Dominican heritage are seen as disloyal to their roots and betraying their co-members. Alejandro, for example, frames maintenance of a Dominican identity among the American-born as a "racial" issue. Being Dominican is a point of pride for him and it is an identity that must be maintained in the face of subordination and/or possible assimilation:

BB: What does "American" mean to you?
Alejandro: I guess he was born here.
BB: A lot of Dominicans were born here. Like your Cape Verdean friend John was born here--do you call him American?
Alejandro: Yeah. But when a Spanish person is born here, it's kind of different, it would be like, there would be some racial thing going on there where, I'm Dominican and I won't deny anywhere I go that I'm Dominican, I'm proud of it. I have friends like that, they're Dominican but they were born here.... I have a little niece like 2-3 months, I say she's Dominican. For me she's Dominican. But like sometimes my mom will go "She's American" and I'm like "What, what are you talking about? She's Dominican" and I'm like, "Her parents are Dominican, her mom's Dominican, her family's Dominican, her damn grandmother is Dominican, so don't come with this 'Cause she was born here she's American' cause she has Dominican blood in her." So she's Dominican for me. Even though she was born here, for me she's mostly Dominican. Cause she don't have no other kind of blood in her than just Dominican blood. She's going to be raised in America, but she's going to be raised in a Dominican household and a Dominican family view....It's not that I have something against Americans, but I believe that even if you have this bit of Spanish blood in you, you shouldn't deny it, cause that's your blood right there.

This affirmation of Dominican heritage, in part a form of resistance to ongoing disparagement from the dominant society, typically results in unqualified identification as Dominican, at least in interview situations with a White researcher. Second-generation Dominicans, for example, never identified themselves as "Dominican American"--a term I use to capture their dual language and cultural socialization--but simply as "Dominican":

Isabella: I know I'm supposed to call myself American
BB: Are you a citizen?
Isabella: I will be when I'm 18, but I'll still consider myself Dominican.
BB: Do you consider yourself Dominican American?
Isabella: Dominican.

BB: When people ask you what you are, what do you say?
Wilson: Well, I tell'em. I'm Dominican.
BB: Do you say Dominican American?
Wilson: Just Dominican.

Even U.S.-born Dominicans with little experience of life on the island identify themselves as Dominican, rather than Dominican American.

BB: Do you use "Dominican"?
Nanette: I say I'm Dominican. If they ask me where I'm from, I don't say I'm American, I say I'm Dominican.
BB: But you were born here?
Nanette: But I was born here.
BB: So if someone says, "Where are you from?"
Nanette: I'll say I'm Dominican.

The second generation, like the first generation, call themselves "Dominican", but for the second generation being Dominican means being a non-White minority identity in the context of the United States. Although the second generation use Dominican cultural practices and interpretive frameworks to define themselves in terms other than Black/White, they are subject to American social and racial hierarchy, with important implications for the ways they think about themselves and see themselves in relationship to other groups.

4.3 Solidarity with Other Non-White Americans

Dominican Americans' position as non-White is regularly reinforced in interactions with White Americans. Many in the second generation find themselves explicitly categorized in the same social categories as African Americans, regardless of individual differences in phenotype. Maria and Nanette, for example, had attended predominantly African American and Hispanic schools before briefly attending Catholic schools that were primarily White, and they gave similar accounts of their treatment by White students at those schools. Although neither reported being mistaken for African American--Nanette describes her skin color as *india* ['indian-colored'] and Maria describes hers as "very white"--both found themselves grouped with African Americans--and deprecated--by White students and teachers:

Nanette: I didn't want to have problems, I lasted the whole year and I didn't have problems because I refrained myself...there was just a bunch of comments. If you were in the lunch line or something, they would start talking in the back saying, "Oh, why is that Black girl in front of me?" stupid comments but they still get to you. The minorities in that school were all limited [in number]...I knew every Black girl and every Spanish girl there.
BB: They called you Black?
Nanette: Black or Spanish, to them it's all the same thing, I think. Cause that's the way they refer.

BB: When you think of White Americans, what comes to your mind?
Maria: I went to Catholic school, I didn't really mix with White people, it was like they look at me like weird, like I'm Dominican, Spanish. "Oh, we have a Spanish girl, she's Black." I always say that Spanish people are Black. These White girls, they're like, "Look at these Dominican girls, those Spanish Black girls" this and that....in America, there's only White and Black, that's the only colors we have. Spanish people are considered Black, that's the way they consider us, Black. I think Asians is White. I just know Spanish is considered Black. Cause I asked my social studies teacher, she said, "Yeah, Spanish are considered Black." So I was telling you, these White girls started picking on me. I started 7th grade, I was always

in public school over here, I hated it, I didn't want to go over there, Mom made me, I didn't like it cause I didn't see more Spanish people over there.

According to Maria, White Americans grouped Dominicans with Blacks as different from White, and they also thought they were superior to those who they didn't count as White:

Maria: Over here, like more the young people, we always, the Dominican people always be with Black people.
BB: At the same time I've also seen Dominicans who are friends with White people.
Maria: Mmm (doubtingly), that's-- It's hard to find a Dominican person with a White person.
BB: How come, do you think?
Maria: I don't really know. Maybe because we feel so, you know -- not threatened--but we used to feel the way we feel with other people with White people. Cause they act like they're perfect when they're not. Like everything they have in the world is better than anybody else. So, that's why.

Maria thus sees a subordinate position for Dominicans being reinforced in everyday interaction with White Americans.

Alejandro highlights the shared structural position of Black and Hispanic youth in explaining the solidarity he experiences with African Americans and other non-Whites: they live in the same poor neighborhoods and attend the same grossly inadequate schools, their parents face the same problems, and they are subordinate to the White establishment.

BB: Is it harder to be Black or Hispanic? Do people hassle you more if you're Black or hassle you more if you're Hispanic?
Alejandro: I think it's the same in the way that we all being thrown in the same areas. They either want us out of here, all the Hispanics, and just control the Blacks. That's why they deport so many people and everything. I guess it's the same sense. We go to the same schools, and our parents are going through the same things that their parents are, so I think it's the same.

Alejandro sees "they"--Whites in power--as trying to control Blacks and Hispanics, e.g. by deporting Hispanics which makes controlling Blacks easier.

Alejandro believes that Hispanics, like African Americans, are discriminated against in ways that Whites aren't. In addition to facing harassment from security guards in stores and malls, for example, he finds that White employees get preferential treatment at the Burger King where he works. Even though all but one of the managers are African American, and only a few of the workers are White, when there is a dispute between White and non-White workers, the non-Whites are blamed:

Alejandro: I try to do good in my classes and everything and where I work I always try to do a good job. But yo, even at work, there's discrimination. Like White people get more credit or whatever for anything they do, while we, Spanish and Blacks, we always talk about stuff. The first time I didn't say anything because the White girl, she's a friend of mine and everything...but she gets an attitude at people. And she be like ((impatient voice)) "Where's my food" or whatever.....I'm like "Wait for your food" so she be getting an attitude and the one that they scream at is not her, it's the other person.

Alejandro groups "African Americans" with "Spanish" with the first person plural pronoun "we" and distinguishes between a Black/Hispanic group and Whites. He later groups young, low-income African American and Hispanics together as "urban kids" in discussing education. He believes that education is a key to socioeconomic success in America, but that the dominant groups' expectations for "urban kids" are low:

Alejandro: ...you gotta get an education to-- to show these people that you can do things. I been doing it for a while. I don't know if I got tired of it or whatever, but I felt like I was getting nothing for it.....
BB: Who's "them" that you have to show that you can do it?
Alejandro: I don't know, like the government, everybody. We gotta show that-- you know we be doing bad in SAT's and all that, the urban kids, and they say that we're only good at sports, or whatever, we gotta show them that we're good at education too.

BB: When you say "urban kids" you mean?

Alejandro: Spanish, Blacks, Asians-- not Asians, even though they're
   kind of, I don't understand, they got money, they got cars, so I don't
   think they're poor. They be getting into Brown, they smart, yo.

For Alejandro, Spanish and Black youth are co-members of the
category "urban kids," while Asians occupy an ambiguous position:
they are phenotypically non-White, but relatively successful
economically and educationally in the White-dominated system.

   Although Dominican Americans in Providence perceive
themselves as non-White minorities, some find themselves relatively at
ease with White Americans. Rosa and Martin, for example, both
attended Classical High School, the public college-preparatory school
where White students were in the majority. They saw themselves as
able to interact with both African Americans and White Americans in
ways that the two groups might not interact between themselves.
Martin attributed this to the fact that Dominicans are "in between"
Blacks and Whites, and Rosa explained it as a function of Dominicans'
being "part everything" and coming in "all different colors, shapes, and
sizes."

BB: A lot of Dominicans have Hispanic friends but also have Black
   friends and White friends. Between Blacks and White it seems like
   there's a real barrier. Do you think it's easier for Dominicans than
   other groups to have Black friends and White friends at the same
   time?

Martin: It is, cause like they in between. I mean, it depends like what
   kind of people you hang around with, whatever, but usually, the
   Spanish people, cause they're considered like minorities, or at least
   to each other they consider themselves, so they could like relate,
   kind of relate, to the Black people. At the same time, like with
   White people, you can still get by with them too, because they just
   see you differently, it's like you're right in between. It's odd.

Rosa: I love being part everything ...you get along with everybody. You
   don't really have that cultural tension that Blacks have when they
   hang out with Whites and Whites have when they hang out with
   Blacks. Because if you're a Black person and you're hanging out
   with a White person, then to the rest of the Blacks, you're an

"Oreo." If you're a White person and you hang around with Black people, then people say that you want to be Black. That you're a "wigga," a White person who wants to be a Black person.... But when you're Spanish, you're everything. ....you come in all different colors, shapes, and sizes.

Dominican American experiences of discrimination and subordination lead them to see themselves as non-White minorities and to experience solidarity with other groups whom they see as in the same structural position in America. Although they resist many American racial meanings--e.g. one-drop rules of classification--their lives and perspectives are shaped by the hierarchical, racially organized society in which they grow up.

4.4 Relating Language to Power Inequality

Until the 1970's, Marxism dominated social scientific approaches to power and inequality in capitalist societies. Such Marxism focused on economic modes of production, which were considered the fundamental "base" that shaped and determined other social processes. Cultural beliefs and practices, e.g. language, were relegated to the "superstructure," epiphenomena that were at most tangential to core political-economic processes. In the 1970's, both Williams (1977) and Bourdieu (1977) countered this orientation by focusing on culture as a source of inequality and directly addressing the multifarious relationships between power and culture in capitalism. Both argued that it was not just physical control over the means of production and direct coercion that gave dominant groups their power, but also control over culturally constructed representations of social reality. By controlling ways of thinking about the world and social relationships, e.g. by controlling education (Bourdieu and Passeron 1977), dominant groups can co-opt, and in a sense, gain a degree of consent from the dominated. Bourdieu coined the term "symbolic domination" while Williams borrowed Gramsci's term of "cultural hegemony," to describe how subordinate groups, to a degree, implicitly accept as legitimate the power of dominant groups.

Although dominant groups rule partially with the consent of subordinated groups, such groups also *resist* this domination. They thus contest dominant, naturalized versions of reality and definitions that are applied to them at the same time that they implicitly accept aspects of this domination. Through such resistance, oppressed groups gain some control over local representations of reality, but this does not necessarily lead to greater political or economic power. To the contrary, oppositional stances and culture can actually contribute to the reproduction of a subordinated group's sociopolitical marginalization (e.g. Willis 1977, Ogbu 1974).

Because cultural practices and symbolic representations are central to understanding social inequality, language, as the central medium through which social reality is represented and the social order (re)constituted, becomes a logical locus for the study of political-economic struggles. A key feature of language for investigating these social processes is its *indexicality.* Language is a system of both *symbols,* in which the sign-referent relationship is arbitrary, and *indexes,* in which there is an existential relationship between sign and that with which it is associated (Peirce 1940). Language thus signals social information through individual or constellations of syntactic, morphological, phonological, proxemic, or code features. The social meanings of these features are locally determined and negotiated, depending on shared understandings of such elements (Silverstein 1976:48, Gumperz 1982).

It is such social indexes that can serve as a key to understanding how members organize and construct their world. Sociolinguists have exploited this indexical dimension of language to correlate features of speech with social variables, e.g. "r-less" pronunciation and social class (Labov 1966). Speakers' negotiation of these socially indexical forms provides a window into the workings of cultural hegemony or symbolic domination in language. The hierarchies that such forms represent and reproduce are attended to by interlocutors, as is evident in expressed linguistic insecurity of marginalized groups, hypercorrection (Labov 1972b), and subjective reaction tests, e.g. the matched guise tests of Lambert and collaborators (e.g. 1960). In such tests, subjects tend to identify speakers using dominant group forms as superior in many traits--e.g. intelligence and ambition--than speakers of the very varieties used by the subjects themselves, thus having internalized the dominant groups' notions of what is "right" or "correct."[26]

Despite the prestige implicitly and explicitly accorded dominant varieties in such studies, linguistic ethnographic work in non-dominant ethnic/racial/class communities invariably shows members using forms that are disparaged by dominant groups and even ridiculing or censuring members who use forms associated with dominant groups (e.g. Labov 1972a, Basso 1979, Gal 1979, Milroy 1987). Woolard (1985) and Gal (1989:354) use the social axes of *status* and *solidarity* described by Brown and Gilman (1960) to account for this phenomenon. While the varieties favored by the dominant groups are popularly seen as standard or correct and have high status in institutional contexts, the differing varieties used by disparaged groups mark and reproduce local *solidarity* in the face of such disparagement. The linguistic implications of forces of 1) solidarity and 2) status were summarized succinctly by Ferguson and Gumperz (1960:9):

> First: any group of speakers of language X which regards itself as a close social unit will tend to express its group solidarity by favoring those linguistic innovations which set it apart from other speakers who are not part of the group....
> On the other hand: other things being equal, if two speakers A and B of a language X communicate in language X and if A regards B as having more prestige than himself and aspires to equal B's status, then the variety of X spoken by A will tend towards identity with that spoken by B.

While Labov and others have referred to the local valuation of solidarity forms as "covert prestige," such prestige is not necessarily covert among groups, e.g. low-income, non-White teen-agers, for whom solidarity and defiance of the disparaging discourses directed at them is a central fact of daily life. In strictly local terms, linguistic forms that mark and reproduce solidarity among in-group peers can also bring status to speakers.

4.5 Local Understandings of "Black" and "White" Language

Dominican Americans see themselves as non-White, as described above, and many explicitly link language to White and Non-White social identities:

BB: What are your associations with White Americans?
Richard M.: They talk different. They're just like different, they talk different. Like maybe the Spanish and Black, they use like the street language, they use a lot of slang. Some Whites, not all, most of them they don't do that...I don't know how to explain it. Like if you listen to two White kids talking, it'll be different than a Black kid and a Black kid or two Spanish. Like they'll be using, they'll say like "Aw, that homework assignment is wack, I don't wanna do that." The White kid will be like, "I didn't like that homework assignment." You see that a lot.

Similarly, for Rosa, forms associated with AAVE are "minority" language that set Dominican Americans apart from Whites:

Rosa: ...when I step out of that group [Dominicans/Hispanics] and I start talking to White people, they'll talk about different things and in different ways. Hispanics can be very blunt about things and very slang-oriented words. White people, they have good grammar, they speak with good grammar. I notice that a lot, just grammar, they speak right. I think they have a problem when they talk to minorities and minorities are like, "You be wack, yo, you be tripping when you be doing this type of junk."

Differences in language use among social groups involve not just discrete linguistic features, but the style of interaction:

Rosa: African Americans they're really-- I said Dominicans were blunt, well African Americans are really blunt. They just really, it's just really real. I mean they will just say anything that comes to their mind. Like you'll see Black girls calling each other "bitch" in a friendly way, and you'll see Dominicans calling each other *putas* ['whores']...in a friendly way. But you don't see that in White people.

According to Rosa, economic class underlies some of these differences:

Rosa: They [White people] have more money so they speak about different problems and they speak about different things. They'll be like "Oh, I got an 88 on my test. I'm so upset." If you went into a

Spanish group or minority group and said that, they'll just look at you like you're ridiculous. They'll want to smack you.

Isabella sees her own language and communicative style as directly influenced by African Americans:

Isabella: ...some of the things I do I get from mostly African Americans, the attitude, the body language, I might get it from African Americans mostly, the way you talk ((modeling a head movement that she uses when angry, in which she moves her head from side to side while keeping it vertical and her face forward-facing))

BB: Do you use African American words and expressions?

Isabella: We all use the same words like phat, mad cool, or butters. Maybe African Americans think of it, but we hear it and we use it.

BB: Is Black style different from White?

Isabella: I think if you put African Americans and White Americans, they're totally different. At least like Dominicans, they might be between. Or Hispanics. But they're totally different from White Americans. Cause, I think African Americans when they talk or something, they sound with more power, their body language looks like it has more power than compared to a White American.

Given this perceived similarity between Dominican and African American styles of English, it is not surprising that Dominican Americans treat vocabulary and syntax that analysts assign to the category AAVE as unmarked in their own speech. When individuals make such utterances as "She look like a witch" (Wilson), "I love the way...the American be making sandwich" (Janelle), and "We studying for the test" (Alejandro), they do not see themselves as using any language other than their own.

In this regard, the use of AAVE features by Dominican Americans is very different from the "crossing" described by Rampton (1995a, 1995b). Rampton (1995b:485) describes language crossing as members of a group "code switching into varieties that are not generally thought to belong to them." Dominican Americans in low-income neighborhoods in Providence generally do not *have* a discrete variety of English from which to switch into AAVE. As described by Isabella, above, there is no sense of discrete ownership: "We all use the same words.... Maybe African Americans think of it, but we hear it and we use it."

4.6 Use of Marked "Black English" and "White English"

I recorded one example of a student using AAVE as a distinct, marked variety (in bold face below). It does not display any clear sociopolitical meaning, but rather appears to be just a local framing device.

1)
[(JS #1 10:40:45) The teacher is talking in the background during physics class. Janelle is talking about being videotaped and whether or not she will skip a later class]

Janelle: If I want to stay outside, it would be better for him, to record me? Like if I don't want to go to 4th, I can stay outside?
Jose: Uh huh.
Janelle: But- it's kind of col'!
Jose: It's not cold.
Janelle: Why do I want to sit outside? *Para (allí) todos están mirándome.* ['Over there, everyone's looking at me.'] Eva, she was like "Janelle, are you doing something that I don't know, that you haven't told me?" I //was like-
Jose: //Who?
Janelle: Eva.
         (.2)
Jose: Eva? How'd she know?
Janelle: Um- hmm.
Jose: What?
Janelle: Cause like- Cause when he was talking to me and stuff.
         (3.0)
Jose: Eva just wanted to be in it.
Janelle: <You know what I'm saying, B?> ((low voice pitch))
         (4.0)
Janelle: Where you going fourth?

In this final utterance, Janelle's pitch is deeper and her tempo slower, and she uses the address term "B". In reviewing this utterance on videotape, Janelle identified it as "talking like a Black person," highlighting the address term "B", by giving an equivalent expression, "You know what I'm saying, Dog?" Smitherman (1994) defines both "B" and "Dog" as AAVE terms of address used mainly among males and suggests that "B" is a shortened form of the address term "Blood", "a generic term for any person of African descent" (1994:62).

In this case, a variety switch may simply serve as a local framing device to end a repair sequence in a longer sequence in which the two have difficulty achieving common understandings. Jose responds to Janelle's initial utterance with a back channel "uh huh" that does not prove understanding. Jose disagrees with her assessment (Goodwin and Goodwin 1992) that it's cold outside. When she begins to relate her conversation with Eva, Jose initiates a repair (Who?). A gap follows Janelle's response, and after Jose asks how Eva knew, he initiates another repair ("What?") on Janelle's response ("Um- hmm.") Jose's assessment of Eva's motives follows a long gap. Janelle's "You know what I'm saying, B?" follows this assessment without displaying evidence that she is responding to it. Jose does not respond to Janelle's final utterance, and after another gap, she asks him where he is going for fourth period, returning to the issue she initially addressed in this segment of where to go during that period.

Language associated with White identities, in contrast, nearly always carries metaphorical meanings in interaction among Dominicans and non-White peers. Dominican American teen-agers report, for example, that they are censured for "talking White":

BB: What would happen if you talked that way [like White Americans]? What would your friends say?
Carlos: They would laugh at me....They'd be like, why, do you think you're White, and they'll be like that, or just call me a sell-out.

Rosa, who attended predominantly White Classical High School and reported feeling relatively at ease with White Americans, noted that she had to be careful to switch communicative styles as she interacted with members of different ethnic/racial groups because of the threat of such censure:

BB: Do White kids see you as White when you hang out with them?
Rosa: That's definitely something that you're scared to do, scared to
    get too close to White people, because then your culture is going to
    say that you want to be White. "No, no, I don't want to be White,
    they're just my friends." "You too friendly with White people, you
    talk all nice." If you [don't switch styles] when you go back to your
    group, they'll notice it right away and back away from you. That's
    kind of what makes you feel uncomfortable if you want to associate
    with other cultures.

Even when individuals are able to use language to cross social
boundaries, in-group sanctions can deter them from doing so, thus
recreating the boundaries and reinforcing internal solidarity (Gal
1989:354).

   Discourse shifts to a White English style typically mark clear
changes in footing (Goffman 1981). The concept of footing
encompasses widely varying phenomena, from the nuts-and-bolts
conversational management activities described for code switching in
Chapter 3 to more metaphorical identity issues of alignment, stances,
and projected self. While switching to White English can serve local
discourse functions, it also suggests more global sociopolitical stances,
attitudes, and understandings regarding language varieties and social
identities.

   In the following example, Isabella uses White English for direct
quotation, one of the functions commonly attributed to code switching.
Isabella is the animator of her utterance (Goffman 1981:144),
producing words that are, in a sense, not her own in a voice that is not
her own. In the first example, a particular form of female White
English and the characteristics that it indexes are a source of
amusement for Isabella and her classmates.

2)
[(IN #2 12:09:05) Students are looking at fashion magazines during
class when Isabella comes upon an advertisement for a clothing
catalogue called "Girlfriends LA." Vela ("V") is a Laotian American
friend.]
Isabella: ((reading from magazine)) Girlfrien:ds. LA.
Isabella: uu! Vela! I called Girlfriends LA stuff.
Vela: And what'd they say?

Isabella: [I just ordered-]
?:   [(   ]   girlfriend   )
Isabella: ((perky smile voice)) Hi! nuhnuhnuh.   ((back to unmarked
          register)) Some girl talking there. I'm like ((bored, impatient
          register for self-quote)) yeah, yeah.   ((back to unmarked
          register)) Then I said I want to subscribe--

In this segment Isabella and classmates construct differences between
themselves and a stereotype of a White female in Los Angeles.
Although it is Isabella who contrasts the voice of this female with her
own voice, it is an unidentified, non-White female classmate who
prompts this use of a White voice. Isabella is initially responding to
Vela's first pair part with "I just ordered-" when this classmate says
something that leads Isabella to give an account of the conversation.
Isabella uses a relatively high-pitched, breathy voice to animate the
voice of the Girlfriends LA representative. Several female consultants
who had little contact with White Americans characterized female
White English as the kind of talk one hears in television, citing the
program "Beverly Hills 90210" in particular. After animating the
representative's delivery, Isabella further distances herself from the
representative, characterizing her as an anonymous, distant individual,
"Some girl there." Isabella's direct quotation of her own speech (or
internal thought (Romaine and Lange 1998)) is in a locally unmarked
variety of English, and emphasizes her impatience with the speaker on
the other end of the telephone. Isabella is using language to mark social
distance between herself and a stereotype of a young, White Los
Angeles female. This mocking use of White English, which was
triggered by a classmate's turn, serves to mark solidarity between
Isabella and her low-income, non-White classmates.
     In the following example, Alejandro uses White English in
feigning to help organize a Friday evening Catholic youth group. The
groups are nominally in Spanish, using a Spanish language Bible, and
the adult leader speaks little English. The attendees, middle and high
school students range from new immigrants who speak little English, to
some U.S.-raised individuals who speak little Spanish.

3)
[(LD #SM 7:54:00) The student leader has been organizing, in Spanish,
the evening's Bible reading and discussion. The students are sitting in

chairs in a circle, with many empty chairs between the 7-8 individuals who are present.]

Alejandro: Could we get together? Like closer?
    (4.0)
Alejandro: C'mon, man!! ((higher pitch, nasal voice, flapping arms slightly as if in mock frustration))

Alejandro achieves a White English style primarily through phonology, including pronunciation of final /r/, higher pitch, a slightly slower tempo, and a straining sound. In this case, his use of this register coincides with an apparent effort to help get the group to sit in a more intimate, cohesive circle. Although the propositional content of Alejandro's turns are commensurate with group cooperation, his choice of code and register, and the timing of his utterances are at odds with it. At the moment of his utterances, the language of group activities--and institutional authority--is Spanish.

Both in school--especially in Spanish class--and youth group, Alejandro regularly worked to undermine the teacher/authority in ways that were difficult to confront. In Spanish class, for example, he read aloud a Spanish passage with marked American English phonology, after hearing the researcher speak Spanish, setting all his classmates to laughing yet avoiding any censure from the teacher. Another time when a classmate finished a section of her oral report on Venezuela with decidedly (and inappropriately) concluding prosodic features, he led the class in clapping, treating it as if she had finished her report. In these Hispanic American contexts, he gives the appearance of cooperation with authority, while humorously undermining it.

In this case, a White voice that indexes institutional authority is used to mock and challenge that authority. Alejandro's higher pitch (cf. "marking" Mitchell-Kernan 1972) and awkward, limp arm movements also index an implicit effeteness or femininity associated with such forms, contrasting with the implicit masculinity that subjugated groups' varieties have for young males (e.g. Labov 1972a, Willis 1977). Disparaged groups maintain disparaged varieties to resist cultural/linguistic hegemony, but they also appropriate dominant forms for their own ends, assigning local meanings to them (e.g. Basso 1979).

4.7 Linguistic Solidarity and Ascription of Racial Identity

Dominican American youth in South Providence share many structural disadvantages with their African American peers and friends in the same neighborhoods: poverty, substandard schools, marked phenotype-race, exposure to drugs and crime, and a limited number of apparent avenues to social and economic mobility. AAVE serves as a language of resistance to dominant discourses of disparagement and a medium for alternative social understandings for many African American youth (Morgan 1994b), and it serves the same purpose for young Dominicans who face similar structural disadvantages.

Dominican American use of AAVE as a form of resistance to symbolic domination has a paradoxical effect, however: it makes many individuals increasingly subject to another form of symbolic domination, the Black-White racial dichotomy. Use of AAVE contributes to the force and frequency with which individuals are perceived as African American, not only by outsiders, but even those Dominican Americans who are themselves regularly taken to be African American.

While intergroup adoption of linguistic forms often suggests sociopolitical solidarity, it rarely has the effects on fundamental group membership assumptions that it has among Dominican Americans. In Rampton's (1995a) "crossing," for example, South Asian, Afro-Caribbean, and White English youth in England use South Asian and Caribbean speech patterns that are disparaged by the dominant society to display solidarity with each other. Rampton (1995b:508) suggests that individuals may be able to temporarily "inhabit" someone else's ethnicity through such use of linguistic forms believed to belong to the other person's social group and not one's own.

Among the youth studied by Rampton, however, there is no ambiguity as to the ethnic/racial identity that individual youth are able to enact successfully. The social categories at issue--Black, White, and South Asian--are based on phenotype and perceived ancestry, rather than language or culture. These youth are unambiguously assigned to ethnic/racial categories based on immediately apparent differences in phenotype, *regardless* of how they speak. Such crossing may display solidarity and novel, alternative understandings of ethnicity and community, as argued by Rampton, but adoption of linguistic forms associated with a group defined by phenotype does not transform one, even temporarily, into a member of that group. Language plays such a central role in identity ascription only when an individual's phenotype is ambiguous or does not meet stereotypes for particular categories (e.g. Bucholtz 1995). For the majority of Dominican Americans, who are of both African and European descent, AAVE linguistic forms do not just suggest a sociopolitical position to others, as does "crossing," they suggest essential social group membership.

4.8 Spanish as Resistance to Phenotype-based Racialization

Dominican Spanish language serves as a resource for resisting Black-White dichotomization on several levels. In terms of identity ascription in everyday encounters, it is the primary means by which Dominican Americans display an ethnolinguistic identity that can decenter phenotype-based ascriptions. In a broader sense, it encompasses an alternate model of the social world in which African/European phenotype is relatively unimportant in terms of social differentiation, and it links individuals to others who share and recreate this world. Unlike forms of linguistic resistance generally available to African Americans and dominated economic classes in the United States, Spanish provides a link to co-ethnics in other nation-states. In Providence, many young Dominican Americans define their *race* as "Spanish" (see Chapter 5), using a language name as a metonym for a constellation of linguistic, cultural, and phenotypic phenomena.

The significance of Spanish language for countering initial identity ascriptions and communicating an ethnolinguistic identity in everyday encounters is evident in both 1) Dominican Americans' explanations of how outsiders know that they are Dominican/Hispanic rather than, e.g. "Black" or "White", and 2) the common proof procedure that Dominicans use to show others that they're not "Black" or "White": they show that they can speak Spanish.

Dominican Americans from the ten to fifteen percent segment of the Dominican population who are of overwhelmingly European ancestry are sometimes perceived as White Americans, for example:

Martin: I don't really look Spanish.... People don't think that I'm Spanish until I tell them I speak Spanish, or whatever. If they just look at me, "Oh, it doesn't look like he's Spanish."

BB: Do Dominicans tease you and say, "Oh you're White"?

Martin: No-- sometimes that'll happen. Sometimes they don't know I'm Spanish, and they'll say something or whatever and I'll say something back in Spanish but not directly to them, but just so they can hear it, though.... And then I have like my friends, after they've known me for a couple of years, and we'll just reminisce and talk about things from before, they be like "I always knew you were Spanish." I tell'em, "No you didn't. I remember telling you I was Spanish." They're like "For real?" After a while you get used to it, I guess. And they're like "You look Spanish" and I'm like "No I don't. You never thought that before."

A much larger percentage of Dominican Americans are of African descent and are regularly perceived to be African American. Even at Central High School, where Caribbean Hispanics outnumber African Americans by more than two to one, many Dominican Americans are assumed to be African American until they are heard speaking Spanish:

BB: If somebody asks you "What are you?", what do you say?

Janelle: I usually say Spanish, Dominican. I'll usually say Dominican first, cause most people--most people think I'm Black though. A lot of people think I'm Black. A lot of people! ....

BB: Can you think of a specific time when someone thought you were Black?

Janelle: I was in the gym, and usually in school I don't really talk in Spanish, and I was talking to some kid in English, and some girl, I guess she was listening, and I said a word in Spanish, and she goes "Oh my god, you're Spanish." No she goes, "You know Spanish." She thought I was just a Black who knew Spanish. I was like "I am Spanish." She's like, "Oh my god, I thought you was Cape Verdean or Black." I was like "No." A lot of people think I'm Black. I don't know, it's usually just little things like that, just people be like "What are you, Black?" I'm like "No, I'm Spanish."

In this exchange between Dominican American Janelle and an African American classmate, "Spanish" is treated not just as a language, but also as an ethnic/racial identity. Being "Spanish," in local terms, does not mean that one is from Spain, but rather that one is Spanish-speaking and ethnically/culturally/racially Hispanic:

BB: When people ask you what you are, what do you say?

Nanette: I say I'm Spanish. I've had disputes over that one, "What do you call Spanish, you're not from Spain." When you're not Spanish, you don't really understand it, and I don't know if I really understand it myself. When people ask me, I'm Spanish. They're like, "What's Spanish? Where are you from then if you're just Spanish?" Well, there's tons of different Spanish people, but we just come from all different places. But we all speak Spanish, so we're Spanish. And they're like, "But no we speak English, and we're not all English." But it's just so different. There's something different. We all say we're Spanish.

Spanish language in the United States is a defining symbol of common origins in former Spanish colonies, and the label for the language becomes the label for the social identity defined by speaking it (cf. Urciuoli 1991 among New York Puerto Ricans).

In Janelle's reported exchange about being perceived as Black, Janelle and her interlocutor treat the social category "Spanish" as parallel in type to the folk-racial category "Black," but mutually exclusive from it. In local terms, if one is Dominican or Spanish-speaking, one doesn't count as "Black," regardless of phenotype. This African American classmate of Janelle treats Janelle's Spanish language (and subsequent self-ascription as Spanish) as valid evidence that she is *not* Black or Cape Verdean, even though she had initially perceived Janelle to be Black or Cape Verdean.

This treatment of Spanish/Hispanic/Dominican identity as a racial identity in its own right, mutually exclusive from Black identities, is common at Central High School:

Wilson: ...a lot of people confuse me for an African American most of the time. They ask me, "Are you Black?" I'm like, "No, I'm Hispanic." And they'll be like "Oh I thought you were Black or something." Most of the time I'll be talking with them, chilling, or whatever. They'll be thinking that I'm just African American. Because sometimes the way I talk, my hair, my skin color, it's just that my hair is nappy. I use a lot of slang. You can confuse a lot of Dominicans as African Americans by their color. So that's why a lot of people just ask me, "I thought you were Black", "I thought you were this".... Two weeks ago, a friend of mine, I know him from last year, and he didn't know I was Hispanic, so this year, right after school started, I had a Dominican flag on my shirt, and he all of a sudden just started looking at me all serious...and then all of a sudden he jumped to the conclusion: "Hold on, don't tell me, you're Hispanic, you're Dominican." and I was like "Yeah." He was like "I thought you was Black." I was like "Noo."

In this reported exchange, a United States racial identity symbolized by phenotype--"Black"--is again juxtaposed with what many would label an ethnolinguistic identity, "Hispanic," and a national identity, "Dominican." As in the above case, however, Wilson and his interlocutor treat "Dominican" and "Hispanic" as categories parallel or equivalent in type to the category "Black." This local system of classification thus does not necessarily privilege identities based on phenotype--specifically, perceived degrees of European and African ancestry--over those based on other social criteria such as language or national origins. Race is thus treated not as a static attribute of individuals, but rather as a locally achieved identity. Both Wilson's and Janelle's African-descent, or "Black," phenotypes remain constant, but they no longer *count* as Black when they speak Spanish or otherwise display symbols of Dominican identity.

The option that Wilson and Janelle exercise of having African-descent phenotype and a non-Black American identity is novel in the United States. As described in Chapter 1, "Black" in the United States has been a particularly and peculiarly totalizing identity, in which members have been implicitly treated as ethnically, culturally, and ancestrally undifferentiated. This distinctive characteristic of the category Black is a result of the particular ways in which Africans and their descendants were historically incorporated into America. The nature of slavery in the United States, in which African co-ethnics were separated, for example, served to erase African ethnic languages and tribal identities within the first generations, and most African Americans know little about from which specific parts of Africa their ancestors came (Waters 1991:60). Discrimination was historically directed uniformly at individuals of African descent, regardless of individual differences, thus having a leveling effect on differences. As a category that is explicitly defined by phenotype, it has historically been applied to anyone of African descent, even when it fails to capture the social heritage of individuals whose cultures and identities were not formed in the particularly American context of slavery, discrimination, and segregation. Wilson and Janelle's freedom to define themselves as something other than Black, despite explicitly African-descent features, thus represents a transformation of racial categories, if only at the local level.

Success in enacting Dominican American ethnolinguistic identities is heavily dependent on context. In the Providence public schools and neighborhoods with concentrations of Dominicans, the category Dominican is widely recognized and there are many opportunities to speak Spanish, thereby constituting a Dominican framework for assigning identities.[27] In contexts with few co-ethnics and few opportunities to speak Spanish, some individuals are categorically perceived in United States phenotype-based racial terms. Nancy, for example, had been bussed to elementary and middle schools that had few Hispanic students:

Nancy: When I went to [middle] school on the East Side, it was all, basically, African American, not many Dominicans, now it was just that I was going to school with mainly White students. I never went to school with Spanish students. When I went to elementary school, I was just mixed in with African Americans students, at Asa Messer. And Asians. It was a few Asians, some White students, and African Americans...

BB: How did people identify you there if they weren't used to Spanish people?

Nancy: I was probably just one of them, they probably just thought I was, now that I think about it, to them I was just probably Black. And it wasn't an issue, because no one ever asked me.

Valentina had a similar experience when she left Providence to attend the predominantly White University of Rhode Island, where Spanish speakers and Caribbean Hispanics were a small minority:

BB: Do people ask you what you are?

Valentina: They mostly assume I'm Black, they never really ask, but when they hear me speaking Spanish, "Oh, what are you, Dominican? I didn't know that." They get all shocked and surprised because they didn't think that I was Dominican...

BB: Can you think of a particular time that someone thought you were African American?
Valentina: Well, that's all the time.

For Valentina, recognition of her Dominican/Hispanic identity--tied to instances of public Spanish speaking--is the exception, rather than the rule. In addition to shaping others' ascriptions of identity, Dominican Spanish gives Dominican Americans entree to an alternate social world in which language encompasses differing assumptions about social boundaries. English and Dominican Spanish differ, for example, in available terms for describing individual phenotypes and social identities. These linguistic differences are intimately intertwined with differences in social histories. The multiplicity and ambiguity of terms for describing skin color/phenotypes in the Dominican Republic (see Chapter 5), for example, reflect and reproduce a way of seeing phenotypes in a society where phenotypes are not grouped and racialized in the ways they are in the United States.

The ways in which Dominican Spanish reproduces Dominican forms of social categorization are suggested by Wilson's description of the differing ways of characterizing his skin color in Spanish and English:

BB: What Spanish word do people in the Dominican Republic use to describe the color of your skin?
Wilson: That's, um, I'm not going to say a trick question, but it's something that you can put a lot of words towards it, like they'll call me indian, they'll call me *moreno* ['dark'], a lot of words, mostly, if I'm dark, any word that means dark they'll use. *Indio* ['indian-colored'], *indio moreno* ['dark indian-colored']. Any word that means you're dark brown or black.
BB: What about if you're speaking English to someone, how would you describe your skin color?
Wilson: ((laughing)) Actually, everybody just uses black and white.

While Dominican Spanish allows for description of a wide range of European/African phenotypes without implying social group membership, American English has just two binary terms that refer not just to phenotype but also to racialized social identities.

Individuals of African descent in American have historically been categorized based on phenotype and treated as ethnically undifferentiated. Dominican Americans in Providence successfully resist this form of classification by defining themselves in terms of national and/or ethnolinguistic origins rather than phenotype. Their use of Spanish language is a salient, everyday way of constituting communicative contexts in which they do not count as Black. This linguistic enactment of race highlights its processual and contingent nature, thereby undermining the dominant Black/White dichotomy, which rests on assumptions of inherent and unchanging difference.

4.9 Intragroup and Contextual Variation

In this chapter I have highlighted Dominican American solidarity with African Americans, a function of shared structural disadvantages, and related this to use of AAVE. I have also argued that a distinct Spanish/Dominican identity--indexed through Spanish use and represented by the linguistic metonym "Spanish"--is claimed, which differentiates them from African Americans and resists Black/White racialization.

Dominican American identities are much more multi-faceted, however, including competing folk-racial, ethnolinguistic, national, class, and regional allegiances and ascriptions. Even individual identities are not monolithic, as individuals invoke and enact varying identities across different situations. In the following utterances, for example, American-born Maria identifies herself implicitly and explicitly in many different ways: as American (1), Hispanic (9), Black (2), Spanish (2,3), from New York City (4,7), from the Southside of Providence (5), 100% Dominican (6), Dominican-Puerto Rican (8), descended primarily from ancestors from Spain (10), and "very White" in color (10). The variation in these self-ascriptions, which are drawn primarily from interview talk with the researcher, but also from interaction with peers, illustrates the way that seemingly contradictory facets of identity co-exist within individuals and are situationally invoked:

1) People who come from DR think it's gonna be easy here, but it's gonna be more difficult. And us Americans, we know what you have to go through.
[Regarding overblown expectations of life and wealth in America among new immigrants and would-be migrants.]

2) I always say that Spanish people are Black.
[In terms of the Black/White American folk-racial dichotomy, Hispanics don't count as White, so they are grouped with Blacks.]

3) "You have anything to tell me, you tell me here. I'm Spanish, but that don't mean you're perfect ['better'] than me."
[Maria is recounting the words she used in a confrontation with a discriminatory White student at a Catholic school she attended.]

4) I'm from New York, and New York girls, New York people...if you say anything, they're going to come up to you and they're going to hit you. They're too rough, that's the way I am. My mom says, "You're too rough." I say, "Lady, I come from New York, how do you expect me to be?"
[Discussing her confrontational style for dealing with White Americans she suspects of discrimination.]

5) I'm from Southside.
[At a South Providence church youth group meeting.]

6) I'm still Dominican, no matter what. I could have a green passport. 'Are you Dominican?' 'Yes.' 'Are you 100%?' 'Yeah, I'm 100%.'
[In discussing the fact that she has a blue United States passport rather than a red Dominican one]

7) I'm more like New York, I'm Dominican but I was born in New York, so I have New York attitude.
[In describing differences between herself and her parents' generation.]

8) BB: How do you describe your race or culture?
Maria: Sometimes I say I'm like "Mud." "Mud" means
Dominican-Puerto Rican.
[Her biological father has one parent who was originally from
Puerto Rico.]

9) When we go to restaurants to eat, we Hispanics, everybody look
at us like weird. I just look at them right back.
[Describing discrimination by White Americans that she and her
family face.]

10) Cause like my family, most of them from Spain....and my mom
she's dark, but my mother's not dark, she's light. Like this
[indicating arm], this is only a tan, but I'm very white, very white,
I'm almost as white, I think I'm almost whiter than you [the White
researcher]. I don't know. I was a white baby. My sister, the little
one, she's very white. My brother, he's whiter than me.
[Describing to the researcher the range of phenotypes exhibited by
Dominicans.]

These multiple self-ascriptions reflect just some facets of identity--
those related to ethnic/racial identity and socio-geographical
allegiances--that one individual Dominican American can invoke over
a short period of time. Their range suggests the complexity and
sometimes contradictory nature of forces influencing the way
Dominican Americans define themselves. While Maria calls herself
"American" in differentiating herself from newly arriving Dominican
immigrants with naive expectations of America, she considers herself
"100% Dominican." At the same time she defines Hispanics--and
herself by extension--as "Black" in terms of American racial hierarchy,
she draws attention to her white skin and Spaniard ancestry, which are
prestigious in traditional Dominican circles.

Because all individuals have multiple characteristics and
allegiances, it is the situational activation of commonalties and
differences that is characteristic of identity groupings (Evans-Pritchard
1940, Moerman 1965). Cohen (1978:387-8) explicitly defines ethnicity
in terms of "a series of nesting dichotomizations of inclusiveness and
exclusiveness" that operate at different levels at different times:

Group A can be labeled A in relation to B, C, and D. But among themselves, A people are keenly aware of subgroup differences in which groups X, Y, and Z all understand the ethnic distinctions among themselves and the possibility of greater or lesser differences in the future, depending upon a large range of factors.

When asked by a White American researcher in an interview context, "When people ask you what you are, what do you say?", Dominican Americans invariably highlight their Dominican or Hispanic/Spanish identity. Non-White identities marked by phenotype are easily perceived by others and are unilaterally invoked and treated as relevant by others. In intergroup encounters in the United States, Dominican Americans define themselves as "Dominican" without qualification, even if they are United States-born and -raised. They thus use the same term to identify themselves that is used to identify Dominicans who have never left the island, even though the two groups differ significantly in cultural experiences, beliefs, and practices (see Chapter 5).

In intra-group situations, however, Dominicans and Dominican Americans invoke numerous sub-boundaries among themselves. On the island, for example, Dominican Americans who are seen as Americanized and inauthentically Dominican are disparagingly referred to as *dominicans* /dominikins/ (adopted from the English word "Dominicans") rather than *dominicanos,* or as *dominican yorks* (Dominicans from New York/America). Adolescent and young adult Dominican Americans who adopt stereotypical hip hop fashions in dress, language, and behavior are disparagingly referred to on the island as *yos* /dʒos/ (a Dominican Spanish pronunciation of "yo's"), because of their frequent use of the interjection "yo".[28] Adoption of low-income, non-White, urban youth culture--the type most readily available to many Dominican Americans and a means of expressing opposition to United States ethnic/racial hierarchies--leads to negative evaluations in the Dominican Republic where there is less understanding of American social stratification and racial dynamics.

To many outsiders, Dominican Americans and Dominicans may both count simply as Dominicans, but among themselves the differences are noted and in many contexts treated as relevant. Although members of the second generation identify themselves to outsiders simply as "Dominican," their parents, recent immigrants, and those who haven't left the island see them as different from those who have grown up on the island. Even though parents and recently arrived relatives regularly point these differences out to them, many in the second generation are surprised by the culture shock they experience upon visiting the island. This culture shock can even occur among those who did not leave the island until the beginning of adolescence. Jose M., for example, had not been to the Dominican Republic for nine years after emigrating at age 13. He found himself feeling like a stranger in the Dominican Republic--a feeling he had previously associated only with his life in America--when I talked to him shortly after he returned from a Christmas visit:

BB: What do you call yourself?
Jose M.: It's funny because before I went to the Dominican Republic, like I was so proud to say I'm Dominican, Dominican. But then when I went there, it was like, I hadn't been there in nine years, and everything is so different. I feel so different from everybody. Like people are so fast and things are so disorganized. Like I felt like out of place. I swear. And people are just there to rip you off for the money and stuff. I don't know, I feel Dominican, but not really Dominican like really from there. I feel like I'm a little bit like a stranger over there too. I'm more Americanized. That's probably why. Cause I'm used to more like making the line to go pay a bill or something instead of trying to jump around and push, I'm not used to that. I had a good time, but it was also-- it was annoying sometimes. And the guys are like so-- I went with my girlfriend and they wouldn't stop staring. Like if you walk with a girl they're like this ((demonstrates conspicuous staring))...It's like they get them naked with their eyes and stuff.

Other consultants experienced differences on a less stark and more pleasurable note, e.g. emphasizing the relative spontaneity of social life in the Dominican Republic. Regardless of whether experiences are positive or negative, however, such visits invariably activate awareness of differences between American socialized and island socialized Dominicans.

Among Dominican Americans, being Dominican involves minimally having parents from the Dominican Republic and following some cultural practices associated with the Dominican Republic. Classical High School graduate Nancy, for example, defined herself as feeling "very much Dominican" even though she spoke virtually no Spanish and had never been to the Dominican Republic:

Nancy: I think we've always had the culture, because I live very much like a Dominican, we ate the rice and beans, the music was always going on, we went to the festivals and the Church, even though we didn't speak Spanish at home, we were very much Dominican. That's why I feel very much Dominican. Raised the same way, all the rules and all the strictness and all that stuff.

The significance of language as a diacritic (Barth 1969) of Dominican identity in America varies among individuals and across contexts. Jose M. points out that there can be a disparity between the perceptions of Dominican Americans and Dominicans from the island (cf. Zentella 1990b among New York and island Puerto Ricans):

BB: To say that you're Dominican, do you need to speak Spanish?
Jose M.: Not really. You might say to a White person or somebody of another race that you're Dominican, and they might be like, "Oh yeah, okay, you're Dominican." But then if you see a real Dominican, and you cannot even speak Spanish or you don't know this or that, they be like "And you're calling yourself Dominican? You don't deserve that title."

Dominican American ethnicity, like other ethnicities, is not homogeneous but rather a repertoire of social identities (Kroskrity 1993) variously available to members of the Dominican American community, various aspects of which are situationally made relevant in members' lives.

4.10 Code Switching in a Multivariety Setting

Language behavior and social identities in the context of code switching have often been treated as dichotomous, focusing on two languages and the ways in which alternation between these languages corresponds to expression or enactment of one of two identities.[29] As shown in Chapter 3, the linguistic resources of Dominican Americans comprise not just two codes but forms from multiple and syncretic varieties, and as shown in this chapter, the identities variously available to Dominican Americans are multiple and multi-faceted.

In the remainder of this chapter, I will explore a few of the many relationships between Spanish/English code switching and the construction of Dominican American identities.[30] As seen in examples in Chapter 3, code switching is frequently unmarked in Dominican American interactions, serving various conversational management functions, but *not* representing metaphorical extensions of Dominican worlds (Spanish) or United States ones (English). There are, however, also times when these codes/varieties are used as metaphorical extensions of specific sociocultural interpretive frameworks, institutions, understandings, and activities, as described by Blom and Gumperz (1972) in their original distinction between situational and metaphorical code switching.

These switches do not follow simple dichotomies in which Spanish represents a Dominican "we" and English represents a United States "they," however. In the following examples, Spanish is used to represent the voice of a stigmatized Dominican Other (as opposed to Dominican *American*); a Hollywood version of African American communicative behavior is used to display intragroup Dominican American solidarity; and White English is used to index the lack of urban cool associated with rural Dominican living. These associations between language varieties and social identities are not static or preset, but are negotiated in talk. Because interlocutors display to each other their ongoing understandings of the social worlds they are constructing, some of these meanings are available to the analyst observing their talk.

4.10.1 Example 1: "He's like a hick, he talks so much Spanish"

In the following segments Isabella and Janelle use language to display shifting stances toward Spanish language and various Dominican/Dominican American identities. In the first segment Isabella gives an account of how she came to be dating a recent Dominican immigrant, Sammy, and why she is going to break up with him. Her explanations of why she eventually found him to be undesirable--including a code switched direct quote--reveal the

negotiation of code meanings and identities in the construction of a
Dominican American identity.

[(JS #2 11:56) Isabella and Janelle are sitting outside, skipping class,
discussing their weekend plans. Isabella has been dating Sammy for
about 10 days.]

Janelle: I though Sammy was going to come Friday
Isabella: He's coming Sat- Friday but I'm going to break up with him
            before that. So // (   )
Janelle: //Why?
Isabella: I don't like him, Janelle.
Janelle: Why did you go out with him in the first place?
Isabella: Because he was ma::d cute! he he he! //But he (   )
Janelle: //You are stupid
Isabella: *Mira* ['Look/You see'], I used to see him at the club. >Look
            at Hector.< I used to see him- in- Tropical with his brother
            (   ) I used to be checking that kid out, yo.
Janelle: (   )
Isabella: And then- I saw him (   ) at ('s) with the guys. And
            then I'm like, whoa, you know, I had to (whatever). And
            then I started going out with him. And I couldn't believe that
            he would like me because he was so cute.
Janelle: Uh huh.
Isabella: And then I got to know him? And I'm like-- ((wrinkles
            face))
Janelle: u::::::! ((of disgust)) ((both laugh))
Isabella: He's like-- I don't kno:w. He's- he's so jealous.
Janelle: Oh
Isabella: This kid is sickening! He- he tells me to call him before I go
            to the club. He- I'm like, I don't have time to call you, pick
            up the phone, call you while my friends are outside beeping
            the horn at me so I can jet with them to the club. And he's
            like- I don't know, he talks- he's like a hick, he talks so
            much Spanish! And he //(   )
Janelle: ((looks away))   //O::h!
Isabella: No, but he speaks Spanish, but- I- the reason- I talk to him-
            when he talks on the phone he speaks English a lot because I
            speak English. more. I tell him, speak English, speak

English. (I go *loco* ['honey']), ((wrinkled face)) *lo::ca*,
lo::ca. He goes, you know, *ni:ña* ['girl'], and you know, and
I don't want to hear it.

Janelle: You should have found that out before you went out with
            him.

Isabella: I know, he's rushing into it, he thinks- he's already looking
            to the future....

Sammy is initially described as very attractive ("he was mad cute";
"he was so cute") and desirable, but then subsequently construed as
very unappealing. This lack of appeal is constructed in terms of a
constellation of associated traits that are sequentially revealed and
interactionally assessed. This construction of negative traits begins with
a very general characterization of his personality, proceeds through a
specific trait (jealousy), and ends with highly specific examples of his
linguistic behavior--animated (Goffman 1981) by Isabella--that index
negative social attributes.

Sammy's biophysical cuteness--a desirable trait--contrasts with
aspects of his person that were revealed to Isabella as she got to know
him. Janelle co-constructs this social situation of cute but undesirable
males by completing Isabella's assessment (Goodwin and Goodwin
1992) and then joining Isabella in laughter.

Isabella: And then I got to know him? And I'm like-- (wrinkles face)
Janelle: /u:::::/! (of disgust) ((both laugh))

Isabella's "like" in this case serves to introduce a reported affective
state (cf. Romaine and Lange 1998) that she experienced after getting
to know Sammy. By appropriately completing Isabella's turn, Janelle
proves her attendance to Isabella's talk, displays her understanding of
Isabella's unstated, historical internal state, and displays alignment with
Isabella's displayed stance toward Sammy and, perhaps, the type of
male he represents.

Isabella then specifies a particular personality deficiency from
which Sammy suffers--"he's so jealous"--and gives an example of the
effects of this jealousy, his displeasure that she went to a club without
first calling him. In this same turn, Isabella specifies two further,
negative characteristics of Sammy: "he's like a hick" and "he talks so
much Spanish."

Janelle responds to these final two assessments with an emphatic "O::h!" and vertical head nods, suggesting a shared understanding of the undesirable nature of a male who is like a hick and speaks so much Spanish. Isabella, however, treats some aspect of Janelle's second-assessment ("O::h!")--perhaps her turning away--as problematic ("No, but...."). The fact that Sammy is like a hick and speaks so much Spanish is not the last word on him and why Isabella is breaking up with him. Isabella then describes specifics of Sammy's language use--that he speaks a lot of English on the telephone at Isabella's insistence. She then enacts, through direct quotation, particular Spanish forms--*lo:ca, lo:ca* and *ni:ña*--that Sammy uses. Isabella wrinkles her face and uses a slightly nasal voice quality, drawing out the /o/ of *loca* and the /i/ of *niña*. In later viewing of this videotape, Isabella translated *loca* as "honey" and *niña* as "girl", i.e. address forms of endearment. She said that she didn't like being addressed with these terms in Spanish, although there was "nothing wrong with them," and that she wanted boyfriends to use their English equivalents.

The use of code switching to set off quotations from surrounding talk has often been noted as a function of code switching, and many have noted that the code used for the quotation is not necessarily the same one that the speaker originally used. In this case, the code match between the quoted speech and Sammy's original speech is of significance. Code switching here is not just a means of marking off the directly quoted speech, but a means of indexing social attributes and displaying stances associated with a particular use of a code.

This code switch for direct quotation--and the prosodic and visual features of the quoted speech (cf. Mitchell-Kernan 1972 on "marking" among African American)--serve to index negative attributes: a stereotyped island Dominican backwardness that is inappropriate for an American urban youth context, and, perhaps, traditional Dominican gender roles associated with island Dominican male identities. Isabella identifies Sammy as jealous, like a hick, and speaking so much Spanish, all in the same turn at talk. Consultants as well as literature on Dominican gender roles (e.g. Pessar 1984, 1987; Grasmuck and Pessar 1991, 1996) suggest that Dominican males have traditionally exercised a great degree of control over their girlfriends'/wives' interactions and social contacts outside of the home. For Isabella, Sammy's addressing her as *loca* and *niña* may invoke a traditional Dominican social framework for their relationship, a framework that she wishes to avoid.

As described by Ochs (1992), linguistic indexicality of social identities is often *indirect*. Language frequently directly indexes activities, acts, or stances, which, in combination with other linguistic and social features of a context, serve to constitute social identities. In this case, Isabella code switches to display a particular stance toward particular Dominican male ways of talking to her, a stance that is at least partly shared by Janelle. This stance, in turn, serves to index aspects of a particular Dominican American teen-age female identity, which is distinct from other Dominican and American identities.

Much of the literature on code switching has emphasized the in-group connotations of the code used by the non-dominant/minority group in informal and family situations. In this case, in contrast, Spanish is being used to mock a fellow Spanish speaker and differentiate between a positive self and a disparaged other, even though the other is a fellow Dominican immigrant and Spanish speaker. Although Isabella had lived in the Dominican Republic until age 6, was a fluent Spanish speaker, and had a monolingual mother, Spanish language is treated as indexing *negative* attributes in this interaction.

4.10.2 Example 2: "They're friends *de Santo Domi:ngo, del ca:mpo*"

The meanings of code use and individuals' relationships to them are locally negotiated, as are the aspects of individual identities that are invoked and highlighted. In the prior segment, for example, Isabella and Janelle align themselves by defining themselves in opposition to characteristics of a recent male immigrant. In the following segment, Isabella and Janelle implicitly and explicitly reveal multiple stances toward codes and the Dominican Republic, and Isabella differentiates herself from Janelle, implicitly claiming greater authenticity. In this case, Isabella's relatively greater familiarity with the language and institutions of the island are treated as favorable characteristics of a positive social identity.

[(JS #2 12:39:33) Isabella and Janelle are outside skipping class and have been talking about a couple that just walked by. Isabella tries to ascertain the relationships between Daniel and Sammy, the boyfriend she was disparaging in the prior segment of transcript, by asking Basil, who is standing nearby.]

Isabella: And I go out with his-

    (.5)

Isabella: (→B.) Sammy and Daniel are cousins? ((Janelle looks away))

Basil: They're friends

Isabella: They're friends

Basil: They know each other //(   )

Isabella: //(*de*/from) *Santo <Domi:ngo>*,
            ['the Dominican Republic']

Janelle: Are they really- //they're brothers, ( )?

Isabella: //*<del ca:mpo>* ['from the countryside']

Janelle: *Son hermanos?*   ['Are they brothers?']

Isabella: (→B.) *Son hermanos* ['Are they brothers?']

Basil: They used to go to school together.

Isabella: They used to go to school together in *Santo Domi:ngo. En el-* (.) *asilo.* ['...the Dominican Republic. At a (.) boarding school']

    (2.2)

Isabella: *el-* (.8) ((Isabella frowns)) *colegio.* ['a (.8) private high school.'] >Yeah, that.<

    (.2)

Janelle: I know, I hate that with *colegio*. It sounds like- (.2) some Catholic- or I don't know ((Isabella quietly mouths *colegio* during Janelle's turn))

Isabella: I used to- (you know-) Oh, //(now) I understand

Janelle: //(   ), hmm.

    (.2)

Isabella: You're a bootleg, //I forgot.

Janelle: //(yeah, man)

Janelle: But what?

Isabella: I used to- I used to- when I //used to go over there?

Basil: //(going inside)

    (.5)

Isabella: (→B.) Get out of here!

As in the prior segment, Isabella adopts a marked, slightly nasal pronunciation as she switches into Spanish (*Santo Domingo, del campo*). This register--her version of a rural Dominican variety--is distinct from the variety that she uses in code switching with friends (e.g. in her subsequent *Son hermanos?*) or speaking Spanish to her mother. Although she is not using Spanish for direct quotation here, she is still assuming the voice of a recent Dominican immigrant from the countryside, inspired by her perceptions of Sammy, to talk about Sammy. This change in footing makes clear that her "alignment, or set, or stance, or posture, or projected self is somehow at issue" (Goffman 1981:128). Isabella uses this code switch with marked prosodic features to distance herself from Dominican *campo* identities.

Rural areas of the Dominican Republic contrast sharply with the urban centers in wealth, infrastructure, and education. While luxury cars, satellite dishes, first-class hotels, universities etc. can all be found in the major cities of Santiago and Santo Domingo, many rural areas lack electricity, pavement, safe drinking water, etc. and illiteracy and poverty rates are high.[31] Dominican Americans' characterization of individuals as "hicks" or references to the *campo* do not necessarily mean someone is actually from the countryside, but that they display what is perceived as a lack of urban American sophistication.[32]

Isabella hesitates in specifying the institution where Sammy and Daniel met, with a cut-off and a beat of silence before saying *asilo*, which, she later told me, she thought was a kind of school. (It can mean "boarding school" or "old-age home.") After a gap of 2.2 seconds, she self-corrects with *"El-* (.8) *colegio"*, again with a cut off and a pause after *el-*. Before saying *colegio* she displays a dramatic frown as if trying to come up with a word or concept with which she was unfamiliar, even though *colegio* is the everyday word for (private) high school in the Dominican Republic. Her subsequent accelerated pronunciation and code switch ("Yeah, that") help instantiate a separate speech activity, a comment on *colegio* that displays her stance toward it, one of distance and unfamiliarity.

Janelle treats Isabella's utterance as displaying this outsider stance toward *colegio*, by addressing that aspect of Isabella's turn in her own turn. Janelle's "I know"" is not oriented toward the propositional content of Isabella's turn, but the social stance (e.g. "These are strange words and institutions") that she displays in it. Janelle is aligning herself with Isabella in this outsider perspective on island Dominican institutions, and she gives an example of her own unfamiliarity and confusion regarding the word *colegio*. In her next turn, Isabella begins to give an account of when she used to go "over there" (the Dominican Republic), but then cuts herself off to address Janelle's associations of the word *"colegio"* with "Catholic" ("Oh, ( ) I understand."). Rather than displaying alignment with the stance displayed by Janelle, she chooses to socially differentiate herself, identifying Janelle as belonging to a separate social category based on Janelle's displayed stance toward *colegio* and Catholic: "You're a bootleg, I forgot."

Dominican Americans in Providence who speak little Spanish and are unfamiliar with institutions and geography on the island are sometimes accused of being "bootleg" Dominicans. The term bootleg, commonly used to identify products such as cassette tapes or CD's that are illegally produced or distributed, suggests a lack of authenticity. Thus, "bootleg Dominicans" are those individuals who are Dominican by parentage but who lack the traits of true, authentic Dominicans. Paradoxically, Isabella publicly displays her own unfamiliarity with the Dominican secondary school system through hesitation and metadiscursive comment ("Yeah, that"), but then differentiates herself from Janelle in terms of linguistic/cultural knowledge and authenticity. Isabella had spent her first six years on the island and visited several times. Janelle, in contrast, was American-born and had been there only once to visit, as a small child.

Isabella's identification of Janelle as a "bootleg" is preceded by Isabella's incipient reference to trips to the Dominican Republic. After the bootleg comment, Janelle other-initiates repair ("But what?"), leading to Isabella's self-repair of her uncompleted utterance: ("When I used to go over there?"). Isabella's reference to trips to the Dominican Republic is consistent with her ascription of Janelle to the category bootleg, both serving to differentiate between authentic Dominicans with knowledge and experience of the island and inauthentic ones. Even within a single sequence of talk, Dominican Americans display shifting stances to the island and Spanish language, which can be both a source of stigma and positive identity. As is evident from this segment, social categories, their linguistic indexes, and the ways individuals fit into them are not static but are negotiated. These categories and meanings are constructed both referentially and indexically.

4.10.3 Example 3: *Loca, loca, eeeee, epa*

In the following segment, which begins less than a minute after the end of the one transcribed above, Janelle and Isabella display their understandings, both referential and indexical, of what it means to be a "hick."

[(JS #2 12:40:58) Janelle and Isabella are sitting outside. Janelle has noticed some students staring in her direction. Their attention is likely attracted by the spectacle of her being videotaped.]

Isabella: I like Bulivan's dress. ((gazing at a fellow student))
Janelle: I know.
Isabella: If it was sleeveless, it'd be nicer.
Janelle: What's up with them people looking over here, them hicks? And stuff.
Isabella: <No: hicks>. ((deep pitched, husky voice; assuming slack-faced, dull stare))
Janelle: What do you call a hick? Cause Jose says a hick is someone ridiculous, somebody stupid. Isn't a hick someone who just came back from the country and they can't really dress, they can't speak English? And they, you know,
Isabella: They be like *loca, loca, //e:::::: pa, epa::: , huepa:* ["honey, honey, he:::::::y, alright!, alri::::ght!, alri:ght!"]
Janelle: //Yeah, right?
Isabella: (//   )
Janelle: //See that kid? He looks like he's White and Black?

Janelle uses the term "hick" to refer to a group of students who are staring across the school grounds in her direction. Isabella then intones "No, hicks," taking on the voice of a hick by using a deep-pitched, husky, slow tempo pronunciation and assuming a slack-faced stare. Although this is not a code switch, it is clearly a variety or register shift, demonstrating the constant and immanent heteroglossia of language. She is using English code to take on the voice of a category of speaker who would most likely be speaking Spanish or English with marked Spanish phonology. Both the propositional content of her utterance as well as her marked pronunciation index a stance in which hicks count as the Other.

Janelle then checks her understanding of the meaning of the word "hick," contrasting her understanding with that of her friend Jose, who understands "hick" only in terms of its local connotations of "stupid" or "ridiculous." Janelle offers a candidate understanding of a hick in referential terms: as someone who just came from the (Dominican) countryside, is not acculturated to urban American youth clothing fashions, and can't speak English. Isabella displays her common understanding of hicks not through reference but by giving a representative direct quotation of their speech: *loca, loca, e:::::, epa, epa, huepa.* She squints and scrunches her face, using a nasal, slightly high-pitched register.[33] Janelle displays alignment with Isabella's characterization ("yeah") and once again requests confirmation that her candidate understanding of hick is correct ("right?").

In these three segments, Isabella and Janelle use language both referentially and indexically to situationally invoke commonalties and differences between themselves and others, and between each other. Enactment of these varying "dichotomizations of inclusiveness and exclusiveness" (Cohen 1978:387) is the basic realization of identity, marking who counts the same and who counts as different.

4.10.4 Example 4: C'mon, dude

In the following segment, Alejandro uses a variety of Spanish and English linguistic resources that index varied facets of his Dominican American identity in rapidly shifting fashion. As in the above cases, his code switching and assumption of different voices rely on metaphorical meanings of codes and styles in ways that are much more complicated than suggested by 'we' vs. 'they' codes and identities.

[(LD #SM 8:30:44) Jonathan, Alejandro, and Samuel are sitting next to each other in a larger circle of about 12 members of a Friday evening Catholic youth group. The adult group leader is discussing, in Spanish, upcoming summer activities for the group.]

GL: *El viernes ellas empiezan, el viernes el cuarto de julio.*
         // *Entonces*.....[They're starting Friday, Friday the Fourth of July. So...']

Alej.:   //((chanting)) I ain't gonna be here! /u::/ DR! ((Slaps hands with Jonathan after /u::/, then bobs his shoulders in a *merengue* style))

(1.5)

Alej.: (→J) *Al estilo* Will Smith, *al estilo* Fresh Prince. Kpsh:::. ['Will Smith style, Fresh Prince style'] ((Slaps hands with Jonathan, then does a synchronized over the shoulder pointing gesture with thumb accompanied by /ʃ/ rushing sound))

(4.5)   ((Group leader continues discussing, in Spanish, the schedule of summer meetings.))

Jon.: (→ S)   You going to DR?

(.5)

Jon.:   You're (   )

Alej.:   You gonna be in this *campo*

Jon.:   (   )

Alej.:   C'mon dude ((holding up his hands, palms forward; assuming a goofy expression))

Jon.:   No phone, they got telegraph ((mimes tapping and makes beeping noises))

Alej.:   *No, jugando Nintendo* ((mimes staring at handheld game and playing slowly)) ['No, playing Nintendo.]

Jon.:   *Con palitos* ((mimes tossing sticks into the air)) ['With little sticks']

Alej.:   I want- I want to go to the beach- ((White voice; facing forward))

Alej.: (→ J) Oh, *el papá mío me dará cinco mil* (*tubos*)- *cinco mil pesos, loco.* ['Oh, my Dad is going to give me five thousand (   )- five thousand pesos, man.']

Jon.:   In DR?

Alej.:   He:ll, yea:h! *Me dan- me dan más entonces.* ['They're going to give me- give me more later.']

Jon.:   *Allá?* ['There?']

Alej.:   For the first- for the first fifteen days *cinco mil pesos.* ['...five thousand pesos.]

Alejandro's first utterance follows the adult leader's mention of the Fourth of July, a date when Alejandro will be in the Dominican Republic. He turns to Jonathan, one of his best friends, who is also going to spend the summer in the Dominican Republic, to celebrate his and Jonathan's impending trips.

In one sense this is a code switch in that his most recent utterances have been in Spanish and the referent that triggered his utterance was in Spanish. In another sense, this interaction with Jonathan and Samuel is a separate activity from the group leader's talk, a form of "subordinate communication" that does not interfere with her "dominating communication" (Goffman 1981:133). Participants themselves treat this communicative activity as distinct from the dominant communication by relaxing normally exigent turn-taking rules (Sacks, Schegloff, and Jefferson 1974), and extensively overlapping with the group leader's talk.

Alejandro's use of English here, though not a paradigmatic code switch, carries local metaphorical meaning. As described above, games and Bible-study activities that involve the whole group are generally carried out in Spanish, and the adult leader speaks little English. English dominant individuals will speak to each other in English or both, however, and bilingual male members of the group often use English to resist the Bible-reading and discussion activities in Spanish, subverting the activities that Spanish helps to constitute. In this case, Alejandro's use of English serves to metaphorically resist the ongoing official group frame, the leader's discussion of upcoming activities.

In his next turn, Alejandro switches to Spanish, but a syncretic form with nonce borrowings of English proper names--"Will Smith" and "Fresh Prince"--unassimilated to Spanish phonology. Jonathan and Alejandro both treat this utterance as a cue to engage in a second handslap and an over-the-shoulder pointing gesture with the thumb, which they execute in unison. This gesture comes from the network television show "The Fresh Prince of Bel-Air" that stars African American rap artist Will Smith. The gesture is used by characters to signal departure. Alejandro is thus using Dominican Spanish with English borrowings to coordinate a gesture drawn from a Hollywood version of African American male youth behavior to celebrate an upcoming trip to the Dominican Republic.

After turning briefly back toward the group leader, Jonathan turns toward Samuel, directing a question at him in English ("You going to DR?"). This activity is topically tied to Alejandro and Jonathan's immediately preceding interaction--impending summer trips to the Dominican Republic--which was visually and acoustically available to Samuel, but Samuel is only now ratified as a participant in this talk (Goffman 1981).

The choice of code to address Samuel is marked because Samuel is a recent Dominican immigrant who speaks little English. He had just minutes before volunteered to the entire group that he couldn't follow activities when English predominated, and in both the school and church group contexts that I observed, Alejandro and Jonathan addressed him otherwise only in Spanish. This use of English violates basic expectations of situational code choice (Blom and Gumperz 1972) that Alejandro and Jonathan otherwise follow.

Samuel does not audibly respond to this question, but Alejandro and Jonathan's subsequent turns suggest that Samuel gave an affirmative visual response, perhaps a vertical head nod (he was off-camera). It is possible that being addressed in English deterred him from responding verbally.

While Alejandro and Jonathan jointly celebrated the fact that they were both going to the Dominican Republic, they treat Samuel's upcoming trip as grounds to make fun of him. Their subsequent turns addressed to Samuel are in English and have a derogatory tone, e.g. Alejandro tells him "You gonna be in this *campo*," switching only on a word for which English equivalents fail to capture the appropriate connotations.

Following Jonathan's inaudible turn, Alejandro switches to a marked White English variety, "C'mon, dude." He uses a relatively high pitched and slow tempo voice, and he uses the term of address "dudes" which Alejandro and other Dominican Americans I observed did not use. While speaking he holds his hands up even with his shoulders, palms forward and directs his gaze forward as if performing a role for others to view.

While White English is the prestige standard in educational, business, and many institutional contexts in the United States, as shown earlier, it also has negative connotations in some local Dominican American contexts. In this case, White English, with its local connotations of boring effeteness, is being used to represent the lack of sophistication and urban youth excitement of life in a remote Dominican *campo*.

Jonathan then claims in English that in Samuel's *campo* they do not have telephones, only telegraph, and he mimes the tapping on a telegraph key. Alejandro counters that they don't even have that contact with the outside world there--that the most exciting activity there is to sit by oneself and play Nintendo, and he mimes playing with a small, self-contained game. Jonathan suggests that individuals there don't even have Nintendo for entertainment, just little sticks, and he mimes tossing little sticks up into the air and catching them.

Alejandro continues in White English, his upper body stiff and upright, facing forward rather than to the side toward Jonathan or Samuel, his voice slightly high pitched and strained ("I want to go to the beach-"). These prosodic and visual features suggest that he is enacting a role, perhaps a mocking of Samuel or similar individual stuck in the *campo*. Alejandro had described to me his extensive plans for going out to nightclubs that summer and for going to various beaches. Dominicans are proud of the island's beaches, and middle and upper class urban youth, like Alejandro, regularly visit them in the summers. In contrast to Samuel, both Jonathan and Alejandro could expect a summer not just of socializing with relatives, but of enjoying urban entertainment such as nightclubs and taking trips to various beaches.

Alejandro cuts off his own speech, breaking off the White English voice and the teasing frame by turning to Jonathan, sitting less upright, and using the disjunct marker "oh" to display "sudden remembering" (Jefferson 1978), and describing the spending money that he will receive in the Dominican Republic. Referring to the limitations of Samuel's summer entertainment options may have triggered pleasurable anticipation of his own summer plans. Alejandro and Jonathan no longer address Samuel, directly or indirectly, but engage in talk of spending money, a relative's vehicles in the Dominican Republic, and plans for summer activities there. In contrast to the immediately prior code switching, in which code and variety switching had clear metaphorical implications, this code switching is the unmarked sort common among bilingual Dominican Americans in everyday talk.

4.11 Unmarked Code Switching and Identities

Bilingual Dominican American youth use interpenetrating linguistic resources from both Spanish and English in ways that defy both assumptions of linguistic homogeneity (e.g. Chomsky 1965) and dominant, implicit ideologies of linguistic purity and prescription (Milroy and Milroy 1985). Such linguistic ideologies (Schieffelin, Woolard, and Kroskrity 1998), often highly naturalized, shape both behavior and the ways in which that behavior is interpreted, making it difficult to distinguish between an analyst's prejudices and the phenomena under investigation. The naturalization of such ideologies led Weinreich (1953:73), for example, to confuse his own idealization of behavior with individual linguistic facility[34]:

The ideal bilingual switches from one language to the other according to the appropriate changes in the speech situation (interlocutors, topic, etc.), but not in unchanged speech situations, and certainly not within a single sentence.

My data, like that from many other studies among Spanish-English bilinguals in the United States (Poplack 1981, Duran 1981, Amastae and Elias-Olivares 1982, Lipski 1985, Zentella 1997), show that individuals regularly *do* switch languages in relatively unchanged speech situations. Poplack (1982:259) sees generalized use of intrasentential code switching not as a mistaken mixing of forms, as implied by Weinreich, but as "an overall discourse *mode*" in its own right. Poplack argues that it is precisely those individual New York Puerto Ricans who use intrasentential switching who tend to have the greatest bilingual skills.[35]

> precisely those switch types that have traditionally been considered most deviant by investigators and educators, those that occur within a single sentence, are the ones that require the most skill. They tend to be produced by the "true" bilinguals in the sample: speakers who learned both languages in early childhood and who have the most contact with the monolingual English-speaking world. (1982:261)

Dominican Americans in Providence, like the New York Puerto Ricans studied by Poplack, do not have a linguistic ideology that idealizes compartmentalization of codes, and in everyday intragroup situations Dominican English and Dominican Spanish do not have the politically charged metaphorical connotations that they have in other multi-lingual/multi-variety situations (e.g. Heller 1992).

Comparative studies of code switching highlight the roles played by groups' political economic position and language ideologies in code switching practices and interpretation. Poplack (1988), for example, shows that contrasting patterns of code switching between two communities--a New York Puerto Rican one and a Ottawa-Hull French Canadian one--correlate to contrasting political economic positions of the two groups. Even though the genetic relationships between French and English are very similar to the genetic relationships between Spanish and English, the communities switch very differently.

Bilingual New York Puerto Rican switches tend to be smooth and seamless, i.e. unmarked, while French-English switches tend to be highlighted, or marked, through repetition, hesitation, intonational highlighting, and even explicit metalinguistic commentary.

In their behavioral flagging of code switches, Poplack's Ottawa-Hull French Canadians approach the ideal of bilingual behavior described by Weinreich (1953):

> If he [the bilingual] does include expressions from another language, he may mark them off explicitly as "quotations" by quotation marks in writing and by special voice modifications (slight pause, change in tempo, and the like) in speech. There is reason to suspect that considerable individual differences exist between those who have control of their switching, holding it close to this ideal pattern, and those who have difficulty in maintaining or switching codes as required. (1953:73)

While Weinreich attributes such differences to individual linguistic facility, Poplack (1988) argues that the forms of code switching in particular communities are a function of larger sociopolitical forces. Whereas bilingualism is seen to be emblematic of New York Puerto Rican identity--differentiating members from island Puerto Ricans and non-Puerto Rican Anglophones--Ottawa-Hull French Canadian bilingualism is not associated with a social identity distinct from that of local monolingual French Canadians. For New York Puerto Ricans, syncretic use of two languages is both an emblem of a distinctive identity and a practice that draws in immigrant newcomers. In the French Canadian situation, there is no stream of newcomers to incorporate and no distinctive identity bridging disparate communities that needs to be enacted or maintained through language.

Gal (1988:247) links specific code switching ideologies to their broader political economic and historical context. She suggests that groups with similar structural positions will display similarities in code switching meanings and practices. Second generation Italian labor migrants in Germany (Auer 1984, 1988) and New York Puerto Ricans, for example, share a position that includes "legally assured opportunities for circle migration, discrimination and lack of social mobility linked to relatively late entry into a contracting economy"

(Gal 1988:257). In both communities, code switching follows a distinctive pattern in which switches are frequent and unmarked, and more often used as contextualization cues (Gumperz 1982, 1992) to signal and achieve changes in footing (Goffman 1981) than to communicate metaphorical meanings. Dominican Americans share a similar political economic position to Italian and Puerto Rican labor migrants--although even more marginal because of phenotype and migration obstacles--and they share similar frequent, unmarked code switching behavior. This pattern is very different from the ones found in bilingual communities in other historical and political economic positions (Gal 1988:251-8).

The fact that much Dominican American code switching is locally unmarked, however, is not the same as saying that it has no meanings. In terms of identity, it is important to distinguish between *discursive functions of particular code switches* and the more global *sociopolitical functions of code switching as a discourse mode* (cf. Myers Scotton 1993b:149). The syncretic conversational practice of unmarked Spanish-English code switching is a key index of ethnic, racial, and political economic identity for Dominican Americans.

As described above in section 4.8, it is precisely individuals' use of Spanish--*which occurs most commonly in the context of code switching rather than extended Spanish language narratives or interactions*--that is central to ascriptions of ethnolinguistic, as opposed to phenotype-racial, identity for Dominican Americans. The interaction transcribed below illustrates how displays of Spanish language are available not only to bilingual ratified participants (Goffman 1981) but also to monolingual English speakers who have aural access to an interaction. In this particular segment, Isabella even addresses a monolingual English speaker in Spanish--without triggering any apparent interactional trouble--as she carries on two simultaneous interactions in which Spanish and English turns interleave and overlap.

[[IN #1 9:30 Isabella is sitting between Aisha (Nigerian/African American) and Ana (Dominican American) in word processing class as they sit in a row facing computer monitors.)

Aisha: (→I.)   I never centered a table horizontally. Have you
                 //done that?]
Ana: (→I.)   //*Mira qué hora tú tienes (ahorita)?* ['What time do
                 you have (now)?']

Isabella: (→Ana) *Eh?* ['Huh?']
Ana: (→I.)   *Qué hora tú tienes?* ['What time do you have?']
Isabella: (→Ana) I'll have to check my beeper
Aisha: (→I.)   Have you?
Isabella: (→Ais.) *Qué* ['What?']
Aisha: (→I.)   Have you ever centered a table, horizontally?
Isabella: (→Ais.) Nope.
Aisha: (→I.)   //Fi:gu:res
Isabella:(→Ana) //*Son las nueve treinte uno*. ['It's nine thirty-one']
                  (→Ad.) >Shut up<
Ana: That means what? Ten- nine forty..
Isabella: U:m (.) the bell rings (.3) yep.

Isabella's bilingualism and code switching are so publicly apparent that even when she initiates a repair of Aisha's "Have you?" with a Spanish *Qué*, Aisha does not treat it as marked or incomprehensible, but responds as if Isabella had used English (e.g. "What?") by repeating her question.

When Dominican Americans code switch at Central High School, "bystanders" are virtually always present who will be "able to glean some information" from the interaction, "for example, the language spoken" (Goffman 1981:132). At Central High School, code switching is not limited to certain domains or locales, and speakers are often discursively unaware of code switching, making displays of Spanish language readily apparent to others. According to Goffman (1959), individuals "give" impressions, i.e. try to make particular impressions, but they also "give off" impressions, i.e. others form impressions about them that may or may not correspond to the impressions individuals are trying to make. Although code switching may occur out of discursive consciousness and involve no marked linguistic choices for individuals, it is an activity that shapes the impressions of others, i.e. the identity ascriptions they make. In the presence of those who do not have prior knowledge of individuals' Dominican American identities, code switching as a discourse mode always has meaning and implications for achieving social identities.

Code switching as an unmarked discourse mode serves not only to counter phenotype-racial ascription, but also to construct a positive self in a political and economic context that disparages Dominican American phenotypes, language, class status, and ethnic origins (cf.

Zentella 1993). Code switching is an act of identity (LePage and Tabouret-Keller 1985) in a society in which English monolingualism, solely European ancestry, and middle class status are unmarked. Dominican American use of Spanish in code switching serves to include and incorporate the ongoing stream of newcomers (including family) from the Dominican Republic.[36] At the same time, second generation use of English differentiates them from such newcomers in ways that they situationally make relevant through code switching, as shown above. Their use of syncretic, multi-variety language also represents an implicit rejection of the ideology of assimilation. The offer implicit in the United States ideology of assimilation--e.g. work hard and acculturate and you will advance economically and socially--may be specious for many non-White immigrants. Even if the second generation acculturated by compartmentalizing codes--or becoming monolingual English speakers--their phenotypes would prevent their assimilation to unmarked White American identities with attendant privileges.[37]

4.12 Conclusions

The identities of Dominican American high school students in Providence reflect their socialization in both Dominican social circles and a low-income, multi-ethnic urban American environment. The second generation grow up in a context in which their language, culture, and phenotypes are marked and disparaged by the dominant White groups, and they learn to think of themselves as non-White based on these experiences and being co-categorized with other non-Whites, e.g. African Americans. This non-White identity is evident in the ways Dominican Americans define themselves (e.g. as Dominican rather than American), in their relationships to White and non-White groups, and in their language. For young, urban Dominican Americans, AAVE forms serve many of the political/identity functions that they serve for young African Americans in a similar structural position--as a means of resisting disparaging discourses and representing an alternative social world.

Paradoxically, Dominican American use of AAVE--a form of resistance to White linguistic hegemony--makes many individuals of African descent increasingly subject to another form of hegemony: the

Black/White racial classification system in the United States. Dominican Americans use Spanish language, particularly in the context of code switching, to resist such classification and enact an ethnolinguistic identity. While English-Spanish code switching is generally an unmarked intragroup behavior among Dominican Americans, it remains a marked behavior to the numerically and politically dominant groups of Americans who are monolingual English speakers. This code switching differentiates Dominican Americans from other groups with whom they might be identified or confused: island Dominicans, White Americans, and African Americans.

CHAPTER 5

Dominican American Understandings of Race and Social Identity

5.1 Introduction

Immigration from the Dominican Republic to the United States brings together people with different social histories and with very different constructions of race and ethnicity.[38] In the United States, a White majority has maintained a color-line for centuries, and notions of race are dominated by dichotomous categories of "Black" and "White," which are popularly seen as discrete categories representing fundamental difference. In the Dominican Republic, in contrast, roughly three-quarters of the population is of both European and African ancestry, and there is little sense of social identity associated with perceived relative degrees of African and European ancestry. Dominicans growing up in the United States are thus confronted with often-contradictory Dominican and American frameworks for construing individuals' "racial" identities.

As described in Chapters 1 and 4, language, rather than phenotype, is a key to the way Dominican American high school students in Providence--and many of their peers--see their identities in everyday life. The Dominican second generation variously define their race as "Dominican," "Spanish," "Hispanic," or "Latino," thus using terms that can also refer to national, linguistic, and/or cultural identity, but not, traditionally, to phenotype. In local terms, not only Hispanics, but also

Puerto Ricans, Cape Verdeans, Mexicans, and Vietnamese can count as races. For groups who entered America in the post-Civil Rights era, there are many forms of social differentiation--e.g. based on language or national origins--that are more salient than presence or absence of African ancestry. *This Dominican American recognition and enactment of non-phenotype racial identities highlights the incipient transformation of social categories in America. As the post-1965 non-White, non-Black immigrant American population grows, American notions of race and what constitutes significant social difference are being reframed.*

In this chapter, individuals' accounts of their identities and their explanations of race reveal significant divergences between their ethnic/racial categorization system and the dominant American ones, undermining popular and social scientific differentiation between race and ethnicity. The role of Spanish language in the maintenance of non-Black second-generation identity is highlighted by comparing Dominican American identities with second generation identities among African-descent immigrants who lack Spanish language and colonial heritage. These groups are much more likely than Dominicans to identify as Black or African American in the second generation. Historical Dominican notions of race and social identity are then described because they provide Dominican Americans with one framework for self-definition. Finally, discontinuities between first- and second-generation Dominican immigrants in cultural orientation and understandings of race are explored. Contrasting the two generations' frames of reference serves to highlight the effects on the second generation of socialization within a racialized American society. While the Dominican ethnicity of the first generation represents continuity of identities and cultural and linguistic practices from the Dominican Republic, Dominican identity in the second generation is partly a "reactive ethnicity," in which significant aspects of identity are a reaction to being defined as a minority Other in a hierarchical society. Second generation concepts of race and identity are thus presented as hybrid, drawing from both their Dominican heritage and their structural position in the United States.

5.2 Dominican American Notions of Race/Ethnicity

In the United States today, race is popularly treated as implying distinctions based on, or at least symbolized by, physical appearance, while ethnicity is taken to imply distinctions based on national origin, language, religion, and other cultural markers. From a social science perspective, the boundary between "race" and "ethnicity" is diffuse, however, and referents of the English word "race" have varied across time. Various immigrant groups in early 20th century America, e.g. Jews, Italians, and Slavs were referred to as races (Waters 1990), while now they are more commonly described as ethnic groups. The commonalties of descent, whether cultural or biological, implied by both race and ethnicity often overlap, i.e. groups that share common language, culture, and religion often share a degree of common biological ancestry.

"Race" in late 20th century America is often used in an even narrower sense to refer to the American social categorization system whereby some individuals count as Black and others count as White based on perceived ancestry. The salience and distinctiveness of these categories lie not in the distinctive nature of group members but in the starkly coercive social history out of which these categories grew. While other groups, e.g. Asians, are commonly recognized as "races," the American history of slavery, segregation, color-line maintenance, and discrimination makes the contemporary categories of Black and White qualitatively distinct from other racial categories in terms of cultural meanings, accumulated structural inequality, and salience in popular consciousness.

Dominican Americans did not experience the specific social history out of which American Black/White social categories were formed, and they do not treat the categories Black and White as necessarily of a different, or superordinate, type than social categories based on other criteria. For Dominican Americans, the term "race" does not just refer to distinctions based on, or symbolized by, phenotype, but also to linguistic and national-origin distinctions. This expansion of the concept of race decenters the dominant, naturalized American notion of race and suggests its historical and geographic specificity.[39]

This lack of differentiation between Black/White race and other forms of social identity is evident both in the ways Dominican

Americans talk about themselves and others, and in the ways in which they use and define the word "race." In both interview and more discursive contexts, Dominican American high school students use the same labels to identify their race and their culture/ethnicity, for example. In response to the question, "If people ask you, 'What are you?' what do you say?," Dominican American high school students answered "Dominican", "Hispanic" or "Spanish", and occasionally "Latino." When asked specifically how they identify their race ("If someone asked you, 'What's your race?', what would you say?"), students used the same four categories that they used to describe their culture and ethnicity. They most commonly described their race as "Spanish" or "Hispanic", and sometimes as "Dominican" or "Latino." Individual Dominican Americans never characterized their race to me in terms of White or Black.

Most Dominican Americans are aware that the majority of Dominicans are of both European and African ancestry, but they do not define their race in terms of Old World (Europe/Africa) origins, but rather in terms of much more recent linguistic/cultural/national origins in the New World. For Dominican-born individuals, race can be nothing more than where they were before they came to the United States:

BB: What does "race" mean to you?
Wilson: If they're asking "What race are you" I just say what I am, Dominican, Spanish. It means like where you're from.

For American-born individuals, race is typically defined in terms of where one's parents or grandparents were before they came to America:

Martin: Where you're originally from, like your parents and your grandparents and things like that, that's what I take for your race.

Local theories of biological descent are intertwined with socio-geographical allegiances in this Dominican American notion of race. In describing how American-born Dominicans should be identified, Jose invokes the notion of "blood," a biological notion, but he traces such blood back only one or two generations, more similar in time depth to contemporary social science notions of ethnicity than dominant, contemporary American notions of race:

> Jose: If they ask you what's your race, like where are your parents from and stuff like that, then you would tell them, my parents, they come from the Dominican Republic, before I was born here, so my blood is from Dominican Republic, my blood is Hispanic....

In contrast, Black and White Americans typically define themselves in terms of much more remote ancestry. Americans whose ancestors have been in North America for nearly four centuries are still categorized based on African or European ancestry, i.e. African American or European American.

For the many Dominican Americans who define their race as "Spanish," "Hispanic," or "Latino," linguistic, cultural and/or geographic commonalty underlie their notions of race:

> BB: What do you understand when you hear the word race?
> Maritza: I guess, race, I kind of like picture a map in my head, say Hispanic, is all towards Central America and South, if I look up North, then there's America, Americans. Basically, I guess, where countries are.

> BB: Hispanic includes everybody, right?
> Wilson: Hispanic is all the Spanish-speaking countries.
> BB: Would you be the same race as someone from Guatemala?
> Wilson: Yeah.

At the same time that "race" is used to refer to a pan-ethnic group such as "Hispanic," it can also be used to refer to national-origin groups. Frangelica, for example, refers to Dominicans, Puerto Ricans, and Mexicans as being of different races:

> [In discussing parents' attitudes toward different groups.]
> BB: What about Puerto Ricans?
> Frangelica: To date? No, no. That's another race they do not like....They really like you to stay in the group, because if you stay in the group, if you ever want to retire, you don't really have the disagreement as to where to go, who stays with the kids. Like my

uncle, he married a Mexican woman, now he realizes that's not what he likes, he likes his own race. He wants to go to the DR and she doesn't want to go.

The term "race" is also used to refer to non-Hispanic national-origin groups. In describing how people don't know how to classify her when they first see her, Frangelica refers to Haitians and Cape Verdeans as "races":

Frangelica: Sometimes some of them get confused, like, 'What are you?' Some have confused me with this race, I don't know what it is, Haitian. They have confused me in a lot of ways. Cape Verdean, that's the one.

Dominican Americans also use "race" to refer simultaneously to historical American racial categories ("American Indian" and "Black") and social categories defined by national-origin ("Portuguese" and "Cape Verdean"):

Jose: Like my girlfriend is mixed, she has like five different races. Her father is American Indian and Black, and her mother is Portuguese, Cape Verdean, and I don't know the other one.

Notions of race dominated by Black and White have played a fundamental role in structuring and representing American society for several centuries. For post-1965 immigrants who did not share these centuries of social history, forms of social differentiation based on language, culture, and national origin are frequently more salient than Black and White. As the post-1965 immigrant second generation becomes the American next generation, their alternative notions of race and their resistance to received categories are contributing to the ongoing transformation of American racial categories.

5.3 Second Generation African-descent Identities in the US

Resistance to American phenotype-based racial categorization among the Dominican second generation is virtually categorical, in sharp contrast to the patterns of acculturation dominant among non-Hispanic

African-descent immigrants. Historically, such immigrants have merged into the African American population by the second generation (Bryce-Laporte 1972). In the post-1965 immigration, such non-Hispanic immigrants have continued to adopt an African American identity by the second generation, although identification may partially co-vary with socio-economic class (Waters 1994). Reviewing research on the ethnic/racial identities of such non-Hispanic African-descent immigrants highlights the distinctiveness of the Hispanic/Dominican American pattern of resistance to Black-White racialization, and it thus helps to isolate the role of Spanish language and ethnolinguistic heritage in making such resistance possible.

Most studies on the identities of post-1965 Afro-Caribbean immigrants have focused on the first generation. Such works (e.g. Foner 1987, Zephir 1996, Stafford 1987, Charles 1992) emphasize the first-generation individuals' dismay at being assigned to a subordinate folk-racial identity based on their phenotype. The "Black" identity assigned to them in America effectively disregards their language background, national origins, and culture, i.e. what they see as the bases of their social identity. The first generation overwhelmingly reject this folk-racial categorization as "Black American" instead emphasizing their ethnicity as Haitians, Jamaicans, Trinidadians, etc. Many in the first generation actively disaffiliate themselves from African Americans:

> [I]f race unites Jamaicans with American blacks, ethnicity divides them. Jamaicans ... feel they are different than, indeed superior to, indigenous blacks and they conduct their social life mainly with other Jamaicans. Ethnicity...while it draws them together with their fellow Jamaicans (and often other West Indians), it drives a deep wedge between them and American blacks. (Foner 1987:213-214)

Such synchronic studies on the first-generation yield results that emphasize the maintenance of ethnic identity and resistance to American folk-racial categorization. Given that the subjects of the studies are immigrants who left their countries as adults, it is not surprising that they reject the American folk-racial categorization that denies them their primary socialization, e.g. language and national origins. Inattention to generational differences leads to conclusions--

e.g. "Haitian immigrants, in general, show no tendency toward assimilation" (Zephir 1996:69)--that are directly contradicted by studies that look at social identification across generations. Woldemikael (1989), for example, sharply distinguishes between the identities of first- and second-generation Haitian immigrants in Evanston, Illinois. While the first-generation maintain Haitian identity and practices, the second generation increasingly conform

> to [racial] expectations of American society rather than those of the Haitian community....with increasing interaction with their black American peers, younger-generation Haitians become less distinct from black Americans. This means Haitians become black Americans in the second generation. (Woldemikael 1989:114)

This pattern of assimilation to an African American identity in the Haitian second generation is also found by Stepick (1998) in Miami.

Waters (1994) finds a type of segmented assimilation among the second generation of non-Hispanic African-descent Caribbean immigrants in New York City. While most of these second generation immigrants have become African American identified, i.e. see themselves as essentially the same as native-born African Americans, some remain relatively ethnic-identified, e.g. as Jamaican or Jamaican-American. This smaller group who are ethnic-identified tend to come from families of higher social and economic class and attend better schools. They share their parents' belief that Afro-Caribbean immigrants are different from African Americans and superior in many respects, and that with perseverance they can succeed socio-economically despite racism. They have enough contact with White Americans and middle-class Americans to know that many Whites and socially mobile Americans share this view that they are more industrious, disciplined, and education-oriented than African Americans. They attribute their hard work in school and opportunities for mobility to the discipline and culture of their immigrant ethnicity. They tend to have friends who are Afro-Caribbean and White American (Waters 1994).

The much larger group who identify as African American are more likely than their immigrant-ethnic identified peers to come from poorer families, live in lower-income segregated neighborhoods, and attend substandard schools with almost no native-born White Americans. Unlike their parents and ethnic-identified peers, they see positive characteristics among African Americans such as working hard and struggling against racism. They do not realize that many White Americans and socially mobile Americans consider African-descent immigrants to have superior work and education values relative to native African Americans. They have little contact with White society on a personal level, but are well aware of American racism against people of African descent. They tend to adopt an African American peer culture of racial solidarity and opposition to school authority (Fordham 1996, Ogbu 1974). These students' experiences of discrimination and their assessments of negligible opportunities for social mobility lead them to reject their parents' ideology of individual social mobility and accept peer analyses of blocked social opportunity (Waters 1994:189).

The Dominican second generation display neither the relatively uniform identification as African American described by Woldemikael (1989) or the slightly variable assimilation to African American identities based on socioeconomic class described by Waters (1994). The Dominican second generation identify virtually categorically as Dominican, Spanish, or Hispanic. Unlike these other African descent immigrants, Dominican Americans have been able to maintain an ethnic/ethnolinguistic identity in the second generation despite the dominance in America of a phenotype-based racialization system (cf. Rodríguez 1989, 1993 among mainland Puerto Ricans).

The primary factors which enable Dominicans in the second generation to resist American folk-racialization include the following: 1) Individuals of Dominican nationality/ethnicity do not fit into a single American phenotype-based racial category. 2) Dominicans on the island have traditionally seen themselves as a Spanish and more-or-less White population, and certainly not as African or Black. This framework for self-identification as *not* Black is passed on to the second generation in America. 3) Speaking Spanish a) sets Dominican Americans apart from most native-born Black and White Americans, b) qualifies them for membership in the widely recognized category "Hispanic," and c) contributes to the maintenance and vigor of an ethnolinguistic community which in turn validates traditional Dominican ways of thinking about social identities such as race.

Compared to Haitian and West Indian immigrants, who are relatively uniformly identified as "Black" in America, Dominicans exhibit a wide range of phenotypes in a smooth continuum from those associated with Europe to those associated with sub-Saharan Africa. Many Dominicans are of overwhelmingly European descent and are never perceived as Black in the United States, and many others, who are of predominantly European descent, do not match popular stereotypes of African American phenotype. In terms of United States phenotype-race categories, Dominican Americans are a more heterogeneous aggregate group than Haitians or Jamaicans, who can more uniformly be assigned to the single category "Black."

A second difference between Dominicans and non-Hispanic African-descent immigrants is that Dominicans have traditionally considered themselves European and not Black or African. (This topic will be addressed more fully in section 5.4 below). Dominican national identity has been defined in part through opposition to Haiti: Dominicans perceive Haiti as a Black and African country against which they see themselves as White and European. Popular and official Dominican minimization of African heritage stands in stark contrast to popular Haitian discourse on African ancestry. The African and slave past of Haiti is a unifying aspect of national identity in Haiti because of pride arising from the revolution of 1791-1804 that resulted in an independent, Black-ruled Haitian nation state (Charles 1992:108).

A third factor, the Spanish language of the Dominican Republic, is a key to the ongoing reproduction of a Dominican identity, both on the island and in the United States. In the Dominican Republic, adoption of Dominican Spanish by immigrants *to* the island has historically been a key to the relatively rapid and complete assimilation that has been characteristic of such immigrants (Del Castillo and Murphy 1987). For Dominicans on the island who are phenotypically indistinguishable from individuals who count as Black (e.g. Haitians and West Indians), "the ability to speak Spanish like a Dominican becomes the ultimate symbol by means of which they establish their Dominican identity" (Gonzalez 1975:113). Just as they do in Providence, Rhode Island, individuals in the Dominican Republic thus use Spanish language to show that they are Dominican and "not Black."

Spanish language and colonial heritage aligns Dominicans with peoples from other former Spanish colonies, both before and after immigration:

Citizens of countries of the Hispanic Caribbean view their nations...as subsets of the linguistically determined macroculture area of the Hispanic Caribbean, which is in turn a subset of Spanish America. Language thus allies this island region more with Latin America than with the rest of the Caribbean. The implication of ethnic homogeneity is reinforced by the imposition of "La Raza" by Spain (in other words, the new mestizo/ethnic/cultural population in the colonies) and "Hispanic" by the United States, as the founding and current colonial powers in the region. (Davis 1994:120-1)

Spanish language has thus served as an index of commonalty for categories--"La Raza" and "Hispanic"--even as the political economic centers have shifted over time.

Following immigration, the Spanish language of Dominican Americans and their parents sets them apart from Black and White Americans in ways that the languages of many other African-descent immigrants do not. Among the Anglophone West Indian second generation, for example, language does not provide such a clear line of demarcation between immigrant ethnics and Americans whose parents and grandparents are native-born. Second-generation Anglophone West Indians can grow up as monolingual English speakers because their parents can understand American English, even if it is not the variety the first generation use among themselves. Caribbean varieties of English are thus not as salient as markers of solidarity between first and second generations and among the second generation, as Spanish is, because these English varieties do not isolate and differentiate individuals from the surrounding English-speaking population as fully as Spanish does.

For the Haitian second generation, Haitian Creole, and to a lesser extent French, contribute to the constitution of a distinct identity, but this ethnolinguistic identity does not have the support of the massive community that Spanish does. While there are Haitian ethnic enclaves in New York and Miami, for example, their ethnolinguistic communities are dwarfed by the Spanish-speaking and identified one. There is no ethnolinguistic category such as "Hispanic" to which to assign Francophone/Creole-speaking immigrants from former French colonies. While some Haitians, particularly from the educated elite, may define themselves as "French" (Stafford 1987; Schieffelin and Doucet 1994), few Americans will ratify them in that identity. This lack of recognition of a "French" identity is apparent in local contexts in Providence. In speaking to a Laotian American friend in class, for example, Janelle characterizes two Haitian classmates as "Black kids" who were "talking French":

"A lot of Black people know French. Yesterday two Black kids came into my class talking French." (JS #1 9:28:50)

For Janelle, the defining feature of these francophone African-descent students is their Blackness. Their phenotype thus precedes their ethnolinguistic identity, reversing the ordering of these criteria, as documented in Chapter 4, in Dominican American self-ascriptions. The words that Janelle uses to characterize these students--"Black people who know French"--contrast sharply with the way she identifies herself in a report of an incident in which she herself was perceived as Black:

...she goes, 'You know Spanish.' She thought I was just a Black who knew Spanish. I was like 'I am Spanish.'

In the local categorization system, African-descent individuals who are native speakers of French count first and foremost as Black, rather than French, while African-descent individuals who are native speakers of Spanish count first and foremost as Spanish.

The language of Dominicans--in contrast to that of Haitians--is a defining criterion for assignment to a widely-recognized, pre-existing United States social category. It enables access to a thriving ethnolinguistic community with its own churches, restaurants, stores, Spanish language media, and community organizations, a world that exists in many ways parallel to, and in many ways separate from, Anglophone society. Participation in this immigrant ethnic community has important implications for the trajectories of acculturation of second-generation immigrants (Portes 1995). A thriving community validates the customs, language, and beliefs of the first generation, reinforcing a common cultural memory and identity for the second generation. Without this community reinforcement of linguistic and cultural identity, parents' customs, practices, and expectations can seem irrelevant and out of touch with the social realities faced by the second generation, resulting in faster acculturation to American ways.

Spanish language is thus a key to the second generation's maintenance of Dominican cultural frameworks for social categorization in the face of dominant American phenotype-based racialization practices. Spanish language competence enables participation in Spanish/Dominican social networks with Spanish monolingual adults and grandparents, and newly immigrated monolingual Dominicans. It facilitates the maintenance of ties to relatives on the island and permits greater involvement with Dominican society on visits to the island. Incorporation into these social networks in the United States and Dominican Republic helps Dominican Americans maintain aspects of a Dominican cultural frame of reference for social categorization. Socialization into Dominican ways of thinking about identity that run counter to historical American racialization practices, e.g. that Dominicans constitute a race and that they are not Black, is thus reinforced through Spanish language.

The Dominican second generation differ dramatically from other African-descent immigrants who assimilate to Black American identities in the second generation. Dominican American maintenance of a distinct ethnicity and resistance to phenotypic racialization is made possible by social and linguistic conditions in both the Dominican Republic and the United States. The Spanish language of the second generation marks boundaries between them and other American groups, and it connects them to an immigrant and ethnolinguistic community in which their Dominican and Spanish identities, rather than their phenotypes, are of primary significance.

5.4 Race and Identity in the Dominican Republic

Many of the ways in which Dominican Americans see their racial/ethnic identities are a result of socialization into ways of thinking about identity that are prevalent in the Dominican Republic. Many in the second generation, for example, identify their race in the same terms used by their parents and by those who haven't left the island, i.e. as "Dominican." An overview of the way Dominicans on the island think of themselves, and, in particular, how they treat African and

European ancestry, can explain much about the way Dominican Americans see themselves.

African ancestry plays a very different role in social categorization in the Dominican Republic than it does in the United States. In the United States, the presence/absence of African ancestry in a predominantly European population is treated as a primary emblem of difference among individuals. As described in Chapter 1, the one-drop (Davis 1991) or hypodescent (Harris 1964) rule means that those who are perceived to have any African ancestry are assigned to one category regardless of other ancestry, and those who are perceived to have only European ancestry are assigned to another. Boundaries between these two social categories are vigorously maintained and have widespread social repercussions. Historically, for example, individuals have lived, gone to school, and married with other individuals assigned to the same category. Although individuals belong to many social categories, e.g. based on regional origins or socio-economic class, membership in these presence/absence of African ancestry categories has preceded other social category memberships for defining an individual.

Segregation, discrimination by those who count as White Americans, and a social hierarchy between the two social categories have encouraged individual members of each category to emphasize their differences from those perceived to be in the other category. Cultural and linguistic differences that have arisen and/or been maintained between the groups serve to naturalize the categories and lead members of each group to see themselves as essentially different from members of the other category. Even though the assignment to a category is ostensibly based on ancestry/phenotype, membership in one category or the other has become popularly associated with language, culture, and even intellectual aptitude and morals, i.e. one's essential nature.

In the Dominican Republic, in contrast, there is no binary division among Dominicans into social categories based on the perceived presence/absence of sub-Saharan African ancestry. Dominicans do not have a notion of race that differentiates among Dominicans in the way the American folk-notion of Black/White differentiates among Americans. For Dominicans, Dominican nationality, Dominican ethnicity, and Dominican race are more or less the same thing (Davis 1994:119). When I surveyed Dominicans in the Dominican Republic, *Cuál es tu raza?* ['What race are you?'], they answered *dominicano/a*

['Dominican'] without regard to individual phenotype, and many treated it as a statement of the obvious. This virtually categorical identification as *dominicano/a* occurred despite the placement of the question in my survey immediately after a question referring explicitly to skin color: *Cuál es el color de tu piel?* ['What color is your skin?'], which elicited various descriptors of skin color. Although the Dominican Republic is a country of immigrants, both voluntary and involuntary, few Dominicans define themselves as the descendants of a particular immigrant group, but rather simply as Dominican, nationally, ethnically, and racially (Del Castillo and Murphy 1987).

In the Dominican Republic, gradations in African/European phenotype are recognized and hierarchically perceived, but are not treated as indicators of primary social group membership. Individual differences in phenotype are seen much more as *individual* attributes than as markers of a broader social identity (Oquendo 1995). In contrast, differences in socio-economic class, regional origins, and urban vs. rural background are all highly salient symbols of difference and identity in the Dominican Republic, and they are often used to represent essentialized social categories. Individuals on the island often identify themselves as inhabitants of particular regions or cities, for example, and there is strong regional and class variation in language use (Lipski 1994, Canfield 1981, Henríquez Ureña 1940, Alba 1990a, 1990b, Sabater 1975).

Individual differences in phenotype, i.e. relative degrees of African/European phenotype, do not co-vary with language, culture, religion or other markers of social identity (Davis 1994). There is no "Afro-Dominican" style of Spanish corresponding to AAVE, for example, and no sense of ethnicity or group identity based on, or symbolized by, relative degree of African/European ancestry. A Dominican American professional in his forties described how individual differences in phenotype can be acknowledged, and even disparaged as individual attributes, without racial essentialism:

> People [in the Dominican Republic] will make jokes about white people, black people, fat people, gay people, sometimes in a very crude manner....but the people there don't take race as--not not as seriously--they don't think of race as being the humanizing aspect of you. They see it as a characteristic of you as an individual, something that doesn't make you less of

a human being. So when they joke about the fact that you ugly, and that you black and ugly, it's like-- that's superficial, that's not like 'you're black and ugly and you're also less of a human being'.

Like being "fat" or "ugly," being "black" is a negative *individual* attribute, not one of social grouping.

Although perceived degrees of African and European phenotype are not racialized in the ways that they are in the United States, phenotypes associated with African and European ancestry are not valued equally. African phenotype is considered less attractive than more European phenotype, for example. Relatively straight hair is called *pelo bueno* ['good hair'] and relatively kinky hair is *pelo malo* ['bad hair'] (Badillo and Badillo 1996; cf. e.g. Cleaver 1973, Gaskins 1996 on 'bad hair' among American Americans). The Miss Dominican Republic beauty pageant is dominated by contestants from the roughly 10% of the Dominican population that is overwhelmingly European in ancestry.[40] Employment advertisements for positions with public contact, e.g. bank tellers or flight attendants, often specify that they seek individuals *de buena presencia* ['of good appearance'], which Dominicans understand as excluding individuals of relatively African phenotype (Alarcón 1994:303).

There is also a correlation between phenotype and class: the oligarchy are white and more or less endogamous, resulting in maintenance of a color line between the oligarchy and the rest of the population; the elite and upper classes are disproportionately light; and the very poor are disproportionately dark. The phenotypes typical of the lower classes and the middle class vary substantially by region (Davis 1994:122). This correlation between phenotype and class is not a categorical form of hierarchy. Although the oligarchy is white in phenotype, for example, not all phenotypically white individuals are in the middle and upper classes, let alone the oligarchy (Gonzalez 1975), and leading military and political figures have historically ranged across a spectrum of phenotypes (Hoetink 1985). In the 1996 presidential election, the winning candidate was of a phenotype associated with both European and African ancestry, and the runner-up was of a phenotype associated with overwhelmingly African ancestry.

Dominicans have terms for a variety of phenotypes, ranging from those associated with just European ancestry, e.g. *blanco* ['white'], to those associated with just African ancestry, e.g. *negro* ['black']. A relatively large vocabulary exists to describe individuals with particular constellations of hair texture, skin color, and facial features, e.g. *jaba(d)o* refers to an individual with relatively light/white skin but with hair and facial features associated with African phenotypes (Cambeira 1997). Such terminology differs across Hispanic Caribbean societies (e.g. Stevens 1989; Hoetink 1967, 1975; Oostindie 1996), and even within the Dominican Republic individuals vary in their conceptions of the particular phenotypes to which particular terms refer. The three categories used to describe skin color (*color*, as opposed to *raza*) in the *cedula*, the national identification card, are *blanco* ['white'], the broad *indio* ['indian-colored'], and *negro* ['black']. According to 1981 *cedula* data, 16 percent of the Dominican population was *blanco*, 73 percent was *indio*, and 11 percent was *negro* (Haggerty 1991:xxviii).

These color categories are not objective descriptions of skin color, but rather cultural constructions, and their situational meanings reveal much about the way Dominicans think about phenotypes. For a small circle, including the elite who are primarily descendants of relatively recent (19th and 20th century) European immigrants, *blanco* signifies categorical European ancestry. More generally, *blanco* includes individuals whose physical appearance approximates a stereotypical European phenotype of relatively straight hair, relatively light skin, a relatively aquiline nose, and relatively thin lips (Dominguez 1978). *Blanco* is a relative category in a country in which only a small part of the population does not have some African ancestry, so individuals who count as *blanco* in the Dominican Republic would not necessarily count as phenotypically "White" in the United States.

Judgment of an individual's color is also dependent upon the context in which it is made. The positive social connotations of "Whiteness" lead many Caribbean Hispanics to identify themselves as white for the public record regardless of their precise phenotype (Dominguez 1978:9). Judgments of color are also heavily dependent upon the nonphysical attributes of an individual, as they are elsewhere in Latin America. Money, education, and power, for example, "whiten" an individual, so that the color attributed to a higher class individual is often lighter than the color that would be attributed to an individual of the same phenotype of a lower class. Since members of the elite are expected to be *blancos*, they are often labeled as such regardless of phenotype. This can problematize research based on self-reports in census data or surveys (e.g. Massey and Denton 1989, Grasmuck and Pessar 1996) that find that "whiter" Caribbean Hispanic immigrants to America are more successful economically than "darker" Caribbean Hispanic immigrants. In Hispanic Caribbean terms, if one is socioeconomically mobile, one doesn't count as dark, so such causal or correlational claims between self-reported color and socioeconomic success can be tautological.

Most Dominicans identify their color as some form of *indio* ['indian-colored'], a term applied to individuals with a phenotype suggesting a combination of African and European descent. The category *indio* is often broken down into *indio claro* ['light indian-colored'] and *indio oscuro* ['dark indian-colored']. Individuals describing their own *indio* color in the Dominican Republic will become even more precise, using such terms as *indio oscuro claro* ['light dark-indian-colored'], i.e. on the light side of the dark-indian continuum, or *indio medio claro* ['medium light indian-colored'].

Few Dominicans self-identify their color as *negro* ['black'], regardless of how dark or African in phenotype they are. The label *negro* is synonymous with being poor or low-class, and it is stigmatized. Terms such as *moreno* ['dark-skinned'], and *indio oscuro* ['dark indian-colored'], or even *indio oscuro oscuro* ['dark, dark indian-colored'] are thus used to describe the skin color of those Dominicans who are of overwhelmingly African ancestry. As with other color categories, one's assignment to the skin-color category *negro* is based not just on phenotype but also on other social criteria. Individuals from the upper classes cannot count as *negro*, because it is synonymous with being lower class, and class is socially more significant than phenotype in the Dominican Republic. While a very dark-skinned Dominican of high social class might not be labeled *blanco*, he/she can be described as some form of *indio* (e.g. Rout 1976:287). The Dominican poet and intellectual Blas Jimenez--a dark-skinned member of the educated elite--recounts identifying himself as *negro* when applying for a passport. The flustered civil servant insisted that Jimenez could not be *negro* because he was not impoverished and starving.[41]

Stigmatization of Blackness by Dominicans on the island does not imply feelings of self-hatred because Dominicans do not think of themselves as being Black, but rather as Hispanic and more-or-less White. Racial categories and identities in the Dominican Republic--as they are everywhere--are social constructions rather than reflections of biological or phenotypic realities. In the United States, for example, the historical American one-drop rule has made individuals with perceived, recorded, or imagined African ancestry count as "Black." Into the 1980's, individuals in Louisiana who were "1/32 Black," i.e. had one great-great-great grandparent who had counted as Black, were themselves counted as Black for legal and official purposes (Dominguez 1986). In the Dominican Republic, a very different one-drop rule is in effect: any perceived or imagined European ancestry makes an individual *not* Black, and perhaps even White. By this standard, only a small percentage of Dominicans count as Black.

Dominican self-perceptions of themselves as a more-or-less White extend back for centuries. According to Moya Pons (1996:15-16), when French travelers visited Santo Domingo in the 1700's, they were surprised to discover that the dark-skinned local inhabitants identified themselves as *blancos de tierra* ['whites of the land']. For the many Dominicans of African descent, this distinguished them from the slaves whom they saw as the only *negros* on the island. The relatively small numbers of European colonists and the lack of a color line in mating behavior resulted in a population that was successively less White. At the same time, however, Dominicans disassociated themselves more and more from slaves and Haitians to the West, leading Moya Pons (1996:16) to conclude, "while the Spanish colonial population was becoming blacker the Dominican mentality was becoming whiter."

Dominican understandings of their color, race, and nationality have been constructed in contradistinction to Haiti, both historically and in contemporary times (e.g. Moya Pons 1995, 1996; Silié 1989). Two 19th century Haitian occupations of the Dominican side of Hispaniola served to galvanize a sense of Dominican national identity when it was still a colony, and Haitian war crimes at the time served to vilify Haitians in the popular memory. The primary Dominican Independence Day remains the anniversary of the revolt against Haitian occupiers in 1844 rather than the 1861 independence from Spain.

Today, Dominicans differentiate between themselves and Haitians in terms of color/race, culture, language, and religion. For many Dominicans, Haitians are Black/African while Dominicans are White/European, Haitians speak an Afro-French Creole while Dominicans speak Spanish, and Haitians practice African voodoo while Dominicans are Catholic (Duany 1994:67, 69). Haitians are racialized as the Other; for many Dominicans, the only *negros* are Haitians (Silié 1989:170).

The dictator Rafael Trujillo, who ruled the country from 1930 to 1961, made it official ideology that the country was White, Hispanic, and Catholic. In 1937 thousands of Haitians in the border area were massacred at his command, which was officially treated as an act to save Dominican race and nationhood from Africanization and Haitian invasion (Moya Pons 1996:22). The construction of a White national identity posed problems for Trujillo himself, who was of both European and African descent. Trujillo took care to powder his face white, and he discouraged public appearances by his brother whose relatively more African phenotype could not be disguised with face-powder (Rout 1976:286). In the 1960 national census under Trujillo, census workers were instructed to record as *blanco* any individual who was not unequivocally *negro*, resulting in official figures to support the official ideology that the country was overwhelmingly White.

Trujillo's racist, anti-Haitian sentiment continued to be promulgated at high levels after his death by his follower, Joaquín Balaguer, who was president of the Dominican Republic from 1966-1978 and from 1986-1996. In 1983, Balaguer published a nationalistic, anti-Haitian book, *La Isla al Revés: Haití y el Destino Dominicano* ['The Island Reversed: Haiti and Dominican Destiny'] much of which is copied from his 1939 book *La Realidad Dominicana* ['The Dominican Reality']. The book, which cites primarily nineteenth century sources on race, warns of being overrun by lazy, unclean, un-Christian, amoral, fast-reproducing Afro-Haitians. Balaguer reaffirmed *hispanidad*--the doctrine that the Dominican Republic is a European, Spanish, and Catholic nation--with the building of the Columbus Lighthouse (*el Faro a Colón*), a huge monument in the capital to Christopher Columbus. Symbolic of the European and Christian conquest of the Americas, its long axis points between Spain and South America. Its Catholic and European symbolism was validated within a week of its inauguration, by a visit from the Pope who held an outdoor mass at it (Davis 1994:121).

The obfuscation of the Dominican African heritage has been accompanied by an aggrandizement of its Native American, or Taíno heritage. Emphasizing Dominican Taíno heritage is compatible with Dominican nationalism, a non-African Dominican identity, and anti-Haitian sentiment. The popular and official construction of significant

Taíno ancestry provides an explanation for the *indio* ['indian-colored'] skin color of most Dominicans without invoking their African ancestry or the stigma of slavery. Identification with the aborigines of the island was encouraged by 19th century romantic *indigenista* writers, who sought roots of Dominican culture in an idealized Indian past (Duany 1994:69). An 1882 Dominican novel, *Enriquillo*, for example, depicted a noble, Christian-convert, European-clothing-wearing Dominican Indian chief of the 1500's. This tradition of idealizing Native Americans as opposed to Africans/African Americans extends as far back as Bartholomew de Las Casas' 1519 suggestion that Africans rather than Native Americans be used for forced labor in the New World, because the aborigines had souls and could be saved whereas Africans couldn't be saved (Fennema and Loewenthal 1987).

This Spanish-Taíno version of the Dominican past is in conflict with the historical demographics of the islands given by scholars. According to Moya Pons (1995:37), European diseases, forced labor, and armed attacks killed over 99% of the aboriginal population within 30 years of Columbus' 1492 arrival, leaving fewer than 3,000 Taíno. In contrast, by the late 18th century there were over 450,000 African and African-descent slaves on Hispaniola, comprising over 90% of the population of the island (Fennema and Loewenthal 1987).

Despite the virtual extirpation of the Taíno more than four centuries ago, they still play a strong role in the popular and official construction of Dominican identity. Contemporary junior high school textbooks describe the Dominican people and culture as a mix of Spanish, Taíno, and African influences, thus privileging the role of the Taíno, whose contributions to Dominican society were relatively few and minor (Del Castillo and Murphy 1987). It was only in the last twenty years that a statue representing an African joined the two representing a Spaniard and a Taíno in front of the Dominican *Museo del Hombre Dominicano* ['Museum of the Dominican People'] in the capital city (Hoetink 1985)[42.] In Providence, Rhode Island, Dominican Americans generally consider themselves to be part Native American, or Taíno, and one consultant described one of her grandmothers as "full-blooded" Taíno.

Today in the Dominican Republic, construction of an aboriginal heritage, rather than one of colonialism and African slavery, distracts attention from divisive historical social relations and serves to unify the Dominican people (Fennema and Loewenthal 1987). The power of this

constructed national identity to obscure the history of slavery among
Dominicans--but not in Haiti--is captured in Wilson's explanation (in
Providence, Rhode Island) of why some people in the Dominican
Republic have dark skin:

> Haiti is in the same island as Dominican Republic. That's one
> reason why there's a lot of dark Dominicans, cause as you
> know, people from Haiti are from Africa, they're really from
> Africa, from Africa to Haiti, and being in the same island...

Even though Wilson is aware of his own African ancestry ("I know our
background, most people come from Africa, Spain, and American, so
we're all mixed. I say that I've got African blood, Spanish blood,
American blood..."), his African ancestry counts as different and less
direct than that of Haitians. His statement that "people from Haiti are
from Africa, they're really from Africa, from Africa to Haiti" suggests
that Dominicans aren't really from Africa, and if they have African
ancestry, it's not because their African ancestors traveled directly from
Africa to the Dominican Republic in the way that Haitians went
directly from Africa to Haiti. In a literal and physical sense, this is not
accurate: African slaves were brought from Africa to the Spanish part
of Hispaniola just as they were brought to Haiti (Moya Pons 1995). In
terms of Dominican perceptions and ideology, however, the link
between Africa and the Dominican Republic is remote and obscure.
The heritage that Dominicans see as defining their identity is Spanish
and European.

5.5 Generational Differences in Racial Understandings

In a pattern typical of immigration, first generation Dominicans who
arrive in America as adults maintain strong material, affective, and
behavioral ties to their country of origin, while subsequent generations
become increasingly acculturated to the United States. Those who grew
up on the island typically maintain important personal relationships
with family and friends who have remained, send remittances, and even
maintain business interests in both countries, traveling back and forth
or residing parts of each year in each country. Many in the first
generation see themselves as staying in America just long enough to

better themselves economically, e.g. to save enough money to buy a house or establish a small business in the Dominican Republic. Many plan to retire in the Dominican Republic as soon as their children are grown. These first generation immigrants, who have multiple, ongoing ties in both countries, have been the inspiration for monographs on Dominican migrants as a transnational community, e.g. *The Making of a Transnational Community* (Georges 1990), *Between Two Islands* (Grasmuck and Pessar 1991), *One Country in Two* (Guarnizo 1992), and *The Transnational Villagers* (Levitt 2001).

In contrast to their parents, who see their sojourns in the United States as temporary (even when they frequently do not prove to be), the second-generation high school students who were born in America or who arrive by early elementary school generally see themselves as staying permanently. Individuals who grow up in the United States become accustomed to the highly developed public infrastructure, economic opportunities, and individual freedoms. Frangelica, who arrived in America at age five, for example, planned on staying in America even though she had fallen in love during a summer vacation on the island. Rather than moving to the Dominican Republic to join her boyfriend, whom she planned on marrying, she had begun the arduous process of getting him a visa to join her in America. Despite multiple ties to the island and well-developed Spanish skills, Frangelica couldn't see herself settling there:

America means to me an opportunity to get a good job and make dollars, it means getting sick and calling 911--down there you don't have 911. It means feeling free and being able to do not anything you want but being able to do something and knowing you have a right to. It means eating everything good, and going to stores--shopping, down there I can't picture myself going shopping, down there, there are hardly any mall, and if there is a mall it's probably really expensive. It means no mud, and light ['electricity'] and water, every day. Not just once in a blue moon, but every day. I'll stay here. That's what I told my father. I'll stay here. If I go down there, I'll go to visit.

The second generation see their futures in the United States, rather than in the Dominican Republic, and their expectations and behavior reflect this socialization. In contrast to the second generation, adult migrants tend to view and experience their current lot not in terms of the ideals and expectations of the majority society but rather in terms of the ideals and expectations of the 'old culture' (Suárez-Orozco and Suárez-Orozco 1995:325). This tendency is important for understanding differences in identity between first- and second-generation Dominican immigrants because of the hardships faced by Dominicans in America. Dominant groups in America have historically disparaged individuals who count as Spanish speaking, labor migrants from less-developed countries, not-White, of apparent African descent, and of low income. Both first- and second-generation Dominicans face stigma in the United States from being defined in these ways, but such disparagement has very different implications for identity development in the second generation than in the first. First-generation identities are forged on the island and maintained by isolation in the United States, while second-generation ethnicity develops in a context in which various American social and cultural frameworks are central.

Voluntary, first-generation migrant adults are a particularly select and robust group, those with the resources and ambition to try to make a better life for themselves, their families, and their children. Research on Dominican migration through the 1970's showed migrants to be largely middle-class and urban, rather than impoverished proletariat or peasants (Grasmuck and Pessar 1991; Guarnizo 1992; Ugalde, Bean and Cardenas 1979). Middle-class urban Dominicans, in contrast to the rural and poor, have historically had the resources to reach America, legally or illegally. For adult migrants, the life that was experienced growing up on the island provides the primary frame of reference. Grasmuck and Pessar (1991), for example, have shown that Dominicans who migrate to America as adults use a Dominican frame of reference for judging their own social class, perceiving themselves to be middle class while working in jobs that would lead most Americans to classify them as poor or working class. Consumer goods such as color television, refrigerators, and automobiles, which are common among the American poor and working-class, are beyond the reach of even many middle-class households in the Dominican Republic. Having acquired such consumer goods, first generation Dominicans, using an island frame of reference, can construe themselves as middle-class. Although the migrant stream became more diverse in the 1980's in response to continuing economic decline in the Dominican Republic, migrants remain urban and well educated by Dominican standards (Grasmuck and Pessar 1996). The positive social identities that such adult immigrants bring with them to America can provide emotional resources to cope with subsequent hardship.

Adult first-generation Dominican immigrants in Providence are able to maintain a Dominican cultural frame of reference in part because they are socially isolated from non-Hispanics. Dominicans who immigrate to the United States in their 20's or later typically do not become fluent English speakers by the time their children are in high school (cf. Heskamp 1959), and many avoid situations requiring English, relying on their children, relatives, or friends to interpret. In Providence, Dominican immigrants are able to shop, socialize, attend services at a variety of churches, listen to any of several radio stations, watch TV, find work, and negotiate social services in Spanish. In the jewelry factories where many first-generation Dominican adults find employment in Providence, Spanish, not English, is the language of the factory floor. Ongoing immigration, driven in large part by family networks utilizing the 1965 Family Reunification Act, results in a constant influx of newly arriving relatives and friends from the island. The vibrancy of this community contributes to the maintenance of Dominican customs, language, and beliefs by shielding immigrants from extensive contact with non-Hispanic America.

The second generation, in contrast, grow up in a context in which various United States social and cultural frameworks are central. As described in Chapter 4, the second generation's structural position as a non-White, American minority is central to the ways they perceive themselves, which makes being "Dominican" in the second generation very different from "Dominican" in the first generation. While the Dominican ethnicity of the first generation represents continuity of identities and cultural and linguistic practices from the Dominican Republic, Dominican identity in the second generation is partly a "reactive ethnicity," in which significant aspects of identity are a reaction to disparagement and being defined as a minority Other. At the same time that historical Dominican notions of race clearly inform the understandings of the second generation, their understandings of race and identity are different from those of their parents, a result of their socialization in the United States.

5.6 Generational Attitudes toward Black and White Americans

The differences in the social experiences of first- and second-generation Dominican immigrants result in very different generational attitudes toward other social groups. Many in the first generation symbolically align themselves with White Americans, admiring what they perceive as their educational/vocational discipline and socioeconomic success, while many in the second generation see White Americans as a discriminatory group that consider Dominicans inferior. Generational differences in attitudes toward African Americans and African-descent immigrants are particularly pronounced. While members of the first generation are highly critical of African Americans, the second generation often align themselves closely with African Americans, who are their peers and friends at school. Many Dominican Americans report that they feel more comfortable with African American peers, in general, than they do with Hispanic peers who aren't from the Caribbean, e.g. Mexican and Guatemalan immigrants.

First generation prejudice against those who count as Black is highly salient to members of the second generation. Repeatedly, teenagers I talked to accused their parents of being prejudiced against African Americans, and many didn't understand why their parents spoke negatively about them. When interview questions alluded to parents' perceptions of other social groups, consultants regularly turned the topic to discussion of their parents' negative beliefs about African Americans:

BB: Do your parents ever talk about other groups, e.g. White Americans, Black Americans, Puerto Ricans, Guatemalans, Asians?
Eva: They'll sit there and like they'll talk about some crazy stuff, they talk about all sorts of people and it's sickening cause they'll be like- I don't care, I think my mother is a racist, cause she said something about, she asked me to ma-- she wants me to understand that it's not that she's racist, it's that most African Americans don't really do

good, most of them if you see them selling drugs or something, that's what she thinks, that's her opinion, she thinks that most Africans-Americans don't do good. And she'll be like, "No you shouldn't look for the baddest person, you can do better," if I was to find somebody that I want to be with that's African American, she'll be like "You better check if he sells drugs this-that-and-the-other cause you could get in trouble for that. But she thinks that mostly Puerto Ricans and Africans-Americans, they really don't do good. Most of them are selling drugs or using drugs, that's what she'll probably say. She hasn't really talked about White people. In a way, my family has had so many bad luck with White people, though, not to be mean or nothing, cause most of the time they'll like, like if we was to be in the bank or something, they'll like, they won't attend you, cause there's some people that are like that or there's cops that'll stop you and stuff, stupid stuff like that. I don't have nothing against nobody, I like all sorts of people. The only thing she'll probably say is don't get married with the wrong person, ...I don't know why she got that crazy idea that most African Americans are no good.

Eva doesn't understand her mother's prejudices against African Americans. These prejudices are particularly incomprehensible to her because her mother does not talk in similar terms about White Americans, who regularly discriminate against members of her family.

The anti-Black sentiments of the Dominican first generation have multiple roots. As described above, Blackness is deprecated in the Dominican Republic and associated with Haitians, a racialized Other. Immigrants also bring with them negative stereotypes of African Americans, based on media representations and what they hear from friends and relatives in the United States. Teen-agers I interviewed in the Dominican Republic, who had not had personal contact with African Americans, associated them with gangs, fighting, crime, poverty, and success in sports.

Newly immigrated Dominicans, hoping to make a better life for themselves, have little incentive to affiliate themselves with a group that is widely perceived to be among the least socially and economically mobile in America. African Americans and first generation economic immigrants, regardless of race/ethnicity, who encounter each other in low-income, segregated neighborhoods typically have different experiences and beliefs regarding the nature of racism, discrimination, self-reliance, and opportunities for social and economic mobility in America. Even first-generation immigrant groups that have self-consciously Black or African-descent identities frequently disaffiliate themselves from less socially mobile African Americans. Waters (1994:797), for example, found negative stereotypes regarding African Americans among the Anglophone West Indian and Haitian immigrants she interviewed in New York City:

> The immigrants see themselves as hard-working, ambitious, militant about their racial identities but not oversensitive or obsessed with race, and committed to education and family. They see Black Americans as lazy, disorganized, obsessed with racial slights and barriers, with a disorganized and laissez faire attitude toward family life and child raising.

Both traditional Dominican attitudes toward Blackness and the immigrant ideology of self-reliance and socio-economic mobility encourage the first generation to differentiate themselves from African Americans.

Many first-generation Dominicans also have few opportunities for deeper personal contact with non-Hispanics. Alejandro characterized his parents' social reality as consisting of work and home in explaining their stereotypes about American groups:

BB: Do they ever talk about White Americans?

Alejandro: They say whatever they listen ['hear'], so they say that Black people are bad. That's what they think. They think that everybody is bad. White people are bad, Black people are bad...you know, they have such a different way of living. Their way of living is work and home. For the kids, it's like school, and they see that it's different, cause they see that the Black students and the Spanish students, and they mix...

With limited interpersonal contact, the first generation base their impressions of African Americans in part on public displays of indecency and delinquency, e.g. drinking and drug dealing, that they observe in their low-income neighborhoods. Many attribute crime and the torn social fabric of their neighborhoods to African Americans. This attribution of a negative otherness to African Americans is not always consistent with the behavior of the first generation toward individual African Americans they encounter. Many students reported that their parents made blatantly racist statements against African Americans as a group and criticized the second generation for talking, dressing, or acting "Black," but that their parents treated African American friends that they brought home respectfully and on an individual basis.

Even though many in the first generation have little personal contact with either Black or White Americans, they are ready to express opinions of both groups to their children:

BB: Do your parents ever talk about their experiences in America with different groups of people, with White Americans for example?

Maritza: They consider White Americans to be very polite. They speak of them very highly. Compared to how they speak about, like Black people? They're not prejudice or anything, but they speak, I guess they prefer, I guess they are prejudiced, I don't know if I should call it prejudism, but...they kind of prefer White people, more, I don't see why.

BB: Do Blacks seem less polite?

Maritza: I don't know. I guess because-- I don't know why. I don't know. I won't say why. I always disagree on that aspect.

BB: Do they say anything in particular? Can you think of an example of what they might say?

Maritza: For example, my Dad, he could be like driving, and the light is green, and there goes a Black person walks, they're like "You don't see White people doing that" whatever. I don't like the way they talk like that. I think if they had a little bit more education, they wouldn't speak like that, because if they learned about Africans being slaves and stuff, they wouldn't really think of Blacks as bad as they do.

Maritza explains her parents' attitudes toward African Americans as a function of their lack of education. Neither had attended school beyond the 7th grade in the Dominican Republic, and both were employed in factories in America. Maritza suggests that if they knew about African Americans' past as slaves they would better understand their present situation in American society.

Both Dominican and American racial frameworks are evident in Maritza's understandings of race. Maritza and her parents are almost certainly the descendants of African slaves: she reported that people generally perceived her to be African American until they heard her speaking Spanish, and she said that her parents, despite speaking little English, are even mistaken for Black Americans at times. She empathizes with historical oppression of African Americans, displaying an American framework for understanding race--but she disassociates herself and her parents from similar, historical oppression, thus displaying a Dominican understanding. For Maritza, historical slavery is relevant only to understanding African Americans and not Dominicans.

Parents' attitudes toward African Americans also become evident when Dominican teen-agers such as Maritza date African Americans:

Maritza: I recently broke up with him [an African American boyfriend], but I went to my prom with him, and my aunt, she saw the picture, she was like, "No." I hate it, I don't like that. She said "If you're thinking about getting together with someone, make sure that it's someone good-looking, cause your kids are going to look like him." But I bet you that if the person was American [i.e. White], Dominican, it would be a different story. It all narrows down to racism. That's what I think about it. My parents, my Dad, he would straight out say, okay, no, he doesn't like Black people. My mom would kind of say it, but then when she met him, it was kind of different. She had like a different point of view after. So that's why I think usually they'll speak bad about someone. You don't know, just because they're Black or any other color, you can't talk about them because you don't know who they really are. I hate that so much, I do.

Maritza's aunt expresses a form of anti-African-descent sentiment that is commonly heard in the Dominican Republic. Phenotypes popularly associated with sub-Saharan African descent are considered much less attractive than those associated with European descent. Maritza, however, has a very different attitude toward the beauty of Black phenotypes:

BB: When you imagine having a husband someday, what background do you think he might have?
Maritza: You know, for some reason, I want to marry a Black American. One, because I'm attracted to them...And also to show my parents, "See this is not what you thought."

Maritza thus rejects the Dominican ideology in which relatively more European phenotype is equated with beauty and higher social class. Her desire to marry a person explicitly defined as Black (versus, for example, an African-descent individual defined as Dominican and *indio* ['indian-colored']) would be almost unheard of in the Dominican Republic, where it would be tantamount, in traditional Dominican terms, to saying "I want to marry someone relatively unattractive and low class."

Dominicans on the island who are relatively dark have traditionally been urged by family members to *mejorar la raza* ['improve the bloodlines'] of the family by finding a lighter-skinned mate so that offspring would be relatively lighter, considered more attractive, and associated with a higher social class. The first generation in America also encourage their children to marry someone relatively light:

Rosa: They... say, "Marry a White person. Don't marry anyone uglier ['darker'] than you, marry a White person. Get some White blood into it." Dominicans tell you to marry someone light.

To members of the second generation, who have a different understanding of phenotype, social hierarchies, and racial politics based on their American socialization, this glorification of fair skin can seem absurd:

Rosa: They really push it, light-skinned Dominicans, "Oh he's so cute, *él es bien fino* ['He's really elegant/refined'], high class," just cause he's white and cute, he's light-skinned, they just look up so much to people that are Dominican or Spanish and they look White. They think of it like a step up in society. I just can't believe that. They think of it as a step to a higher class when you look White.

While the first generation symbolically align themselves with White Americans, the second generation understand that Dominicans are in a similar structural position to African Americans. They realize that racism can just as easily be aimed at Dominicans as at African Americans, and that the dominant groups in society do not differentiate among non-White groups in the ways that first-generation Dominicans do. Maritza argues that this common experience of subordination from Whites should deter Dominicans in the first generation from discriminating against Blacks:

Maritza: ...they shouldn't be prejudiced against them [African Americans] or racist against them. Cause you see how some White people are racist against Blacks? Sometimes they see us also as Blacks, or Spanish people. They kind of have the same idea about us, not the same, but they relate to us as the same people. I don't think we should be racist against Blacks.

Many in the second generation are also more ready than their parents to acknowledge their African ancestry. They find their parents' criticisms of other African-descent groups to be hypocritical in light of the African ancestry of most Dominicans:

Rosa: Dominicans talk about Black people in a negative way, and that really gets on my nerves. I really can't stand that. Because they're part Black. They took Africans to the Dominican Republic and they're just mixed with everything. I think Dominicans have absolutely no right to talk about anybody because they're everything....when she's [Rosa's mother] talking about Black people or any other culture, she's talking about herself. I think that's really wrong and Dominicans do that all the time.

The first generation's disparagement of African Americans is often accompanied or introduced by invidious comparison with White Americans:

Maria: I told my Mom she's prejudice, because she always says "White people this, White people that. You don't see White people wearing those kind of clothes." I'm like "Mom, nowadays, everybody wears those kind of clothes." She's like "Black people this, Black people that," I'm like "No, mom, you are so prejudice." She's like "No, I'm not prejudice, I'm not prejudice." I'm like, "Mom, my grandmother is dark, she's dark. You know, Mom, I'm not (   ), but she's Black no matter what. It's bad when people are known as Black. Cause we Hispanics are Black. She's like "No." "We're Black, so I don't know what you're talking about." I just leave her. She's like "White people this, White people that, White people work." I'm like, "No *mami* ['mom'], I know White people, it don't matter. I know Black people, it don't matter. Everybody's the same thing." She thinks that Black people are the ones that go do gangs and all that.

BB: She says Whites do what?

Maria: She say that Whites are people that are responsible, they think about working, going to school... And I don't consider it like that.

The social construction of racial identity can become particularly clear in such intergenerational conflicts. Because the two generations are raised in different social contexts and use different cultural frameworks to view themselves, racial identity and solidarity is sometimes better predicted by generation than actual phenotype. Maria, for example, describes herself as "very white" and "almost whiter than you" [the White American researcher]. Despite her relatively light skin color and her self-ascriptions of being "very white," Maria identifies strongly as non-White, and in some senses as Black:

Maria: In America, there's only White and Black, that's the only colors we have. Spanish people are considered Black, that's the way they consider us, Black. I think Asians is White. I just know Spanish is considered Black. Cause I asked my social studies teacher, she said, "Yeah, Spanish are considered Black".... when my Mom talk about Black, I'm like "Mom you're talking about Hispanics," [she says] "Yeah, I know, but it's different, they're Black." She's starting to leave that....I just tell her I'd appreciate her not to talk about Black people in front of me.

Maria considers herself "Black" in some senses despite her light skin. Maria's mother, in contrast, aligns herself with White Americans despite having hair, facial features, and skin color that lead to her being perceived at times as African American. Her mother's prejudice against African Americans and her symbolic identification with Whites has led Maria to accuse her of thinking she's White:

Maria: I consider that [anti-Haitian racism in the Dominican Republic] very bad, that's one of the reasons I don't really like the DR, "You people think you're so White," "Mom, you think you're really White." She's like, "I don't think of myself as White." I'm like, "I don't want to hear it."

The first generation see themselves as having little in common with African Americans. They do not think of themselves as Black or of African descent, and discrimination based on lack of English or on immigration status is much more salient to most than discrimination based on phenotype (cf. Itzigsohn and Dore-Cabral 2000). Life in America for many is a sojourn in a land of economic opportunity that consists of work, family, and little beyond the immigrant community. Those who immigrate as adults maintain a Dominican frame of reference for viewing themselves, and many plan on retiring to the Dominican Republic. Isolation from American ethnic and racial discourses prevents them from seeing themselves in a structural position similar to African Americans, which might otherwise lead to greater solidarity.

The second generation, in contrast, grow up as non-Whites in a society in which Whites are at the top of the economic and ethnic/racial hierarchies. Those who attend public schools in Providence have ongoing contact with African Americans, and the essentialized ethnic/racial stereotypes of their parents do not hold for the individuals the second generation encounter and become friends with. The social reality the second generation face of being non-White, low-income, and urban is shared with other American and immigrant groups, contributing to intergroup solidarity. Exclusion and discrimination by White Americans thus leads the second generation to see their identities relative to Black and White Americans in very different terms than their parents, even as they maintain an ethnolinguistic, rather than Black/White, understanding of their own identities.

5.7 Dominican American Ways of Seeing Phenotype

At the same time that members of the second generation resist American racialization, many implicitly adopt dominant American assumptions about relationships between phenotype and social identity.

Whereas Dominicans on the island use physical descriptors (e.g. *blanco, moreno, indio*) to characterize individuals' phenotypes and skin color, Dominican Americans frequently use national/ethnic/folk-racial labels (e.g. "Dominican," "Spanish," "Black") to characterize physical appearance. A Dominican with relatively fair skin might thus be described by a Dominican American as "Looking Puerto Rican" in Providence, whereas he/she might be described as *indio claro* ['light indian-colored'] or *blanco* ['white'] on the island. For the second generation, phenotype is not just an individual physical characteristic, but also a key to judging the social identity of others. United States racial organization of the social world thus influences second-generation social perception even as the second generation resist phenotype-based racialization when it is applied to them.

Individuals of varying European/African phenotypes encountered in the Dominican Republic are assumed to be Dominican unless there are clues, e.g. linguistic, behavioral, or dress, to suggest otherwise.

Wilson: If you're there [in the Dominican Republic], everybody is just one color. Like over there, there's a lot of Dominicans with brown eyes, green eyes, blue eyes, blonde hair. Everyone knows he or she is Dominican, they don't consider as White. She can be white, but they won't say "Look at this White girl." They'll just look at this Dominican person. So everybody over there is just like one.

Individual differences in phenotype are thus treated as individual attributes rather than social group attributes.

The second-generation shift to use of stereotypical national/ethnic/folk-racial phenotypes disregards the phenotypic variation within social groups. Although Dominican Americans are discursively conscious of the range of phenotypes exhibited by Dominicans, they report mistaking Dominicans for African Americans, Puerto Ricans, and occasionally White Americans. Whereas the phenotypically-European Dominican in the Dominican Republic is generally taken to be Dominican, that same individual is initially perceived by Dominican Americans as White in the context of the United States.

Jose M.: There are Dominicans that can look White. I know a Dominican girl, I thought she was White....She talks White, I never even saw her speaking Spanish. I didn't even know she was Spanish.

More common among Dominican Americans is to mistake other Dominican Americans for Black/African American:

Alejandro: Once I seen this kid, I thought he was Black, I could've swear to god he was Black, and I seen him with my friend talking Spanish, we were like, "Where you from, man?" He's like, "I'm Dominican." We're like, "Hell, no." He's like, "I'm Dominican." A lot of people are like that.

Maria: A lot of girls from the Dominican Republic they look like Black girls. And guys look like Black guys. They're actually Dominican....they start talking Spanish, and I be like "What, you talk Spanish?" they be like "Yeah."

Even Dominican Americans who are regularly perceived to be African American themselves, e.g. Janelle and Maritza, mistake other Dominican Americans for African Americans until they hear them speak Spanish.

BB: Some Dominicans look like they could be Black Americans.
Janelle: They do, yo. Some kid in our school, that kid Kristin? He is so dark, I thought he was Black. Then he talked to someone in Spanish, I was like--
Jose: Yeah my cousin, he looks Black....
Janelle: He looks Black
Jose: When you speak to him, he won't have no accent or anything? But he's Dominican, pure Dominican. He got his hair, is kind of rough, so that makes him look like he's Black.
Janelle: Black. He looks Black.

BB: Who think you're Black? White Americans, Dominicans...?
Maritza: Black Americans. It's kind of, it's kind of different, because they should know their own people. I would know who's Dominican. Actually, no, there was this guy, he's Dominican, and I thought he was Black. And then when I heard him speak Spanish, I was like, "He's Spanish! He's a Dominican."

Puerto Ricans are also a reference point for perceiving and describing phenotypes. They are popularly stereotyped as more European in phenotype than Dominicans, with the result that Dominican Americans with lighter skin in Providence are often assumed to be Puerto Rican until they are heard speaking Dominican Spanish or they explicitly identify themselves as Dominican:

BB: What do you say you are?
Martin: Dominican
BB: Do you ever say Hispanic or Latino?
Martin: I just say I'm Spanish, they're like "Where from?" They usually think Puerto Rico. I'm like, "No Dominican." I usually have to break it down for them.

Maria: People think I'm Puerto Rican because of my color, because a lot of Puerto Ricans are light....

Janelle: Usually Puerto Ricans are lighter
Jose: Sometimes you could get mixed up, like "You're Puerto Rican." "No I'm Dominican." A lot of people confuse me and say I'm Puerto Rican....the Puerto Ricans, they got a more lighter color than Dominicans. Usually they're real, real light.
Janelle: Most Dominicans are dark.
Jose: The Dominicans they're dark, they got a darker color.

This use of phenotype as an indicator of social identity also leads Dominican Americans in Providence to perceive members of *other* social groups as Dominican, particularly Cape Verdean Americans, who share Iberian and sub-Saharan African ancestry with Dominicans. A Cape Verdean American student at Central High School who was friends with Dominican students, for example, reported that he was regularly mistaken for Hispanic/Dominican:

BB: Do people ever ask you what you are?
John: Most of the people, they think I'm Spanish, and they start talking Spanish to me, but then I say "No hablo español" and then they say, "Oh you're not Spanish?" and then I say "No" and then they ask me what am I, and then I say "Cape Verdean."

Socialization in America thus not only affects the ways in which individual Dominican Americans see themselves, but also the ways in which they see others. Stereotyped phenotypes become so strongly identified with particular social identities that Dominican Americans mistake each other for members of other social groups, even though they are discursively aware of the diversity of Dominican phenotypes. Even as the second generation resist American racialization of their phenotype, they have internalized the American assumption that phenotype is an indicator of social identity.

5.8 Conclusions

Dominican American constructions of race in Providence reflect socialization in both Dominican social circles and a low-income, multi-ethnic urban American environment. Unlike non-Hispanic African-descent immigrants, who generally identify themselves as "Black" in the second generation, Dominicans in the second generation think of themselves as "Dominican" or "Spanish"/"Hispanic"/"Latino." Spanish language is a key to claiming and enacting these ethnolinguistic identities. In everyday life, Spanish language enables participation in a vibrant, growing ethnolinguistic community, which helps to preserve a common cultural memory and distinct sense of Dominican origins. This encourages the second generation to see their roots as remote from the American history of social relations out of which American Black/White racialization practices have grown and promotes the maintenance of culturally distinctive frames of reference for self-definition.

At the same time, second-generation understandings of race are a function of growing up in a United States context in which specific racial and ethnic hierarchies are central to social categorization. Unlike their parents, for example, the second generation experience significant solidarity with African Americans, based in part on their common experiences of subordination and discrimination. This United States socialization also leads many to associate phenotype with specific social identities in ways that do not occur on the island.

The notions of race maintained by Dominican Americans and their everyday linguistic enactment of Spanish/Dominican identities highlight the processual, constructed nature of racial categories. As the overall post-1965 immigrant second generation comprises a larger and larger proportion of the United States population, received constructions of race will be increasingly challenged by groups whose understandings and enactments of identity do not fit the historically available categories.

CHAPTER 6

The Interactional Negotiation of Race by an African-descent Dominican American

6.1 Introduction

In the multi-ethnic, multi-phenotype, multi-lingual context of Central High School, language is central to the social identities that individual Dominican Americans claim and that others ascribe to them.[43] In this chapter, one Dominican American's negotiation of social identities during a single class period is analyzed. Through skillful use of multiple language varieties, the student, Wilson, is able to situationally highlight Dominican, American, and African American facets of his Dominican American ethnolinguistic identity. The ambiguity resulting from Wilson's African-descent phenotype and his facility with multiple language varieties make his identity a topic of explicit discussion during this class period. Analysis of Wilson's talk and interaction reveals much about the local roles of language and phenotype in the negotiation of identity. As previously described, for example, language is shown to situationally precede phenotype as a criterion for racial classification, and racial identities shift across linguistically constructed contexts.

At the same time that language gives Wilson the freedom to highlight ethnolinguistic facets of identity, however, language is also used to impose restrictive identities. In segments of talk and interaction presented here, Wilson's African-descent phenotype is repeatedly invoked by his classmates in both English and Spanish, and treated as relevant, sometimes jokingly, to his identity. Association of African-descent phenotype with social identity is so pervasive in the United States that it implicitly informs social assumptions, even among Dominican Americans who claim identities outside of the Black/White dichotomy. Language is a medium that affords individual social actors the freedom to highlight various aspects of identity, but it is also a medium through which constraining, hegemonic forms of inscription, e.g. social classification based on phenotype, are invoked and reconstituted.

Spanish language serves Dominican Americans both as a direct index (Silverstein 1976, Ochs 1992) of Spanish social identity, as well as an interactional tool with which to negotiate identities. Local treatment of Spanish language as a direct index is evident in the metonymic social category "Spanish," as described in Chapter Four. Many linguistic forms also serve as *indirect* indexes of social identity, however, as they index and reconstitute identities via the performance of particular speech acts and activities and social stances (Ochs 1992). As shown in Chapter Four in terms of Dominican authenticity, this indirect constitution of identity through language is an interactional process. Individual social actors can use language to align themselves with others (i.e. communicate co-membership), or differentiate themselves from others (i.e. mark social boundaries), marking multiple and shifting "we"/"they" dichotomies at various levels of specificity (Cohen 1978).

Wilson and his classmates use both English and Spanish resources creatively, selectively invoking Dominican and American interpretive frameworks and social affiliations in ways that belie one-to-one correspondences between code, cultural framework, and social identity (cf. Duranti and Ochs 1997). Dominican individuals can thus use English to invoke a Dominican interpretive framework, for example, and they can use Dominican Spanish, ostensibly a language of solidarity, to highlight intra-group differences.

The use of language as a tool to construct identities has important implications for the analyst who seeks a window into members' phenomenological world:

> In examining talk the analyst is immediately confronted with an organization which is implemented on a turn-by-turn basis, and through which a context of publicly displayed and continuously updated intersubjective understandings is

systematically sustained. It is through this turn-by-turn character of talk that the participants display their understandings of the state of the talk for one another, and because these understandings are publicly produced, they are available for analytic treatment by social scientists. (Heritage and Atkinson 1984:11).

Heritage and Atkinson (1984) emphasize actors' understandings of the organization of talk, but actors also display understandings of social organization more generally (Goodwin and Duranti 1992:29-30). Since identity is a function of self- and other-ascription, the constitution of identities--through the negotiation of congruent ascriptions--is visible in the turn-by-turn talk of individuals. The micro-level social activities out of which larger scale social constellations such as race and ethnicity are constituted and reproduced can thus be observed.

6.2 Highlighting Facets of Identity Through Language

Wilson and his interlocutors both align themselves and differentiate themselves from each other during this class period. He interacts primarily with three recent Dominican immigrants, a Guatemalan American, two African Americans, and a South East Asian immigrant, and he alternates among linguistic forms that are distinctively Dominican Spanish, American English, Dominican English, and African American English. Both his linguistic forms and his speech activities variously highlight his Dominican heritage, his American socialization, and his affiliation with African American peers. In terms of code choice, he aligns himself situationally with recent Dominican immigrants, for example, by interacting with them in fluent Spanish, but he also differentiates himself from them through displays of his fluent English and American cultural knowledge. He aligns himself with African Americans through his use of AAVE forms and interactional gestures of solidarity, but he also implicitly differentiates himself from them, e.g. by directing *piropos* ['amorous compliments'] in Spanish to Dominican and Hispanic female classmates. Dominican American acculturation does not follow a single, discrete trajectory, and it does not result in a monolithic category but rather multiple and multi-faceted identities. A characteristic feature of Dominican

American identity in Providence is precisely its incorporation of language and cultural practices that are popularly associated with diverse social identities. In the transcripts that follow, I classify the linguistic forms/speech activities Wilson and his classmates use in order to highlight this diversity and juxtaposition.

Transcripts in this chapter are drawn from a video-recording made during the last period of the day, a social studies class. The teacher is absent, and at the beginning of class the substitute teacher explains the assignment that the students are to do in class: read and outline a magazine article about the Chinese assumption of rule in Hong Kong. Few students even pretend to work on the assignment. Most treat the period as an opportunity to move around the room, talk, and socialize. Some students leave the room, and others come in.

[(WR #2 1:13:05) The following segment of interaction occurs five minutes into class. The substitute teacher is talking to the class about the assignment for the day during this interaction. Wilson has been chatting in English and Spanish. Some students are taking seats and others are still drifting into the room. Abbreviations for different language varieties/activities are before each line: 'SP' for Spanish, 'DS' for distinctively Dominican Spanish, 'AAVE' for African American Vernacular English, 'DE' for Dominican English, 'AE' for American English, and 'HE' for Hispanicized English, the variety spoken by recent immigrants just learning English (cf. Zentella 1997:32).]

((Wilson turns to see Gabriella, a recent Dominican immigrant, entering the classroom wearing a mini-dress, and he turns his head to follow her progress across the room.))
 (DS) Wilson : (→Gabriella) *Muchacha diablo! Ssss*   ['Damn, girl!']
                  ((inhales between clenched teeth))
((Wilson turns back to his desk and thumbs through a magazine.))
 (AAVE) Wilson: (→BB) (   ) We just messing around today.
((Claudia, a Guatemalan American, takes a seat diagonally in front of Wilson and turns sideways to look back at him. Wilson turns toward her and sings as he rocks his shoulders to the *merengue* beat.))
 (DS) Wilson: (→Claudia) ((singing))*Dame del pollito, dame del
                  pollito* ['Give me some of that chicken, give me some
                  of that chicken']

(AE) Claudia: (→Wilson) I hate that song. ((She rolls her eyes and turns away from him.))

(DS) Wilson: *Del pollito--.* ['Some of that (good) chicken']

(DS) Wilson: ((Wilson points toward Claudia.)) *Del pollita buena.* ['Some of that good chicken']

((Another student asks Wilson a question that is not clearly audible on the tape.))

(DS) Wilson: *Mira pa(ra a)llá.* ['Look over there']
(.3)

(AE) Wilson: Look over there. ((gestures with head toward blackboard))

(DS) Wilson: ((singing)) *Dame del pollito* ((looking at magazine)) ['Give me some of that chicken']

((Claudia gets up from her chair to move toward the front of the room; Wilson grabs his crushed soda can off his desk.))

(DS) Eduardo: (→Wilson) *Como tú va(s)--* ((Gazing at crushed soda can on Wilson's desk.)) ['Why are you going to--']

(AE) Wilson: (→Claudia) Can you throw that away for me please? ((He holds out his empty soda can toward Claudia, but she doesn't take it.))

(DS) Eduardo: (→Wilson) *Cómo tú va(s) (a) botar esa lata?. Eso vale cinco chele(s) para gente pobre. No ha(s) visto lo(s) viejito(s) recogiendola(s)?* ['Why are you going to throw away that can? That's worth five cents for poor people. Haven't you seen the little old people collecting them?']

(AAVE) Wilson: She left me hanging, yo! hhh hhh ((in-breath of mock sobs))

(DS) Wilson: (→group) ((Turns to recent Dominican immigrants behind him)) *E(s)te viejo sí habla solo.* ['This old guy [the substitute teacher] sure does talk to himself.']

(AE) Wilson: Man! ((thumbing through magazine))

(AE) Wilson: (→teacher) Which article are we supposed--

(DS) Eduardo: ((singing)) *Maria se fue* ['Maria left' (a popular *merengue* lyric at that time)]

In this short segment Wilson switches among varieties of Spanish and English in flirting with females, telling a classmate to look at the blackboard, commenting on class activities to the researcher, making fun of the teacher to friends, and addressing the teacher, among other activities. The linguistic forms and speech activities he engages in selectively highlight different facets of his bilingual-bicultural identity. His use of Spanish to direct *piropos* ['amorous compliments', often undesired by the females at whom they are directed] at Gabrielle and then subsequently Claudia, for example, indexes his Hispanic identity. His *piropo* for Claudia suggests a specifically Dominican identity, as it is achieved through a *merengue* lyric, melody, and physical movement. While *piropos* are common to many Latin American countries, *merengue* is a symbol of Dominican identity both on the island and internationally (Austerlitz 1997, Duany 1994). This *piropo* displays not just knowledge of Spanish code and *merengue* lyrics, but also of the cultural frame in which Dominican popular music lyrics often contain double entendres (*Dame del pollito* ['Give me some of that chicken.']). Claudia displays understanding of Wilson's Spanish utterance and speech activity, but she does not reply in Spanish. In this multi-lingual, multi-ethnic setting, individuals can frequently draw from a range of language varieties to achieve interactional ends. Claudia uses English to state her distaste for the song, and she turns away, effectively rejecting the Dominican communicative frame that Wilson has constituted through referential content, code choice, and visual channels.

The juxtaposition of codes between Wilson's and Claudia's turns also occurs across Wilson's turns, highlighting his bilingualism and dual Dominican and American socialization. When a student asks Wilson an inaudible question, presumably regarding the assignment, he responds initially in Spanish, *Mira pa(ra a)llá*, then reiterates the message in English, after a brief gap, "Look over there," indicating that she should look in the direction of the blackboard where the assignment was printed.

Wilson's use of codes varies with the speech activity that he is instantiating. While he used Spanish to direct a *piropo* at Claudia, he uses American English to request a small favor from her. When she gets up to move toward the front of the room, he holds out his empty soda, asking her if she can throw it away. When she does not take the can and Wilson is left holding it in his outstretched hand, he uses yet another language variety, AAVE, to publicly comment on this rejection ("She left me hanging, yo!"). "To leave someone hanging" is an AAVE expression used to describe the situation when a hand extended for a handshake or hand-slap--a symbol of solidarity--is ignored, and the hand is left hanging in space (Smitherman 1994:153, 110).

Other alternation of code follows a pattern of situational code switching, depending on the linguistic knowledge of potential audiences (Blom and Gumperz 1972). Wilson uses Dominican Spanish to make a comment about the teacher to his Dominican classmates in a way that they will understand but the teacher will not (*E(s)te viejo sí habla solo* ['This old guy sure does talk to himself.']), and he uses English to address the substitute teacher and ask about the assignment for the day.

Wilson thus uses linguistic resources variously associated with Dominican Spanish, American, and, specifically, African American varieties of English in this short segment to engage in speech activities that invoke various Dominican and American frameworks, and involve minimally Dominican, Guatemalan American, and White American audiences. In such interethnic, multilingual contexts, which are the norm at Central High School, Dominican American students can highlight various facets of their socialization. The ability to speak both English and Spanish allows them to situationally align themselves with members of diverse social categories, but it also differentiates them from individuals who are not bilingual. In the following segment of transcript, for example, differences between Wilson and a recent Dominican immigrant in linguistic/cultural knowledge regarding the pronunciation of the name of a local park lead to a temporary breakdown in communication.

JB, who has been in America for several years, is the younger brother of one of Wilson's best friends. During this class period they speak primarily in Spanish, although they have just been speaking English to joke with a student of Southeast Asian descent immediately prior to this segment.

[(WR #2 1:36:05)]
Wilson (DS): *Qué tú va(s) (a) hacer en tu casa hoy loco?* ['What are you going to do at your house today, man?']
JB (DS): *Puede ser que vaya a jugar pelota con Tito.* ['I'll probably go play ball with Tito.']
Wilson (DS): *Con?* ['With?']
JB (DS): *Con Tito.* ['With Tito.']
Wilson (AE): Oh.

JB (DS):   *Que si no iba(s) para /buklin/?* ['Weren't you going to
              /buklin/ too?']
Wilson (SP): *Donde?* ['Where?']
JB (HE):   /buklin/
Wilson (AE/DE): Oh, /bʌklən/. At what time?
JB (HE):   (five)
Wilson (AAVE): Oh wor(d)! I'm gonna go break you up.
JB (DS):   *No me haga(s) reir.* ['Don't make me laugh.']

Both Wilson and JB use characteristically Dominican Spanish in this
passage, e.g. non-inversion of subject and verb word order (*Qué tú
va(s) a hacer...*), elision of syllable-final /s/, and velarization of word-
final /n/, thus marking themselves as co-members of a Dominican
linguistic group. Wilson also uses several varieties of English: the
American English change of state token "oh" (Heritage 1984b), the
Dominican English "At what time?,"[44] and the African American
Vernacular English "Oh word! I'm gonna go break you up."[45]

    JB successfully responds to Wilson's English in this passage, and
Wilson displays understanding of JB's Spanish, but Wilson is initially
unable to understand what JB is referring to when he says /buklin/. JB
assimilates the name of the park to Spanish phonology, using the
Spanish vowels /u/ and /i/ and stressing the two syllables evenly. It is
not so much a difference in language proficiency that leads to this
breakdown in communication, but rather a difference in social worlds.
The park in question, Bucklin, is a feature of the American and English
Providence world in which Wilson has grown up, rather than the island
Dominican/monolingual Spanish context in which JB grew up.
Wilson's American English pronunciation of "Bucklin" may trigger
(Clyne 1967) his subsequent continuation of speech in English ("At
what time?"), representing the first English in this segment beyond the
change of state token "Oh." Differences between Wilson and JB in
their relationships to their Providence environment are thus highlighted
by a temporary breakdown in communication even though they both
share Spanish as a grammatical code and their first language learned.

    Although he interacts primarily with Hispanic classmates in the
above segments of transcript, Wilson uses many forms that are
associated with AAVE. He deletes the copula in addressing the White
researcher ("We just messing around today"), and he uses distinctive
expressions associated with AAVE in addressing Dominican

classmates ("I'm gonna break you up!"), and multi-ethnic audiences ("She left me hanging, yo."). When he does interact with African Americans during this period, his use of these forms is matched with significant, mutual expressions of solidarity toward these classmates. Upon discovering that I was in class to videotape Wilson, for example, an African American classmate said "Wilson? He's cool" (WR #2 1:17:02), at which point Wilson reached out to slap hands with her, a gesture Smitherman (1994:125) defines as showing strong agreement among African Americans. He then pressed his right fist to his chest over his heart two times. Consultants defined this fist-on-chest gesture as indicating deep friendship.

This particular classmate also uses a term of address for Wilson that is frequently reserved for co-members of the category African American:

(WR #2 1:28:17)
Wilson: Andie!
Andie: What up, bro? ((Andie turns to face Wilson.))

"Bro" /bro/ is short for "brotha" ['brother'], which Smitherman (1994:70) defines as referring to any African American male, derived from the traditional "Black Church pattern of referring to all male members of the Church 'family' as *Brotha*." In this case, Andie addresses Wilson in a way that might be used to address fellow African Americans, thus implying a degree of sameness or affiliation with Wilson. (Zentella, personal communication, notes that "bro" can be extended as an in-group term of address for low-income Latinos, even those with relatively light skin). Wilson's use of AAVE and his concomitant alignment with African American peers not only highlight African American aspects of his socialization, but in combination with his phenotype, lead many individuals to perceive him to be African American.

In this multi-lingual, multi-ethnic classroom, Wilson moves seamlessly among varieties of Spanish and English, constituting speech activities that range from giving *piropos* in Spanish, to boasting in AAVE, to negotiating an after school activity in both languages. Language and communicative behavior serve as a resource for him in invoking these various communicative frameworks and alternately highlighting different aspects of his social and linguistic expertise, i.e. different facets of his Dominican American identity.

6.3 Negotiation of Phenotype and Identity

Language is a tool that affords individuals agency in the ways they present themselves, but it is also a medium through which others can impose labels and categories. In the transcripts presented below, Wilson's classmates use language, both in English and Spanish, to repeatedly invoke his African-descent phenotype and treat it as relevant to his social identity. Language minority ethnicity and phenotype-based racial/ethnic minority are the types of ethnicity most closely associated with individual behavior by dominant groups and most easily invoked by others (Mittelberg and Waters 1993). Through skillful language use, Wilson is able to selectively foreground and background his Dominican and American language identities, but he cannot selectively display alternate phenotypes. Wilson defines himself unequivocally as "Spanish" and "Dominican," and these categories are locally available to African-descent individuals--as shown in transcripts below--but phenotype is readily apparent to all and always available for others to invoke.

I examine this negotiation of African-descent identity in three sections, each revolving around chronologically presented segments of transcribed talk and interaction. In the first section, a recent Dominican immigrant jokingly identifies Wilson as Haitian to the researcher and subsequently to a Guatemalan American classmate. In the second section, a South East Asian immigrant student tells Wilson that she had never thought that he was Spanish, but rather assumed he was Black. Wilson and a Dominican confederate then attempt, without success, to dupe her by arguing that Wilson is, in fact, Black. In the third section, Wilson's African-descent phenotype is implicitly invoked in a discussion of relationships between athletic prowess and physical appearance. These segments show that even as Dominican Americans see themselves as outside of the American Black/White racial dichotomy--and successfully resist ascription to the category Black--they remain subject to phenotype-based racial thinking in a variety of contexts.

6.3.1 "He's from Haiti"

Wilson's African-descent phenotype is first invoked during this class by a recent Dominican immigrant, Eduardo. Except for the segment of transcript below, Eduardo speaks almost entirely in Spanish during the course of the class.

[(WR #2 1:10:11) The substitute teacher is discussing the assignment for the day. Wilson has been telling Eduardo in Spanish to hand over Wilson's soda, which Eduardo has been sipping.]

BB: Are you Dominican too?
Eduardo: //(Yeah)
Wilson: //Yeah, he's, he's...((Wilson raises his hand and makes a pushing/throwing gesture toward Eduardo as if dismissing him and laughs.))
Eduardo: He's from Haiti ((gestures toward Wilson)), you know what I mean?
BB: He's what?
Eduardo: From Haiti.

In answer to the researcher's question as to whether Eduardo, like Wilson, was Dominican, they both respond affirmatively. Wilson, however, while acknowledging co-membership as Dominican, distances himself from Eduardo. He twice says "he's," as if beginning to define Eduardo as something other than Dominican, but he does not give an explicit verbal characterization of Eduardo. He does, however, face away from Eduardo toward the researcher and cock his arm two times and make an open-handed pushing/throwing gesture in Eduardo's direction as if to dismiss him. Eduardo stands up, and gesturing with both hands toward Wilson, says that Wilson is from Haiti. When I request clarification of this characterization of Wilson ("He's what?"), Eduardo repeats "From Haiti."

It is highly unlikely that Eduardo thinks that Wilson is Haitian. They have been classmates the entire term, they interact almost solely in Dominican Spanish, and they know each other well enough to share a soda. Asserting that Wilson is from Haiti is more likely a form of teasing, or "cracking on" Wilson. "Cracking" is a popular form of verbal play among Dominican American teen-agers in Providence. "Cracking" is a form of verbal dueling that has been defined as a characteristically African American discourse genre under a variety of names, e.g. signifying, playing the dozens, snapping, sounding, etc. (Kochman 1972, Mitchell-Kernan 1972, Morgan 1998). Characteristic of this genre is the notion of play:

> [play] differentiates the real from the serious by focusing on that which is socially and/or culturally significant (e.g., relatives, sexuality, physical appearance, political figures, class, and economic status) and placing it in implausible contexts. Whether a context is plausible or implausible is culturally determined. (Morgan 1998:267)

In this case, Eduardo is indirectly highlighting Wilson's physical appearance--which has significance in both Dominican and American terms--by referring to it in the context of an implausible claim, i.e. that Wilson is Haitian.

Eduardo's claim that Wilson is from Haiti invokes a Dominican communicative and interpretive framework even though this exchange takes place in America, in English, and involves a White American interlocutor. Although both Wilson and Eduardo might count as members of the category Black in America, incremental differences in phenotype between them (Wilson is more African in phenotype) have meaning in a Dominican context. As described in Chapter 5, having a relatively African phenotype in the Dominican Republic is considered unattractive and a potential source of embarrassment. Calling an individual Dominican a "Haitian" is a way of drawing attention to that individual's African-descent phenotype and insulting him (e.g. Diaz 1996).

What makes this verbal play rather than serious assertion is the implausibility, from a Dominican perspective, of the scenario presented. Wilson does not dress or speak like Dominican notions of Haitians, and he is considerably more European in phenotype than popular stereotypes of Haitians. In many American contexts, in contrast, it is *not* implausible that Wilson could be Haitian. Wilson regularly experiences ascription to non-Dominican/Hispanic categories, so the assertion may not be entirely implausible and may not be taken as unequivocally playful. This could be one reason that Wilson does not verbally respond to this crack on him.

Eduardo simultaneously displays alignment and disaffiliation with Wilson. He aligns himself with Wilson--perhaps unconsciously--by invoking a Dominican interpretive framework for understanding phenotype and identity. Such a shared framework typically serves as a unifying frame among Dominicans in America. Eduardo differentiates himself from Wilson by invoking phenotypic differences between himself and Wilson in a way that denies this common Dominican identity. Thus a shared cultural communicative framework does not necessarily imply speech activities that contribute to solidarity.

Eduardo asserts that Wilson is Haitian twice more during this class period. About 10 minutes into the class, I ask one of the students sitting directly in front of Wilson where she is from, and she replies that she is from Guatemala. Eduardo then interjects, "He's from Haiti, too" pointing to Wilson (WR #2 1:17:13). No one responds to this interjection, however. Three minutes later, Eduardo once again asserts that Wilson is from Haiti, and this time Wilson responds to the assertion:

(WR #2 1:20:07)
Wilson: ((singing)) *dame del pollito* ['give me a little bit of that chicken']
Eduardo: *Tú no dizque ere(s) de Haití? Tú no ere(s) dominicano, Wilson.* ['Aren't you supposedly from Haiti? You're not Dominican, Wilson.']
Wilson: *Yo nací en Haití,* ((Wilson turns to Eduardo, smiling)) ['I was born in Haiti']
Eduardo: //(   ) ((motions toward camera, Wilson turns to camera))
Wilson: //*pero me crié en Santo Domingo.* ['but I was brought up in the Dominican Republic']
((Eduardo holds up both hands, palms forward, with middle and ring fingers curled down—the sign of the cuckold--behind Wilson's head; Wilson turns back toward Eduardo and hits him in the leg with the back of his open hand))   (1.5)
Claudia: So you're Haitian, huh?
Wilson: No I'm Dominican
Claudia: You were born in DR?
Wilson: Yeah
Eduardo: *Nació en Haití* ['He was born in Haiti.']

Wilson: *En Santo Domingo.*   ['In the Dominican Republic.']
Eduardo: *E(s) haitiano.*   ['He's Haitian.']
Wilson: *E(s) mentira, ven acá, a quién tú le va(s)--a quién tú le va(s)
          a creer, a mí o a e(s)to(s) do(s) loco(s)?* ((turning his head
          laterally first to one side then the other, indicating Eduardo
          and an accomplice on his other side.)) ['It's a lie, look, who
          are you going-- who are you going to believe, me or these
          two crazy guys?']
          (.8)
Eduardo: *A mí.*   ['Me.']
          (1.5)
Wilson: *Eh, 'mano* ((looking down at magazine)) ['Hey, man']
Wilson: *Azaros(o)* ((Hits Eduardo sharply on leg with the back of his
          hand)) ['Jerk.'--literally 'You cursed person.']

    In this segment, Eduardo asks Wilson if he's from Haiti, and
asserts that he's not Dominican. As in the previous two instances in
which Eduardo claimed Wilson was Haitian, this question and assertion
are directed in part to an audience beyond Wilson, minimally Claudia, a
Guatemalan American who is sitting directly in front of Wilson and is
turned around to face him. Unlike the previous two instances in which
he did not respond to Eduardo's assertion that he was Haitian, Wilson
addresses this claim. Wilson asserts in Spanish that he was born in
Haiti but brought up in the Dominican Republic. This is untrue: Wilson
was born in the Dominican Republic to Dominican parents and came to
Providence, Rhode Island at age seven. This response, however, serves
to maintain the joking, counterfactual frame instantiated by Eduardo.
Wilson's claim that he was brought up in the Dominican Republic
serves to account for the fact that he speaks and understands Dominican
Spanish, sings *merengue* lyrics, and socializes extensively with
Dominicans. Wilson's smile as he claims that he was born in Haiti, and
Eduardo's cuckold gesture over Wilson's head for the camera suggest
that they are doing a joking speech activity.
    Claudia, however, treats Eduardo's and Wilson's assertions
regarding his identity as serious. She proffers a candidate
understanding--that he's Haitian--that could follow from Eduardo's and
Wilson's immediately preceding claims. Claudia is likely unfamiliar
with the Dominican social framework in which relatively dark-skinned
Dominicans are jokingly accused of being Haitian.

Wilson rejects her candidate understanding and asserts that he's Dominican, thus instantiating a serious communicative framework that contrasts with the joking speech activity that he has co-constructed with Eduardo. The joking line that Wilson is Haitian, initiated by Eduardo, and maintained by Wilson, has been so successful, however, that Claudia displays uncertainty about Wilson's identity despite his new claim that he's Dominican. The condition upon which this verbal play and put-on is predicated--the implausibility of Wilson's being Haitian-- is not being recognized. Because Claudia does not unequivocally recognize this speech activity as play, Wilson is confronted with the stigma of being categorized as Haitian.

Claudia then asks if Wilson was born in the Dominican Republic. She could be checking the veracity of the information--that he was born in Haiti--on which she is basing her conclusion that he is Haitian. She may also be suggesting that one's national/ethnic identity depends on where one was born. If Wilson was born in Haiti but was raised in the Dominican Republic, he might claim a Dominican identity, while others might ascribe a Haitian identity to him. Wilson confirms that he was born in the Dominican Republic, but Eduardo reasserts that he was born in Haiti, thus maintaining the ambiguity surrounding Wilson's identity. Wilson shakes his head and counters Eduardo's claim, saying that he was born in the Dominican Republic.

Wilson switches to Spanish to say where he was born--a turn that repairs Eduardo's Spanish turn, but is directed at Claudia--and he uses Spanish in his subsequent utterance to Claudia. His use of Spanish in this context may be in response to Eduardo's use of Spanish, but it also serves to bolster his claim of a Dominican, rather than Haitian, identity. He uses Spanish to address Claudia, even though she does not speak Spanish in this exchange, and responds to Spanish with English in all recorded instances during the class period. His fluency and his characteristically Dominican pronunciation, e.g. deletion of syllable final /s/, are commensurate with a Dominican, but not Haitian, identity.

Eduardo again claims that Wilson is Haitian. Wilson then looks directly at Claudia and says that it's a lie. He asks her who she's going to believe--Wilson or *estos dos locos* ['these two crazy guys'], Eduardo and a confederate who is sitting behind and to the side of Wilson. Wilson must thus resort to an appeal to his personal integrity to convince Claudia of his claimed identity. His highlighting of his

Dominican heritage through language use does not suffice to achieve congruent self- and other-ascription of himself as Dominican.

In this excerpt, Wilson initially aligns himself with Eduardo by participating in a Dominican joke that could fool an outsider, Claudia. Wilson easily loses control over her ascription of his social identity, however. African-descent phenotype is such a powerful, pervasive, and totalizing criterion for social classification that Wilson has difficulty convincing Claudia that he is Dominican. This occurs despite the fact that Claudia has been his classmate in two classes for nearly an entire term and despite the prevalence of Caribbean Hispanics of European and African ancestry at Central High School. Dominicans are the single largest ethnic group at Central High School, and combined with Puerto Ricans, make up nearly half the student body. Even though Wilson speaks fluent Dominican Spanish and regularly interacts with recent Dominican immigrants, joking assertions that he is Haitian or was born in Haiti are enough to cast into doubt his social identity. In this case, Wilson's phenotype constrains his individual agency to enact identity through language.

6.3.2 "I never thought you were Spanish"

Relatively African-phenotype Dominican Americans such as Wilson face conflicting ascriptions of identity in both Dominican and American cultural contexts. In the Dominican interpretive context invoked by Eduardo, the conflict in identity ascriptions was whether Wilson was Dominican or Haitian. As described in Chapters 1 and 4, it is much more common in an American context for African-descent Dominican Americans to face ascriptions of being Black or African American. This section documents one such ascription and shows the power of language to precede phenotype in altering such ascription.

In this segment of interaction, a student of Southeast Asian descent, Pam, tells Wilson that she didn't think he was Spanish when she first saw him--she assumed he was African American--but she then came to realize that he was Spanish from seeing him speak Spanish. As a joke, Wilson and a Dominican confederate, JB (who discussed meeting Wilson at Bucklin Park, in a transcript above), pretend that Wilson *is* "Black" or African American. Although Wilson never identifies as "Black" or African American, he and JB know that he is regularly perceived to be African American, which creates ambiguity for them to play with. When Pam cites his speaking of Spanish as evidence that he is Spanish, rather than Black, JB and Wilson initially deny that he can speak Spanish and then devise scenarios that could explain his language. They falsely claim, for example, that Wilson's father is Black and that his mother is Black *and* Spanish and was born in America. Wilson and JB are engaged in an adolescent put-on about Wilson's race, ethnicity, and language, but analysis of their talk reveals much about their criteria, and ordering of criteria, for defining a person as "Black" or "Spanish."

[(WR #2 1:34:57) Wilson has just finished explaining to JB, in Spanish, the function of the wireless microphone he is wearing.]

Wilson:	((singing)) Andie Burton is a weird person
	(2.5)
Wilson:	*Me e(s)toy miando yo, 'mano.* ['I have to piss, man.']
	(2.0)
JB:	( )
	(2.0)
Pam:	Yo, the first time I saw you, I never thought you were Spanish.
	(.5)
Wilson:	//Who ?
JB:	//(He's) Black.
Pam:	I never
Wilson:	Cause I'm Black.
JB:	( )
Wilson:	Cause I'm Black.
Pam:	No
JB:	His father //is Black, her mother is-, his mother is uh-
Wilson:	//I'm Black
Pam:	(Can he) speak Spanish?
JB:	No
Wilson:	Cause I was-- //I was
Pam:	//Yeah!
JB:	So why (d- ?)
Wilson:	No, no seriously, I'm Black and I was raised in the Dominican Republic.
	(.5)

Wilson:	For real.
Pam:	Your mother's Black?
Wilson:	My mom? No, my father.
Pam:	Your father's Black, your //mother's Spanish?
Wilson:	//My mom's Spanish
JB:	His mom is Black-- and she's Spanish
Wilson:	Is mix(ed)
JB:	His mom was born over here.
	(2.0) ((Wilson smiles at Pam and throws a piece of paper at her))
JB:	Wilson, don't t(h)row anything to her.
Wilson:	*Excúsa me, se me olvidó, que e(s) la jeva tuya* ['Sorry, I forgot that she is your girl.']
JB:	*Cállate, todavía no.* ['Be quiet, not yet!']
Pam:	English!
JB:	English, yeah!
Wilson:	I said I'm sorry.
JB:	He can't speak Spanish.
Pam:	I saw you were talking to him ( )
Wilson:	I understand, but I don't speak everything.
	(2.2) ((Wilson smiles broadly at Pam))
JB:	I'm teaching him.
	(5.5)
Wilson:	*Qué tú va(s) (a) hacer en tu casa hoy, loco?* ((slaps JB on the back)) ['What are you going to do at your house today, man?']

Pam says that she did not assign Wilson to the category of "Spanish" when she first saw him. It is likely that Pam assumed he was African American: Wilson reported that he was regularly perceived to be African American if people did not see him speaking Spanish, and Pam subsequently treats "Black" as a relevant identity ascription for him. Both JB and Wilson respond to Pam as if Wilson were not in fact Spanish, but African American: JB says "He's Black," and Wilson says "cause I'm Black" two times, but Pam rejects this claim ("No").

JB claims that Wilson's father is Black and begins to categorize his mother, but Pam does not initially address this claim, but rather asks if Wilson can speak Spanish. JB denies that Wilson can speak Spanish ("No"), and Wilson begins to offer an explanation ("Cause I was-- I was"), perhaps an explanation of how he can speak Spanish if he is Black, an explanation that he subsequently offers, that he is Black but he was raised in the Dominican Republic. Pam has rejected JB's denial that Wilson can't speak Spanish, exclaiming "Yeah," i.e. that yes, Wilson can speak Spanish.

Spanish language is being treated in this segment as the key to racial/ethnic identity, preceding phenotype. When JB and Wilson claim that Wilson is not Spanish, but Black, Pam asks if he can speak Spanish. The implication is that if Wilson can *speak* Spanish, then he *is* Spanish, rather than Black. Wilson and JB also treat Spanish language as the key to determining social identity, both for ratification as Spanish and for disqualification from the category "Black." JB initially denies that Wilson can speak Spanish, despite immediately available counter-evidence. Admitting that Wilson can speak Spanish would invalidate JB and Wilson's line that Wilson is not Spanish but Black. One cannot be simultaneously Spanish and Black in the local system of social categorization.

Wilson presents a scenario in which he could be both Black and a Spanish-speaker: he claims he is Black but that he was raised in the Dominican Republic. Pam asks if his mother is Black--JB has already claimed that Wilson's father is Black--and Wilson says that she's not, but his father is, maintaining consistency with JB's claim. Pam offers a candidate understanding of Wilson's parents' identities: that his father is Black and his mother is Spanish. Having a Spanish mother could explain how Wilson would be raised in the Dominican Republic even though his father was African American. In theories of identity based on descent, it might also identify Wilson as at least "half-Black." Wilson, in overlap, identifies his mother as Spanish.

Identifying Wilson's mother as Spanish, however, is incompatible with Wilson and JB's claims that Wilson is Black. Among young Dominican Americans in Providence, there is no "one drop" rule that makes the offspring of an African American parent and a parent of another social group count as African American. When asked in interview questions what they would call such offspring, they did not call them Black, but rather "half-Black, half-x," and fellow Central High School students with one Black parent were typically referred to in precisely such terms, e.g. as being "half-Black, half-Dominican." If Wilson's father were Black and his mother were Spanish, Wilson would not count in local terms as Black, but rather as "half-Black, half-Spanish."

JB then identifies Wilson's mother in a way that could help to maintain the fiction that Wilson is African American: he describes her as Black *and* Spanish and "born over here," i.e. in the United States. Her being born in the United States would explain how she could have a Black parent, and it could make Dominican citizenship and national allegiance remote in Wilson's background.

Pam does not reply to these final assertions. Wilson smiles at Pam and throws a small piece of wadded paper at her, which suggests that the frame that Wilson and JB have created--mock earnest assertions that Wilson is Black--is being recognized as a joking activity. The abandonment of this frame is further evident when Wilson addresses JB in Spanish and he replies in Spanish. This use of Spanish language is salient enough to Pam for her to insist, as she does numerous times during this class period, that they speak English. JB's subsequent claim that Wilson can't speak Spanish is rejected by Pam who has just seen the two conversing in Spanish. Two final claims that Wilson can't really speak Spanish get no reply from Pam, and Wilson drops any pretense of not knowing Spanish by beginning a conversation in Spanish with JB about after school plans (this ensuing segment was transcribed above in 6.2).

The term "Spanish" is used by participants here to refer to both Spanish language and Spanish folk-racial identity. The term "Spanish" is used to refer to a social category four times and a language twice. It is not only Dominican Americans who use the term "Spanish" to describe both language and race/ethnicity. Pam, a teen-ager of Southeast Asian descent, is using it as a social category that she explicitly juxtaposes with African American race/ethnicity: "Your father's Black, your mother's Spanish?" As described in Chapters 4 and 5, "Spanish" is a local social category based on linguistic and cultural criteria that parallels the traditional American phenotype-based racial categories of Black, White, and Asian.

Social classification based on linguistic and cultural heritage captures the local social reality at Central High School much better than Black/White classification. The American phenotype-symbolized racial categories of Black and White developed out of a particular centuries-long social history in the United States. The historical relations between White Americans and African Americans are not of primary importance to the vast majority of students at Central High School, whose families have only been in the United States since 1965, or in the case of many Puerto Ricans, since the 1950's. Binary racial categorization based on phenotype is less immediately relevant in this setting than students' immigrant languages and cultures. Fewer than 10% of the students at Central are non-Hispanic White, and only 16% are non-Hispanic Black, many of them immigrants. In this largely immigrant context, Wilson's immigrant ethnolinguistic identity is a more useful guide to significant attributes about him than his phenotype. Such second-generation Spanish identity at Central High School suggests that one speaks Spanish at home, eats Spanish food, socializes with Hispanics, goes to Spanish nightclubs, has multiple ties to another (nation-)state, translates for parents, etc. Such a second-generation, bi-cultural identity is likely familiar to Pam and may have strong parallels in her own life.

Wilson aligns himself with JB in a playful speech activity that draws on disparities between Dominican and American cultural frames of reference. Their joke depends on making reference to phenotypic differences between Wilson and JB that have great social significance in an American interpretive framework but little in a Dominican one. For JB and Wilson, this readily-available and totalizing American identity is at odds with the way they understand and see him--as Dominican--and it is this discrepancy that they attempt to exploit in order to put on their classmate.

Unlike the prior situation in which Claudia was unsure whether Wilson was Haitian or Dominican, Pam displays understanding of the implausibility of Wilson's being Black. The fact that Pam could not be convinced that Wilson was Black allowed Wilson and JB to remain united in insisting that Wilson was Black. The ambivalence expressed by Claudia as to whether Wilson was Dominican or Haitian, in contrast, left Wilson potentially assigned to a stigmatized category.[46] Wilson was forced to contradict Eduardo, and he eventually called him a jerk (*azaroso*) and hit him.

While Wilson's phenotype remains constant, the social meaning that it has is locally negotiated through language. Wilson and his classmates use Spanish and English to construct Dominican and American interpretive frameworks and joking activities in which he alternately counts as Haitian, Dominican, Black American, and Spanish.

6.3.3 Implicit Reference to Wilson's Phenotype: "You don't look like the guy who plays basketball"

In the three segments of talk just presented, Wilson's ethnic/racial identity is explicitly addressed. The ambiguity of his identity, a function of his phenotype and his multi-variety language proficiency, leads to a number of explicit identity claims: an earnest claim of Dominican identity ("No, I'm Dominican") and playful claims of Haitian (*Yo nací en Haití, pero me crié en Santo Domingo* ['I was born in Haiti, but I grew up in the Dominican Republic']) and Black American ("Cause I'm Black") identities. Wilson actively and explicitly claims, rejects, and exploits for humor these diverse ascriptions. In the three short segments of transcript presented below, racial stereotypes and assumptions inhabit his and his classmates' talk more insidiously. Even as Dominican Americans define themselves outside of the Black/White system of American racial formation, they display racialized assumptions about relations among phenotype, athletic prowess, and fitness for particular vocations.

The following segment of interaction occurs less than a minute after the segment transcribed above and includes the same participants: Pam, Wilson, and JB. Wilson and JB have been discussing, in Spanish and English, plans to get together and play basketball at a park later that day (transcribed above in 6.2). Both have been making boastful predictions of defeating the other when Wilson asks Pam who she thinks to be the superior basketball player.

(WR #2 1:36:16)
Wilson: Do you think he can beat me, playing, playing some ball?
Wilson: Frank! ((gaze directed toward doorway of classroom))
Pam: You don't look like the guy who plays basketball.
Wilson: //Who, him? ((gesturing toward JB))
JB: //Who?
Pam: (→JB) You.
Wilson: //No, he's got--
JB: //I'm (nice) playing basketball.
Wilson: You know what he does, he don't dribble a lot, but he's got a
           nice jumper.

In judging who would be the better basketball player, Pam asserts that JB--in comparison to Wilson--doesn't "look like" someone who would play basketball. She does not make explicit what her criteria are for making this judgment. Height is often associated with success in basketball, but JB is slightly taller than Wilson. Wilson is heavier and more powerfully built, but JB is not frail-looking, and physical bulk is not popularly associated with basketball skill.

One way in which Wilson and JB do differ in appearance is that JB appears to be of overwhelmingly European descent while Wilson appears to be of African and European descent. Success in American basketball is popularly associated with African Americans, who are disproportionately represented among the elite players in college and the professional NBA.[47] Because of this popular and pervasive stereotype, Pam may be associating Wilson's relatively African phenotype with successful basketball playing and JB's European phenotype with lesser success.

It is not just Pam who assumes correlation between European/African phenotype and athletic prowess. In the following segment, Wilson reveals even more far-reaching assumptions about correlations between phenotype and vocational fitness, in suggesting that one can not only "look like" a sports player, one can also "look like" a lawyer:

[(WR #2 1:38:07) Wilson and JB have been discussing their relative strengths as basketball players and the previous night's NBA playoff game. They then return to the issue of Pam's perception that JB doesn't look like a basketball player.]

JB: Why you think I'm not good?
Pam: You don't look like the guy(s) who plays basketball.
Wilson: //Him? Huh? He don't. ((gesturing toward JB))
JB: //How do I--
JB: How do I look?
          (.5)
Wilson: Him, huh, like nothing! He just--
Pam: Yes!   ((laughter from at least Pam and Wilson))
JB: (   )
Wilson: He can be like a, like a lawyer or something, that's what he
          looks like, for real.
JB: What about you?

Pam: Yeah.
Wilson: I look like a straight basketball player=
JB: =Like a--=
Wilson: =or football player.
Wilson: For real baseball player and shit.
JB: Who?
Wilson: Me.
Pam: I hate baseball, it's so boring.

JB requests a reason why Pam doesn't think he's a good basketball player, but she simply reiterates that he doesn't look like the guys who play basketball. Wilson agrees that he doesn't, and JB asks how he looks, i.e. what he looks like if he doesn't look like a basketball player. Wilson uses this as an opportunity to tease his friend that he looks "like nothing." Wilson then amends this characterization by asserting that JB could be a lawyer, that "that's what he looks like."

JB asks Wilson to characterize himself ("How about you?"), and Wilson claims to look like a "straight ['pure'] basketball player or football player. For real baseball player." Wilson does not state his criteria for judging himself to look like an athlete and for judging JB to look like a lawyer, but it is likely that he is making these judgments based on relative degrees of African and European phenotype. Relative degree of African/European phenotype correlates both with athletic success and professional status in the United States and the Dominican Republic. In the United States, African Americans are successful in basketball, football, and baseball--the sports cited by Wilson--in numbers that are disproportionate to their percentage of the population. In the Dominican Republic, sports have also been an area where relatively African-phenotype individuals have excelled out of proportion to their successes in other areas of society. In America, the professions such as law are disproportionately White, and in the Dominican Republic, they are disproportionately dominated by more European-phenotype individuals. Wilson's judging himself to look like a successful athlete and JB to look like a lawyer thus subtly highlights phenotypic differences between the two of them in a way that treats such differences as having wider social implications.

In this local context, looking like a lawyer carries less prestige than looking like a successful athlete. It is a consolation category for those who "look like nothing," for those who do not look like athletes. In this case neither Wilson nor JB had prospects for a career in athletics; neither participated in organized sports, for example. Nevertheless, mere association with athletes by appearance carries prestige. The prestige of relatively African phenotype in this context is at odds with the prestige and privilege otherwise experienced by individuals of relatively European phenotype in both America and the Dominican Republic. Wilson's relatively African phenotype, a potential source of stigma, can also be a source of pride for him, even as it channels his visions of himself (as an athlete) in ways that are unlikely to be rewarded in the future.

Wilson's African descent is implicitly invoked one more time during this class period, in a ritual insult in which JB calls Wilson a "Larry Johnson wannabee":

(WR #2 1:55:38)
JB: (   ) Larry Johnson wannabee.
Wilson: Who?
JB: You.
Wilson: I'm no Larry Johnson wannabee, man. I'm myself-wannabee. ((Wilson leans forward with fists in front of his stomach and flexes his biceps in a body-builder pose. Multiple students laugh.))

"Wannabee" (from "want to be") is a term, associated by some with AAVE (Smitherman 1994:23), for a person who claims membership in a group or a status that he or she has not achieved. It implies that one is pretending to be more than, or different than, one actually is, so accusing a person of being a "wannabee" is always an insult. Wilson responds that he is not a Larry Johnson wannabee, but "myself-wannabee," i.e. he does not copy others or pretend to be something that he is not. This response, which he gives as he strikes a bodybuilder's pose, draws laughter from multiple students.

Accusing Wilson of being a "Larry Johnson wannabee" draws attention to Wilson's African descent. Larry Johnson is an NBA basketball player who was a well-known star early in his career before suffering injuries that made him a much less formidable player. By calling Wilson a "Larry Johnson wannabee," JB may be claiming that Wilson exaggerates his own basketball skills, but Johnson was no longer a star, and it is likely that JB would have compared Wilson to a more prominent player if basketball skills were the sole criterion of comparison. It is more likely that he used Larry Johnson in accusing Wilson of being a "wannabee" because of the strong resemblance in appearance between Wilson and Johnson. Although Wilson was much shorter, he resembled Larry Johnson in terms of stocky build, short hair, face shape, and a distinctive shaved notch in his hairline above the middle of his forehead. Johnson is classified as Black or African American, and if Wilson were not of African descent, his resemblance to Johnson would likely not have been so strong. JB's assertion that Wilson is a "Larry Johnson wannabee" thus depends on, and invokes, Wilson's African-descent phenotype.

Even when ethnic/racial identity is not explicitly addressed in the propositional content of talk, such talk and interaction can reveal many social assumptions. JB, Pam, and Wilson all explicitly ascribe Wilson a Spanish/Dominican identity as opposed to a phenotype-based racial one, but his phenotype is still implicitly invoked. Phenotype-based racial assumptions even enter into Wilson's expressed ideas about individual fitness for particular activities.

6.4 Conclusions

Wilson's skillful use of multiple language varieties and his African-descent phenotype create ambiguity for those who seek to assign him an ethnic/racial identity. His use of varieties of Spanish and English alternately foreground Dominican, American, and African American facets of his ethnolinguistic identity, indexing his agency as a social actor. Language is not just a tool that gives individuals freedom to choose among identities, however, but also a medium through which sociohistorical relations of inequality and reified, essentialist categories are re-constituted and re-imposed. During this class period, Wilson's classmates repeatedly invoke his African-descent phenotype, treating it as relevant to his social identity. When Wilson is presented as Haitian, for example, he has some difficulty in convincing another Hispanic that he is Dominican, despite displays of fluent Dominican Spanish. The relative ordering of importance of language and phenotype is not preset in ascribing identities to Wilson, however, but is locally negotiated. In a second interaction, his Spanish language is treated as such a paramount criterion for ascription that Wilson is unable to convince a non-Hispanic classmate that he is Black despite his African-descent phenotype and assertions of a Black identity.

Wilson defines himself as Dominican or Spanish and outside of the American Black/White dichotomy, but even his own talk reveals racial assumptions about individuals' fitness for certain activities. Language is a medium which affords individual social actors the freedom to highlight various aspects of identity, but communicative behavior occurs in a sociohistorical context in which phenotype has been made to matter, and this association of phenotype with social identity is reproduced in everyday talk and interaction.

CHAPTER 7

Individual Patterns of Language Use and Implications for Ethnic/Racial Identities

7.1 Introduction

The categories "Dominican American" and "Dominican American language," like other social and linguistic categories, imply a discreteness and a uniformity that obscure internal variation. Attention to the variation within categories brings analysis closer to the empirical, individually experienced phenomena upon which second-order analytical categories and theoretical claims are based. The emphasis on individuals and intra-group variation that is particularly evident in this chapter is counter to the tendency in sociology and anthropology to focus analysis on larger-scale constellations or constructs, e.g. "society" (in sociology) or "culture" (in anthropology). The lack of attention to the individual in anthropological theorizing is particularly incongruous with anthropological methods, which often depend on in-depth involvement with a small number of informants (Kroskrity 1993:110-113). Analysis of intra-group variation and attention to the individual can more precisely delineate the social processes that mediate between individual characteristics and practices and larger scale social constellations such as racial and ethnic categories.

In this chapter I analyze relationships among ethnic/racial identities, language socialization experiences, language use, and phenotype for six Dominican American high school students. There are significant commonalties among these students, e.g. they define themselves as "Dominican" or "Spanish"/"Hispanic", and they live in

221

adjoining, low-income, non-White neighborhoods and attend the same substandard segregated school. Linguistically they all share relatively unmarked code switching between Dominican Spanish and a variety of English that includes features variously associated with AAVE, local sociolects, and Spanish-English bilingualism. While they share these experiences and practices, there are also many differences among these six students in life experiences, ethnic/racial identities, and language use. Individuals vary in their use of the multiple Dominican American linguistic resources described in Chapter 3, for example, using them in different proportions and in different contexts. Some individuals are clearly more acculturated to an Anglophone linguistic and cultural context--their English displays little influence of Spanish features and their social networks include many non-Hispanics--while others' social lives are focused more narrowly on the Dominican/Hispanic community. Most significantly in the United States, individual differences in phenotype, ranging from those popularly associated with Africa to those associated with Europe, result in very different issues of racial ascription for different individuals

Attention to such intragroup differences shows that theoretical questions, e.g. "How is individual agency related to structural constraints in the enactment of identity?", have very different answers for different individuals. Those who can speak both Spanish and English without apparent interference from the other language have more freedom to choose among, and successfully enact, American and Dominican identities, for example. Individuals with unequivocally African-descent phenotype have less ability to enact diverse ethnic and racial identities across multiple contexts than those whose phenotype and ancestry are more ambiguous. Attention to such intra-group variation can help reveal local mechanisms in the construction of identities and the tensions and interplay between individual agency and structural constraint in the enactment of identity.

7.2 Social Implications of Individual Language Variation

Dominican American language, as described in Chapter 3, is a constellation of linguistic resources and features that do not fall into a single, traditional linguistic category, e.g. Spanish, English, or AAVE. While no language or culture is "pure" and unaffected by historical contacts (Duranti and Ochs 1997:171), the immediacy of Dominican American syncretism and its use of forms associated with significant social distance (e.g. as between Black and White American varieties of English) make it distinctive. Individual differences in use of these features can thus act as striking indexes of social meanings.

Many individual differences in the language of the six students discussed here are readily apparent to Dominican Americans and other peers. Alejandro and Frangelica, for example, speak English with syllable timing, vowel quality, and low aspiration of stops that lead them and others to describe them as "having a Spanish accent." Maria lived in New York City until age 9, and at age 15 still identified herself as being "from New York." Her language contained structures that Zentella (1997:45-6) identifies as characteristic of (New York) Puerto Rican English, and her phonology diverged from that of the other students. Wilson's phonology includes elements (e.g. "r-less" pronunciation) popularly associated in Providence with a sociolect spoken in an adjoining municipality where Wilson lived for six years with a non-Hispanic stepmother. Janelle and Isabella speak relatively little Spanish in school, using Spanish primarily in code switching and code-mixing with other bilinguals (Isabella) and close Dominican American friends (Janelle). In such exchanges, Spanish language doesn't span more than two consecutive utterances or turns. Frangelica, Maria, Alejandro, and Wilson, in contrast, use Spanish in longer exchanges, typically those involving more recently immigrated Spanish speakers.

Individual patterns of language use reflect individuals' social histories at the same time that they affect the ongoing constitution of social identity and relations. Among Dominican Americans in Providence, for example, individual language use is reciprocally related to social networks. Students who spend time with more recent immigrants maintain or develop their Spanish, for example, while it is those students with stronger Spanish who are able to interact more intimately and extensively with recent immigrants. Central High School is over 60% Hispanic, and with its full program of ESL and bilingual classes, its Hispanic students range from newly arrived monolingual Spanish speakers to bilinguals to third- or fourth-generation American monolingual English speakers. Who socializes with whom at Central High School is intimately intertwined with linguistic abilities.

Individual variation in language use also reflects the complexity and specific circumstances of individual life histories. Proficiency in Spanish and degree of Spanish influence on English do not co-vary directly with individual ages at immigration or their number of years in America or the Dominican Republic. Specific life circumstances such as a temporary family return to the Dominican Republic, living with monolingual English or Spanish step-family, co-residing with monolingual grandparents, or intense involvement in Spanish-language church affect students' language abilities and social identities.

Intra-group language variation can also reflect idiosyncratic, individual social attitudes, or gender, rather than identifiably discrete life events. Frangelica and Alejandro, for example, came to America at similar ages and grew up within blocks of each other attending the same schools, but they differ prominently in use of language associated with AAVE and urban teen hip hop culture. Alejandro's relative embrace of such language and Frangelica's relative avoidance of it correlate with the differences in attitudes they express in interviews toward African Americans and urban teen culture. Such intra-group variation in attitudes and language behavior does not always correlate in obvious ways with other social variables. In America, phenotype-based race is a basic social organizing principle which is often reflected in social affiliations and language practices. In this case, however, Alejandro is relatively European in phenotype and Frangelica is relatively African in phenotype. Individual ways of speaking can thus signal speakers' attitudes toward the social identities associated with particular forms; the use, or avoidance, of particular linguistic forms, in turn, is part of the ongoing enactment of identities.

7.3 Language, Phenotype, and Ascriptions of Identity

Because race based on phenotype has historically been a paramount criterion for social categorization in America, language use often plays a complementary rather than primary role in social assignment to such categories as "Black" and "White." The effect of language use depends both on the language forms and the particular phenotype in question. The frequency and force with which individual Dominicans are assigned to particular categories does not co-vary uniformly with phenotype, but rather is better explained through a combination of phenotype and language use.

The linguistic resources and individual variation in phenotype that affect ascriptions of ethnic/racial identity are represented in Table 2 below. The phenotypes range from those commonly associated with "Whites" or "European Americans" in the United States to those associated with "African Americans," with two intermediate categories. The category "Not White/not African American" includes individuals who do not match stereotypes of European phenotypes, i.e. in terms of skin shade and hair and facial features, but who also do not appear to be necessarily of African descent. The category "Ambiguously African American" includes individuals who appear as if they might have some African ancestry, but who also appear to have considerable European ancestry. By historical American one-drop rules, these individuals would be classified as African American, but in practice, their ancestry is ambiguous. Strangers, for example, ask them "What are you?" or guess at their identity. Such questions are often directed at individuals of "mixed" folk-race in America (Bucholtz 1995; Zack 1993), i.e. individuals whose parents/grandparents do not all count as members of a single phenotype-symbolized racial category.

On this four-stage continuum of phenotypes, Alejandro could be considered "White." His straight hair and light skin, for example, led other students to tease him for being Guatemalan rather than Dominican. Maria could fit in the "Not White/not African American" category. Her hair was wavy and her skin was darker than that of many European Americans, and she was regularly perceived by others to be Puerto Rican. Isabella and Janelle could be assigned to the category "ambiguously African American." Janelle had lighter skin than Isabella but frizzier hair, which she regularly "relaxed" with a chemical treatment. Isabella described her own hair as "soft and curly" relative to African American hair, although she occasionally wore it in an African American style of numerous short braids. Isabella thought her skin color, features, and hair were similar to those of an American friend of hers whose mother was White American and whose father was African American. Both Isabella and Janelle reported having been mistaken for Cape Verdean and African American. Wilson and Frangelica could both fit into the category African American based on phenotype. Both described their skin color as *moreno/a* ['dark'], Wilson described his hair as "nappy" and "bad" [*pelo malo*], and Frangelica chemically relaxed hers. Both reported being mistaken for African American and Cape Verdean.

Table 2: Variation in Phenotype and Linguistic Forms Affecting Ascriptions of Identity

INDIVIDUAL DIFFERENCES IN PHENOTYPE

•European/White (Alejandro)

•Not-White/not African American (Maria)

•Ambiguously African American (Isabella, Janelle)

•African American (Wilson, Frangelica)

AVAILABLE LINGUISTIC FORMS

•Institutionally Prestigious ("Standard") English

•Working Class/Urban/Ethnic Varieties

•African American Vernacular English

•Spanish Influenced English Phonology ("Spanish accent")

•Spanish Code Use and/or Spanish/English Code Switching

If phenotype were the sole criterion used by outsiders for categorization, Wilson and Frangelica would regularly be perceived to be African American; Isabella and Janelle would be perceived to be African American less often, but with the same frequency as each other; and Alejandro would regularly be perceived to be White American. Based on their reports and my observations, however, Frangelica is assigned to the category African American less frequently and forcefully than Wilson, Janelle is much more commonly perceived to be African American than Isabella, and Alejandro reports that he is never perceived as White.

7.4 Role of Language Variety in Racial Ascription

Much of this discrepancy between phenotype and ascribed identities can be explained by individual patterns of language use. Dominican Americans of ambiguously African descent who use a wide range of AAVE forms are more likely to be assigned to the category African American than those who seldom use such linguistic forms, for example. On the other hand, those who are unambiguously of African descent but speak English with readily apparent Spanish phonological features are *not* categorized as African American as forcefully and unambiguously as those with less apparent Spanish features. Variation in language use can undermine others' ascriptions but does not change them categorically. Although Frangelica is assigned to the category "African American" less frequently and forcefully than Wilson, for example, she doesn't report ever having been identified as White American. Similarly, although Alejandro extensively uses AAVE forms, he is never asked if he is African American.

Dominican American language, like phenotype, varies across individuals, and it also varies situationally. In Table 2, I enumerate constellations of linguistic features that significantly affect ascriptions of racial/ethnic identity. These features include those associated with the English forms defined as standard by dominant groups, working class and urban ethnic varieties, AAVE, Spanish influenced English forms, and Spanish code/Spanish-English code switching. The dominant group standard is popularly associated with educated middle and upper class White Americans. "Working class/Urban/Ethnic Varieties" includes features enumerated in Chapter 3 that are common to various low-income and working-class sociolects, AAVE, and the speech of many immigrant enclaves. "AAVE" includes linguistic features popularly associated with urban, African American youth as well as grammatical structures that occur only in AAVE. "Spanish-influenced English Phonology" is meant to represent the fluent English spoken by English-dominant bilingual high school students whose English phonology displays some Spanish patterns. "Spanish code use" refers to the use of Spanish language or the alternation of Spanish and

English. These labels refer to styles or constellations of features rather than discrete codes. All Dominican American speakers in this study, for example, regularly code switch, and use features associated with dominant standard English, various local vernacular forms of English, and AAVE. Speakers, however, do not use these resources with the same frequency as each other and in the same contexts.

7.5 Individual Variation among Six Individuals

In this section I consider individual variation in life experiences and language use. I describe aspects of the six individuals' lives related to language socialization, including: languages of parents/the home, migration histories, immediate social networks, linguistic attitudes, and perceptions of intergroup relations, e.g. understandings of Dominican American identities vis-à-vis White and Black Americans. I describe aspects of the language used by the six individuals at school, focusing on features that are particularly relevant to ascriptions of ethnic/racial identities, e.g. detectable Spanish phonological patterns in English and use of forms associated with AAVE.

7.5.1 Wilson

Wilson came to the United States during the middle of second-grade, joining his father and English-monolingual European American stepmother and older stepbrother. He grew close to his stepmother, considering her in some ways to be his real mother, and he attributes the virtual absence of Spanish phonological features in his English in part to growing up with monolingual English stepfamily. Wilson attended grades four through eight in a primarily white school district, Cranston, bordering Providence. Wilson reported having good friends who were African American, White, and Hispanic in Cranston schools. Cranston residents are stereotyped in Providence as exaggerating the features of the local English variety, e.g. through their consistent r-less pronunciation and the addition of /r/ to words ending in /ʌ/. "Father" thus becomes /faðʌ/ and "area" becomes /æriər/. Wilson included these patterns in his English, e.g. in pronouncing the name of his teacher Mr. "Polka" as /pokər/. This gave his English at times the sound of a specific, Providence sociolect which is locally associated with third- and fourth-generation Italian Americans rather than Hispanics. Wilson's father feared that Wilson would lose his Spanish in an English-speaking home environment and school system, so he made a conscious effort to maintain Wilson's reading and writing. Wilson reported that his father had Spanish books and a small chalkboard, and that they practiced Spanish literacy skills together when he was a child. Wilson attributed his maintenance of fluency in Spanish in part to his father's efforts. Despite these efforts, Wilson's Spanish writing skills were weak when I met him. In transcribing conversations of his peers, for example, he made numerous errors in writing relatively common words. He transcribed *y yo te voy a buscar* ['and I'll go and get you'] as *y yo to boi a bu car*. Many such errors are common among Latin American Spanish speakers, reflecting local pronunciations, e.g. elision of syllable-final /s/ in *bu(s)car)*, or letters with locally identical pronunciations, e.g. 'v' and 'b', 'y' and 'i', resulting in *boi* for *voy*. Other of his spellings appeared more erratic, e.g. *to* for *te* ['you'], *hella* for *ella* ['she'], and *perque* for *porque* ['because'].

Wilson returned to the Dominican Republic for his freshman year of high school, living with his mother and half-sister who had never left the island. Wilson said that his Spanish was not good enough for schoolwork in Spanish, except in courses that didn't depend so much on language, such as math. The year proved to be frustrating because of difficulties with school, but it improved his Spanish to the point that many Dominicans mistook him for never having left the island. It also re-connected him to friends and relatives on the island who were on the verge of immigration to Providence themselves. When he returned to Providence, he and his father moved to a different neighborhood and back to the Providence school district, where Wilson had not been in school for six years. He knew relatively few classmates, which may explain why newly arriving friends and relatives were among his most intimate social contacts. As a high school junior, Wilson identified his three best friends as a newly immigrated cousin, the husband of another newly immigrated cousin, and another Dominican who had recently arrived in Providence and was attending Central High School.

This newly immigrated high school friend, Jonathan, in turn, introduced Wilson to his ESL and bilingual education classmates, who were otherwise partly isolated from the rest of the student body through separate classes and the location of those programs in the basement of the school building. Wilson thus knew, and was known by, many students at Central who spoke little English and who regularly spoke only Spanish with him when they saw each other outside of classes.

Wilson reported that he had many good Black friends (including immigrants) at school but that he rarely saw these friends outside of school. His steady girlfriend, who did not attend Central High School, was a monolingual English speaker who had one Puerto Rican parent and one European American parent.

Wilson's Spanish--like the Spanish of all six students videotaped-- follows the Caribbean and Dominican syntactic and phonological patterns outlined in Chapter 3. A notable sociolinguistic variable in his pronunciation is his regular substitution of /l/ for /r/, which is particularly associated with lower social class in the Dominican Republic. Even in careful speech, when enunciating examples for the researcher, Wilson replaces the /r/ of common words, e.g. *ayer* ['yesterday'], with /l/. While many Dominican Americans variably replace /r/ with /l/, none of the other five students videotaped did it so saliently in careful speech.

Wilson uses typically Dominican vocabulary and expressions, e.g. *un chin* ['a little bit'] and *tú sí jodes* ['you're really bothering me']. His forms of address for friends include *'mano* [from *hermano,* 'brother'], *azaroso* ['jerk'], and *loco* ['man'--literally "crazy person", but used as an interjection in similar ways to the English "yo"], and his greetings include *Dime chulaso?* ['What's up, cool guy'] and *Qué lo qué?* ['What's up?]. These forms are typical among Dominican males at Central High School.

The influence of Spanish phonological patterns in Wilson's English was subtle. With careful listening to tapes it was apparent that he pronounced unstressed syllables more clearly and held them longer than most native speakers, a result of Spanish syllable timing interference. Wilson frequently elides the voiced consonant /d/ following the liquid /r/ ("wor'!"), a pattern characteristic of AAVE, and he simplifies some consonant clusters ("tha's mine"), which is characteristic of AAVE, Southern White speech, and some working class vernaculars. When the Providence pattern of final /r/ elision conflicts with AAVE consonant cluster simplification, as in the popular AAVE youth interjection of affirmation "word", he drops the "d" rather than the "r", following the AAVE pattern. He often uses /t/ for /θ/ in syllable-final position ("wit(h)") and his syllable-initial voiced /ð/ at times approaches /d/.

Grammatically, Wilson uses the Providence second-person plural ("yous are very strange today") and a variety of forms unique to AAVE, e.g. the elision of the copula ("she crazy") and third-person present tense inflection ("she look like a witch"). He regularly uses AAVE habitual "be" ("she be looking at me all nasty"), and he uses the intensifying morpheme "-ass" as a suffix ("punk-ass") following the AAVE pattern (Smitherman 1994).

Wilson uses a wide variety of vocabulary and expressions associated with AAVE and hip-hop, e.g. "word", "break you up", "diesel", "wack", "shooped", "ho", "motherhubbard", "hook you up", "check it," and "yo." He commonly greets peers in English with "What's up?/Whassup?/What up?," and he uses prosodic features that are associated with varieties of AAVE, e.g. falsetto voice and vowel lengthening ("cra::zy mothafucka").

For Wilson, some speech activities are tied to Spanish. I saw Wilson give *piropos* ("amorous compliments" directed toward females) only in Spanish, e.g. *Muchacha diablo! Ssssss Qué muslos que tienes!* ['Damn, girl! Psssst. What thighs you have!']. At Central High School, both linguistic varieties and cultural frameworks for speech activities shift rapidly. Seconds after doing this *piropo,* for example, Wilson bade farewell to a Guatemalan-Dominican American classmate with an expression associated with AAVE, "Check it."

7.5.2 Frangelica

Frangelica was a year older than most of her classmates, and she seemed older than her years in many ways. She lived more or less on her own as her father spent increasingly long periods of time in the Dominican Republic. Work played an important and stabile role in her life. Unlike many of her peers who worked with other teen-agers in short-term fast food jobs with high employee turnover, Frangelica worked evenings 20 hours per week in a jewelry display factory with a dozen women who were all older. Spanish was the language of the factory floor where all but two of the women were from Latin America. The two women who were not native Spanish speakers were from Portugal, and they communicated with the others in a combination of Portuguese and pidgin Spanish.

Frangelica got rides to and from the factory with her upstairs neighbor, a 31-year-old Guatemalan immigrant, whom she counted among her three best friends. She seemed in many ways more comfortable with such older women and their concerns than she did with her high school classmates. She took great interest in her older friends' and relatives' romantic relationships, and she carried pictures, which she liked to show, of their babies. Her own romantic life centered not on high school, but on her older boyfriend in the Dominican Republic, with whom she talked on the phone once a week. When I met Frangelica, she was filling out immigration forms for him to come to the United States. She planned to marry him the following summer.

Frangelica was very organized and business-like about school, which she treated like a job rather than an opportunity for socializing. She displayed little of the adolescent enthusiasm or rebelliousness of many of her classmates, which set her apart from many of them socially. She was critical of students who skipped school ("bunked"), fooled around in class, and did not approach school with the maturity that she did.

She attributed some of her seriousness and responsibility to what she considered a "Dominican" upbringing. She was critical of her younger siblings who had adopted what she thought were indulgent American ways as opposed to more respectful and disciplined Dominican ones:

> My sister was completely raised here. She doesn't listen to my grandmother. She's so into this American culture, she listens to rap, her bedroom is a mess, she's just into American stuff and she doesn't listen. Me, for example, I was raised the Dominican way, and I listen polite, don't disrespect my mother, cause back then, if I disrespected my mother, she would just slap me over the face, automatically. My sister and brother, they get away with everything, he wear his pants up to here [indicating pants sagging off the hips], and if I wear my pants up to there, back then, *oi oi oi*, I would have been dead.

Frangelica's English displayed Spanish phonological patterns that were apparent both to her and her peers. This Spanish influence was most apparent in syllable timing in her English, resulting in speech that sounded markedly slow and careful. Her pronunciation also included simplification of consonant clusters and changes in interdental fricatives, e.g. voiced word-initial "th" is sometimes /d/ and syllable-final unvoiced "th" is pronounced at times as /t/, forms which occur among adolescent and adult English learners as well as in other sociolects. Frangelica also occasionally omits the plural /s/ ("all the market order"), even when it is not part of a consonant cluster ("these are all the recipe"), which is characteristic of AAVE. More distinctively Spanish is the lack of aspiration following the stop of /t/ in "it's", such that "it's" is pronounced as /ɪz/ or /ɪdz/. In the following fragment, in which Frangelica talks to her physics teacher, Mr. B., omitted consonants are surrounded by single parentheses and interdental fricatives replaced by /d/ are in boldface:

(FU #1 11:49:53)
Frang.:   ...So it has an a(c)celeration of eight hun(d)red
Mr B: Hold on...
((Frangelica recalculates on calculator then discusses units))
Mr. B: Okay, it's meters per second squared. 'M' only stands for miles when it's used in 'm' 'p' 'h', otherwise it's meters.
Frang.:   Oh. So i(t')s mph.
((he corrects her use of units and they continue through steps for solving the problem))
Frang.:   Alright. So now I do **d**is one. The time... **d**e distan(ce) is what I'm looking for.

While Frangelica used some expressions that are associated with AAVE, she did not use the lexical items that were frequent in the speech of her peers, e.g. "mad," "butters," "phat," and "yo." Dominican American high school students are generally discursively conscious of this level of language use--vocabulary--and many mentioned that they would use certain words with friends but not in school, suggesting a degree of conscious control over lexicon. Many also defined "Black English" in terms of lexicon, i.e. as a matter of using specific vocabulary or "slangs." The high degree of consciousness that individuals have of these forms makes it possible that the absence of such forms in Frangelica's speech reflected a conscious choice to avoid them. The AAVE grammatical form that was most salient and frequent

in the language of her peers, the habitual "be"--a discrete lexical form--
was also conspicuously absent in my record of her speech.

Avoiding such forms could help Frangelica disaffiliate herself from
her low-income African American peers and the anti-establishment
political stance often expressed through AAVE. The low frequency of
forms associated with African American urban adolescents in
Frangelica's speech correlate with Frangelica's attitudes toward her
low-income African American peers. Frangelica reported having few
African American friends:

Frangelica: I don't have that many African friends. Mostly the
Dominican, White American, Latino. Anything, but not that many
Black American.
BB: Why?
Frangelica: I don't hang around them, I just kind of isolate myself from
them, just there aren't that many in the school system so I could
associate with them. And if they are, they're not the right type I
want to associate with.

Frangelica differentiated sharply between lower-status and educated
African Americans. She said that she couldn't see herself dating an
African American, but then quickly modified her description of whom
she would date based on class:

Frangelica: Because they have this thing for wearing the pants below
the (   ), the beeper, and the car, the forty ['40-ounce bottle of malt
liquor'], the leather jacket, don't work, kids, welfare.... Unless
they're going to college, they're going to school, they dress nice.
You don't have to wear tight clothes [i.e. clothes can have
bagginess associated with urban youth fashion], but dress decent.

She said that she disliked rap music, a sentiment which I did not hear
expressed by any other Dominican American high school student.

Frangelica's relatively conservative language practices extended to
Spanish, in which she didn't use the teen vocabulary and expressions
used by many of her peers. Even in situations where she had reason to
become angry, she avoided profanity. When a Dominican classmate
took her homework paper to copy, she ended up in a tug-of-war over

the paper, but did not use profanity even as her female classmate and friend, Ana, did:

[(FU #1 11:48:30) A very dark-skinned Dominican student nicknamed "*Chocolate*" is copying from Frangelica's homework sheet.]

Frang.: *Qué tú quieres Chocolate?* ['What do you want, Chocolate?']

Ana: *No se lo dé, Frangelica, coño.* ['Don't give it to him Frangelica, damn.']

Frang.: *No, mira, yo no he terminado. Dame, Chocolate, mira me rompes el papel.* ['No, look, I haven't finished. Give it to me, Chocolate, look, you're tearing my paper.']

Chocol.: *Coge lo suave, coge lo suave.* ['Take it easy, take it easy.']

Frang.: *No, no he terminado* ['No, no I haven't finished.']

In addition to avoiding the profanity and teen vernacular expressions used by many of her peers, Frangelica used Spanish expressions not used by other teen-agers--*oi oi oi* (expression of dismay) and *Ay Maria!* ['Oh my God'] (other students used *Ay Dios*). She even used some expressions, e.g. *Woo! Achuchaselo!* ['Oh, freak!'] that other Dominican American teenagers did not understand, let alone use, and that were obscure to some newly arriving immigrants. She reported learning these expressions from her grandmother, and they gave a rural, Dominican adult feeling to her speech. She even adopted a grandmotherly stance at times, e.g. in reprimanding a Dominican classmate who had been missing school: *Tienes que ir todo los dias o si no te garro por la oreja y te doy cocotazos* ['You have to come every day or I'll grab you by the ear and hit you over the noggin.'] Her rural origins and time spent with her grandparents gave her linguistic knowledge that many of her peers did not have. When Spanish words for "pig" were being discussed in Spanish class, for example, she knew not only general terms for "pig" but also more specialized terms for male and female pigs of different ages.

7.5.3 Janelle

Janelle was born in New York City, but lived in a smaller town in upstate New York until she was 9 years old, when she moved to Providence. She reported that she had had numerous friends who were

White American, African American, and Hispanic, at different times in her life depending in part on who was around her. Her elementary school had been mostly White, her middle school was mixed, and Central, of course, was primarily Hispanic. She said her best friends up until high school had been African Americans. Her best friends during her junior year were several Dominican Americans, two Puerto Ricans, a classmate with one Nigerian parent and one African American parent, and another classmate whose parents were from Laos.

She was in the college-preparatory track at school, and her school friends came primarily from those classes, which required fluency in English. She had little contact with more recent immigrants in school. She held no conversations solely or predominantly in Spanish at school, but code switched at times, particularly with Dominican American friends. Her boyfriend at the time was a Colombian American who attended a different school, and she reported that her previous boyfriends had been Puerto Rican and Dominican.

Janelle's English was often indistinguishable to her peers from the AAVE spoken by African Americans in Providence. This was in part because her English pronunciation displayed no obvious effects of Spanish bilingualism and in part because her English included more features of AAVE than any of the other speakers recorded. Although she occasionally used structures that suggested grammatical interference from Spanish, e.g. "Here are mad dogs." ['There are a lot of dogs here.'], she did not speak with syllable timing. Her English pronunciation also included features that were characteristic of AAVE but not other Providence sociolects. She sometimes omitted the off-glide of the diphthong /ay/, for example, rendering it /a/, which occurs in Southern White speech but not in Providence English except in AAVE.

Janelle used many linguistic forms that are common to AAVE and other sociolects, e.g. deletion of auxiliary verbs ("She been waiting like an hour," "She got an attitude") and non-inversion of questions with subject pronouns ("What school he go to?"). She regularly used urban youth vocabulary associated with AAVE, e.g. "mad," "wack," and "phat," she interjected "yo" before and/or after many utterances, and she used the AAVE intensifying suffix "-ass" ("What's up with that big-ass bowtie?").

Janelle's syntax also included features unique to AAVE. She used the habitual "be" in ways that suggested she discriminated between the use of habitual "be" and the standard English "be". In explaining why she wore a particular outfit to a dance practice she explained, "I just wear something comfortable, because it's-- cause it be hot in there. In AAVE, the use of "it's" could suggest that it was only hot that evening, when in fact the asphalt backyard where they practiced dancing was recurrently hot. This self-initiated cut-off of speech and subsequent self-correction suggest that Janelle had practical awareness of the differences in meaning between habitual "be" and the non-habitual copula. While Janelle has practical awareness of the tense/aspect meaning of "be," her use of it suggests that she may not know the social distribution and connotations of the habitual "be" in America. She made this explanation of her clothing to an interlocutor (the researcher, an adult White American) who was unlikely to use habitual "be" or understand the difference between "it be hot" and "it is hot."

Janelle was the only individual recorded using the stressed "bin" of AAVE, and she used it in its archetypal interactional position and meaning. During class, a teacher had repeatedly asked an African American student next to Janelle to remove his portable stereo headphones. The student, with whom Janelle had been flirting, put them on again for the last part of class without the teacher's seeing him. He was wearing the headphones as he and Janelle walked past the teacher to leave class. The teacher asked if he had had the headphones on during class, and the student denied it:

(JS #3 1:35:15)
Ken:	I took it off.
Teacher:	You did?
Ken:	I just now put it on
Janelle:	No, he's lying! He **bin** had it on.

The use of the stressed "bin" serves to emphasize the intensity and validity of a fact (Smitherman 1977:23). Janelle is arguing that it is an established fact, beyond doubt, that her classmate had been wearing the headphones for a period of time before getting up to leave the class.

Janelle's use of Spanish in school was generally limited to single utterances or exchanges that spanned no more than two or three turns, and she code switched primarily with a few close friends. The following is an example of the code switching that occurs interspersed

in longer English interactions between Janelle and her close Dominican
American friend Jose as they sit in class.

(JS #2 10:43:40)

Janelle: Jenadis is the prettiest. Jenadis *después* ['then'] Lala *y*
            después ['and then'] Rosanna, *después* ['then'] Mable.
Jose: Jenadis *después* ['then'] Lala?
Janelle: Yeah
Jose: She's u:::::gly!
Janelle: Nuh uh, she's better than Roseanna.
Teacher: Hey guys, I'm not gonna go over this--
Janelle: My bad.
Teacher: (so) pay attention.
Janelle: ((Gazing at a fellow student's feet.)) *Tiene pies chicitos.*
            ['He's got little feet.']
Jose: What?
Janelle: *El tiene los pies chicitos.* ['He's got little feet.']
Jose: Chang? Cause he's short.
Janelle: So, that don't mean nothing.
Jose: (Yes it does)
Janelle: No it don't.

Even short code switches can index distinctively Dominican (as
opposed to Puerto Rican, Guatemalan, etc.) ethnolinguistic identity
through phonological patterns and lexical choice:

(JS #2 11:12:40)

Janelle: Here look at this-- look at this ((holding up school paper))
Jose: ((Jose pokes her in ribs)) (*a ti*/teeth)
Janelle   Ooww.
Jose: *Es que a tí te duele todo,* man. ['It's just that everything
            hurts you']
Janelle: *Es que* I'm telling you I'm fragile. ['It's just that'] ((Jose
            pokes her in the ribs again))
Janelle: *Y que lo que la vaina!* ['What's up with that shit!']
Jose: You (ain't/aren't) fragile.
Janelle: Yes I am.

In addition to eliding syllable-final /s/, Janelle uses two expressions that non-Dominican Spanish speakers find humorous and clearly indexical of specifically Dominican identities: *que lo que* ['what's up?'], and especially, *la vaina* ['shit'/'stuff'] (Quintero 1998). Poplack (1982) found that it was precisely such bilinguals as Janelle, who were exposed to both Spanish and English codes early in life and had had extensive contact with monolingual English speakers, that did the most intrasentential switching. This matches my findings with Janelle, for example, who switched at a variety of syntactic junctures. In the following two segments, Janelle switches (in order of their occurrence) between a conjunction "cause" and a bracketed first pair part question; between a conjunction "*que*" and subsequent noun clause; between full sentences; between an adverbial phrase (*de balde*) and the rest of a sentence; between a change of state "Oh" and the interrogative "*porque*"; between a main clause and a subordinate noun clause (*que yo voy*); and between a continuer "*Entonces*" and independent clause.

[(JS #2 10:50:10) Discussing whether she needs new immunizations to do her summer job at a hospital.]

Janelle: I don't know if I- I don't know if I have to go again cause--
dizque no es verdad que ['supposedly isn't it true that'] after a certain time- after a certain time you have to do it again? You gotta get shots again?

[(JS #2 10:51:30) Discussing how she had her sister get her brother-in-law give her a ride to a fashion show practice session that turned out to be cancelled.]

Janelle: I hope I don't have fashion show practice today.
Jose: No?
Janelle: Cause yesterday I was mad, *de balde yo fui para allá* ['I went there for nothing/in vain]. I told Benny to take me *de balde* ['for nothing/in vain'].
Jose: (To/*De*) what?
Janelle: I told Benny to take me *de balde*. Raissa goes, "Oh *porqué-* ['why'] she told Benny *que yo voy-* ['that I'm going-'] cause she asked me when's the fashion show? *Entonces* ['Then'], umm I told her July 3. And she goes- wait-

This code switching in Janelle's speech at school is the exception rather than the rule. In classes where she did not have Dominican American friends, Janelle rarely used Spanish, and even in situations where she code switched, she spoke overwhelmingly in English.

Janelle's language use at school--in combination with her phenotype--channeled the ways in which others saw her. Her use of AAVE forms, her multi-ethnic social circles, and the fact that she spoke little Spanish at school and spoke English with no apparent Spanish phonological or syntactic patterns led many to perceive her as African American.

7.5.4 Maria

Maria was born in New York City and is nearly third-generation American on her mother's side, but she has maintained Spanish language as the result of specific life circumstances and events. Her mother came to New York City as an eleven-year-old and speaks fluent English, but Maria spent her childhood years being raised by her monolingual grandmother because of her mother's relative youth and relationship problems between her parents. Various circumstances also led to her spending seventh grade living with her mother and great-grandmother in Santo Domingo. She says that the year in the Dominican Republic greatly improved her Spanish. It also had a critical effect on the use of Spanish in Maria's nuclear family, because her mother met and married a monolingual Dominican when they were on the island. Her stepfather then returned with them to the United States, and Spanish became the language of the nuclear family. Maria reports that she speaks more Spanish than English to her mother but that she speaks *only* Spanish in front of her stepfather, because it would be disrespectful to speak English. Maria's Spanish and ties to the Dominican Republic were once again reinforced the year before I met her. She had problems adjusting to schools in Providence during the ninth grade, so she went back to Santo Domingo for a month, where she attended a school for English-dominant returned-migrants, but she didn't like it so she once more came back to Providence.

Maria's involvement in a local Catholic Church also reinforced her Spanish language ability, and gave it institutional support, including practice in literacy skills. She sang in the Spanish-language choir, attended and acted as student leader of a Friday night Spanish language religious youth group, attended Spanish language Mass, and worked answering the phone several evenings a week in the rectory. Her Friday night youth group at the church was led by a middle-aged Dominican woman who spoke little English. It was structured around reading passages from the Bible in Spanish and discussing their meaning in preparation for the following Sunday's Mass, which would deal directly with those passages. This exposed her to levels and styles of language not encountered in everyday life, and involved both reading and writing: small groups would read and discuss Biblical passages then write a summary in Spanish of the group's ideas.

Maria's best friends were Puerto Ricans and New York-born Dominicans. She said that Puerto Rican boys were often attracted to her and she had dated them. Maria was discursively conscious of the American binary division between people who count as "Black" and those who count as "White," and she saw Hispanics categorized as "Black." Although Maria did not report ever being perceived to be African American, she knew that her mother's mother and one of her uncles were phenotypically indistinguishable from African Americans.

Maria was highly aware of discrimination she faced from White Americans, and she had gotten into verbal confrontations many times over discriminatory treatment. At a Catholic school she attended, for example, her White peers had picked on her and treated her as if she-- and other non-White students--were different and inferior. She reported that White students at that school were asked by teachers to read whole sections of text out loud in class while Black and Hispanic students would be asked to read three sentences. Her confrontation with a teacher over this led to her leaving that school. She also reported being treated as different--and unwelcome--when her family ate in restaurants in primarily white neighborhoods.

Maria's awareness of racial/ethnic hierarchy in America was matched with frequent code switching in school and English speech style that included many AAVE and Spanish structures. She code switched with both Dominican and Puerto Rican friends and used Spanish pronunciations of names in addressing friends, thus displaying her Spanish speaking background across many school contexts.

In terms of AAVE, she frequently deleted the copula ("She like 'You have a ...'") and third-person singular verbal inflection "-s" ("Everybody consider Puerto Ricans, 'Oh your Mom let you do this, your mom let you do that'"), used the habitual "be" ("I talk just like my uncle, that's the way he be talking"), and elided the plural "-s" ("Like us American, we know what you have to go through."). Like her peers, Maria also used a variety of forms that could be multiply determined, e.g. double negatives ("I don't want to be nothing but Catholic") and non-inverted questions with subject pronouns ("Where you bought this?").

Unlike other Dominican Americans that I recorded in Providence, Maria used "be" as an auxiliary *without* a habitual or recurring meaning. She asked a student who was unexpectedly leaving class, "Where you be going?" While this use of "be" collapses a distinction that sociolinguists and creolists have considered a hallmark of AAVE as a syntactic system, it remains a distinctive social marker popularly associated with African Americans. In contrast to Frangelica, who avoided the AAVE "habitual be" in her speech, Maria extended it to novel syntactic contexts, thus increasing its frequency in her speech. This hyper-use of an AAVE form correlates with the explicit solidarity she expresses with African Americans

Maria also used a number of structures that represented convergence between Spanish and English forms. In describing why she went to the Dominican Republic for a month during her freshman year of high school, she used "for" as a conjunction meaning "so that": "I went down there for I could see...if I wanted to stay down there." In Caribbean Spanish, infinitives with pre-posed subjects are often used in place of conjunctions with subjunctive forms. Thus, "I went so that I could see" is rendered *"Yo fui para yo ver."* *Para* has many different meanings with correspondingly diverse translations in English, but the most direct and common translation is 'for,' which could explain Maria's construction, "I went down there for I could see." Maria also duplicated relative pronouns with pronouns, a structure that occurs in Spanish but results in ambiguous meaning in English:

"My uncle$_i$ was the kind of man$_i$ that$_i$ he$_i$ never gave up."

The relative pronoun "that" as well as the immediately following pronoun "he" both refer to the antecedent "man."

Maria's use of prepositions in English also drew on Spanish patterns: "In the Dominican Republic, you don't have to worry for ['about'] bills." The use of "for" rather than "about" can be explained by a literal translation of *por* which is phonetically, semantically, and syntactically similar to "for." Zentella (1997:47) attests this type of interference in Puerto Rican "Hispanicized English," the English spoken by individuals who didn't begin learning English until after adolescence, but it can also occur among American-born and raised Dominican Americans. Maria's pronunciation also included features that are commonly associated with native Spanish speakers who learn English later in life. Her aspiration of some stops was so weak for example that "think" was pronounced as /ðiŋ/, and "it's" was variably pronounced as /ɪz/ and /ɪdz/.

7.5.5 Alejandro

Alejandro came to the United States at the same age as Wilson, during second-grade, but Alejandro's English displayed many more effects of Spanish-English contact than Wilson's. Unlike Wilson, who lived with his father and monolingual English step-family, Alejandro lived with monolingual Spanish parents and two older sisters who were 10 and 12 when they came to America. Although Alejandro had not returned to the island since leaving it, Alejandro was unsure whether his family would stay in the United States indefinitely, and he maintained a strong affective relationship for the island.[48] His father had attended college in the Dominican Republic, and they owned a house in Santiago, which would facilitate their possible return.

Alejandro's English may also have developed differently from Wilson's because of a difference in schools and neighborhoods. While Wilson lived and attended schools in a primarily non-immigrant school district, Alejandro lived in the heart of a Spanish-speaking neighborhood and attended elementary and middle schools that were heavily or majority Hispanic. Two of his three best friends his junior year had immigrated at the same time he had, and had attended ESL and bilingual education classes with him starting in elementary school.

Alejandro's English consistently displayed Spanish phonological features in addition to syllable timing, and his peers identified him as having a "Spanish accent." Although he made clear phonemic contrasts between minimal pairs, e.g. /i/ vs. /ɪ/ and /æ/ vs. /a/--which Spanish speakers who learn English after childhood often fail to do--his vowel and consonant quality often suggested a second-language pronunciation. His pronunciations of voiceless stops, i.e. /p/, /k/ and /t/, for example, were not as explosively aspirated as those of most native speakers of American English. He also pronounced /s/ as /z/ at times when it occurred between voiced vowels, such that "guess" in "I guess that" was pronounced /gɛz/. Some of the phonological features of his language, e.g. /d/ for word-initial /ð/ and consonant cluster simplifications, e.g. "Mis(t)er Cox" and "Tha(t)'s cool", are typical of not only second-language English of Spanish speakers but of other American sociolects such as AAVE.

Spanish grammatical patterns also affected Alejandro's English. He used literal translations of the Dominican Spanish form for the English present perfect to express duration of events that began in the past and continued until the time of speaking, e.g. "I have a long time I don't write letters." The effects of Spanish on his English were also occasionally apparent in use of prepositions ("I go to all the fieldtrips"), some of which were direct translations from Spanish, e.g. "I'm mad with ['at'] her" [*Estoy enojado con ella*] and "They're going in car" [*en carro*] rather than "by car."

The close genetic relationship between Spanish and English facilitates convergent forms because many calques and literal translations are clearly comprehensible in the other language, and even standard in form. Alejandro explained that he didn't usually come to school when it rained by saying, "When it's raining like that, I like to stay sleeping." "Stay" is a literal translation of *quedar*. The Spanish construction "*quedar* ['stay'] + gerund" is typically translated differently, however: as "to continue + gerund." Alejandro's literal translation of *quedar* as "to stay," however, results in a form that is grammatical in English and semantically clear.

Alejandro's English was also strongly influenced by forms associated with AAVE. Alejandro used lexical forms and expressions that are associated with urban African American youth and hip hop culture more frequently than other students I recorded. His description to classmates of a roller-skating trip he went on with other students, for example, is in typical urban teen hip hop terms: "It was fly, yo, it was fly. It was phat, yo." (LD #2 7:41:40). Similarly, his description to African American and Dominican American classmates of his cousin's drug dealing is filled with distinctive lexical items:

[(LD #2 1:11:30)] "My cousin was clocking ['selling drugs'], yo. He left, yo. He got mad loot ['a lot of money'], though.

Yo, my cousin sent mad money to DR ['the Dominican Republic'], yo, because he was clocking ['dealing drugs']. And then like five-oh ['the police'], some guy snitched on all of them, that whole group."

Alejandro used uniquely AAVE verb forms relatively more frequently than the other students who were recorded. He used the habitual "be", and deleted the copula (e.g. "we studying for the test," "that girl from English, that woman cool, yo," "you messing up because you're on camera") and third-person present singular verbal inflection "-s" ("he get all tight"). Alejandro also used grammatical forms that were non-standard in prescriptivist terms, most notably "ain't," more frequently than the other students. Students were generally more aware of "ain't" as a non-standard form than other forms that diverge from prestige prescriptivist standards, e.g. copula deletion. Alejandro's relatively frequent use of "ain't" could represent conscious opposition to prescriptivist standards of school and the dominant society, commensurate with non-White identity and solidarity he emphasized in interview situations and enacted with peers.

Despite his use of many AAVE forms, Alejandro's English was easily distinguishable from the English of African Americans in Providence because of Spanish phonological and syntactic forms in his English. His use of AAVE/hip hop vocabulary and AAVE grammar, however, did align him with African American peers and contribute to the enactment of a non-White urban youth identity. Unlike Frangelica, who used relatively few AAVE grammatical forms or hip hop vocabulary and was not friends with any African American peers, Alejandro extensively used such forms and was friends with a number of African Americans and second-generation African/African-descent non-Hispanic immigrants.

His terms of reference for such non-Hispanic African-descent friends were frequently drawn from AAVE and the language of hip hop, and these terms and his behavior suggested intimacy. In the excerpt below, Alejandro has just explained to a Liberian American friend, Avery, that one of his best friends, John (of Cape Verdean and African American descent), had hit him with a volleyball when his back was turned during a gym class game of dodge ball.

(LD #2 1:36:30)

Alej.:   You don't expect that from your boy ['male friend']. You
            see what I'm saying?
Avery: Isn't John supposed to be your homey ['person from the
            same neighborhood' and, hence, ally]?
Alej.:   Yeah, he's supposed to be my boy. ((John hugs Alejandro))
Avery: Isn't that cute!
Avery: Ever since freshman year we knew each other. ((Alejandro
            touches his chest over his heart with a fist))
Avery: Boy to the bone ['intimate male friend'].

Alejandro refers to John as his "boy" an AAVE term for male friend or
associate (Smitherman 1994). Avery asks rhetorically if John is
supposed to be Alejandro's "homey," who should be an ally rather than
someone who unexpectedly turns on one in a gym class game. When
Avery characterizes John not just as Alejandro's boy, but as his "boy to
the bone," Alejandro touches his closed fist to his chest over his heart, a
gesture used at Central High School to express interpersonal intimacy
and friendship.

Alejandro also uses AAVE to express solidarity/intimacy with
Avery. In saying good-bye to Avery, Alejandro addresses him as "bro,"
short for "brother," a term of address that can express common identity
and is commonly used by African Americans to address African
American males. Alejandro uses the term "bro" along with an AAVE
expression of parting to say good-bye to his Liberian American friend
Avery: "Alright bro, check you out."

Alejandro's Spanish with peers at school, like his English, often
included features associated with adolescent male bravado such as
profanity, playful insulting, and specialized lexicon. This was evident
in the Spanish description of the roller-skating trip that Alejandro had
characterized in English as "It was fly, yo, it was fly. It was phat, yo":

(LD #3 8:43:15)

Alej.:   *Mira coño, mamahuevo, chupacabra* ['Hey, you damn,
            cock-sucking, goat-sucking-alien']
Alej.:   *Diablo loco, la mierda* roller skating *estaba vacaníssimo,
            loco* ['Damn, yo, the roller skating shit was phat (superlative
            form), yo.']
G: *Tú fuiste, loco?* ['Did you go, yo?']

Alej.:	Hell yeah. *Vacaníssima tuvo la mierda esa.* ['That shit was phat (superlative form)']
G:	*Qué?* ['What?']
Alej.:	*Que tuvo vacano* ['It was phat']
G:	*Muchas mujeres?* ['A lot of women?']
Alej.:	Hell yeah
G:	*No te tirate (a) una?* ['And did you screw one?']
Alej.:	Hell yeah

Alejandro's language with his peers, both in English and Spanish, includes features associated with male adolescent joking and posturing. His use of specifically Spanish and AAVE features in this style contribute to the enactment of a particular non-White, urban male identity.

7.5.6 Isabella

Isabella came to the United States during first grade. Before moving to South Providence during middle school she lived in neighborhoods with many White Americans, and she estimated that half of her classmates in elementary and middle school were White. During high school, Isabella's work and school/community activities brought her into contact with individuals outside of South Providence from a variety of social backgrounds, and she appeared more at ease talking with White adults such as her teachers than many of her peers. When an article about Central High School appeared in the local newspaper quoting an African American teacher's criticism of her White colleagues--including accusations of racism toward African American students--Isabella was angered. She thought her best teachers and greatest supporters at school had been White.

Isabella's relative ease with different social groups was matched by her facility with different varieties of language. She reported actively cultivating what she called "proper English," which contrasted with her notion of African American English:

BB: Do you ever speak African American English?
Isabella: I used to. Until my English teacher kept on correcting me, she continued on correcting me so now I speak only proper English, as best as I can. I'm used to it cause every time I say something

wrong, it feels like I said it wrong....cause usually they're like "I ain't gonna do this." I don't talk like that anymore....

BB: Is that just cause of teachers or friends? Why you changed?

Isabella: I changed because my teacher kept on correcting me so I was like, "Fine," then I continued on correcting myself, when I say it wrong, I feel myself saying it wrong, so I correct myself and I say it the correct way. I think it's myself, well probably listening to the teachers, but myself.

BB: So a lot of your English is more like White American English now?

Isabella: Probably. Cause I have a lot of friends that tell me I speak like a White person. They tell me, "You sound like a White girl."

BB: What does that mean?

Isabella: The way I talk. Cause sometimes I may use like long words, big words, they be like "Whaaat?"

A White American teacher had made Isabella aware of prestige standards for English, and she had actively tried to adhere to them in her speech, even though this led to her being teased at times for sounding like a "White girl":

Isabella: I talk the right way I guess, and they make fun of me. Even people I don't even know, like my boyfriend's father, he picks up the phone and I talk to him for a while, and he's like, "Your girlfriend talks like a White girl." His uncle keeps going, "Is that a White girl you're talking to?" ((laughing))

At the same time that she was at ease with White Americans and thought of her speech as containing White characteristics, her social circles were non-White. Isabella's best friends were Dominicans and African Americans, her boyfriend was an American-born Dominican, and she had little contact with White American peers, except through the occasional non-violence workshop. When asked to whom she would feel most comfortable talking at a party where she didn't know anybody, she said she would probably approach African Americans before White Americans, Asian Americans, and non-Caribbean Hispanics.

Isabella spoke English with no obvious Spanish phonological features. Her English variably included phonological features such as simplification of consonant clusters ("Wha(t)'s that?," "Tha(t)'s butters"), substitution of /d/ for word-initial /ð/, and substitution of /t/ for word-final /θ/ which are common to various sociolects. She used the habitual "be" of AAVE, but I attested no examples of copula deletion or elision of third-person verbal suffix /s/ in her speech. She used a variety of urban teen vocabulary associated with AAVE in her everyday talk, e.g. "diesel," "mad," "slamming," "butters," "phat," "crack on," and "nice". She was the only student recorded to use hypercorrected simple past tense forms: "subtracteded" and "misseded".

Despite her reports of consciously avoiding "wrong" forms, she regularly and variably used forms in talk with peers that are non-standard in prescriptivist grammar, e.g. the second-person plural form "yous." When two students simultaneously gave the correct answer in class, for example, Isabella addressed them:

(IN #1 11:11:05)
"Are yous twins or something? Why are you saying the same stuff. What's up with yous? Were yous guys studying this morning?"

Fifteen minutes later, Isabella made plans to meet some classmates after lunch:

(IN #1 11:26:30)
"Where's you guys gonna be? So I can meet yous?"

Isabella alternates between prestige standard ("you," "you guys") and local vernacular ("yous," "yous guys") forms. Her use of prescriptivist standard forms, the salience of "yous" as a non-standard form, and Isabella's professed awareness of "proper English," suggest that she could choose to use the prescriptivist forms categorically. There may be local social incentives in these situations for using non-standard forms, however, social incentives that are more compelling than those for speaking "proper English." Using only prescriptivist forms could result in being teased for "talking White" or for being stuck-up. Strategic use of local vernacular terms could contribute to local solidarity and counteract possible ostracism.

Isabella, like Janelle, generally did not engage in longer conversations in Spanish at school, using Spanish primarily in code switching that didn't go beyond 1-2 turns. As described in Chapter 4, Isabella characterizes peers as "hicks" when they speak Spanish extensively among themselves rather than just in short code switches. She is quicker to identify peers this way than many of her American-born peers, even though she did not come to America until first grade, her Dominican Republic background is rural, and she speaks only Spanish with her monolingual mother and various adult relatives. At school she uses Spanish only in parts of turns or for short turns as in these examples:

[(IN #1 11:24:15) Borrowing a fashion magazine from a Dominican American classmate during class.]

Isabella: *Es el tuyo?* ['Is it yours?'] Whose is this? ((indicating a magazine))
Janelle: Mine.
Isabella: Can I borrow it?

[(IN #1 8:54:04) Chatting during word processing class.]
Isabella: I like your shirt Anna ((English pronunciation)). It's cute. It's different.
Ana: I bought it for fifty cents.
Isabella: Really?
Ana: At a thrift store.
Isabella: Oh, *mi mama- mi mama se va para allá* ['my mom- my mom goes there']

[(IN #2 12:35:15)
Isabella: Let me see that magazine, *es tuya?* ['is it yours?'] ((to a Puerto Rican classmate))

(IN #1 9:31:24
Isabella: I brought my bottle of ge:l. ((taking bottle out of bag))
Aisha: Gel?
Isabella: Gel *de pajón* ['for bushy hair'] ((carefully studies hair in mirror))
Isabella: Pretty darn cool. (.5) It's holding up. (.5) It's drying up. (1.0) Mayday, mayday!

Isabella had a more Spanish-language public persona than Janelle even though she did not engage in longer Spanish conversations. Isabella used Spanish in more situations and with a wider range of people, e.g. with Puerto Rican, Mexican, and South American classmates, not just Dominicans. She used the occasional Spanish word even in conversation with non-Spanish-speakers. When planning what to do during lunch break, she told an African American friend, for example: "I have to go to the *banco* ['bank']" (IN #1 10:37:15). At other times, she spoke Spanish words aloud to no one in particular. As she copied notes off the blackboard in physics class, for example, she enunciated words syllable by syllable, switching to a Spanish pronunciation for the final word: "What- is- the- grav-i-ta-tional *potencial* ['potential']" (IN #1 11:15:20). When a teacher wrote an assignment on the blackboard, she called out *Ay Dios* ['Oh God']. In another class, a teacher's talk about his personal life was disturbing students who were chatting and reading teen-age girl magazines. Isabella called out jokingly, as she thumbed through her magazine: Shut up, *cállate* ['shut up'], *cállate, cállate* (IN #1 12:33:05). In both of these classes, her classmates within earshot were both Hispanic and non-Hispanic.

Isabella also occasionally used markedly Spanish pronunciations of Dominican and Puerto Rican friends' names, e.g. *Frangelica* and *Melissa*. This could include not only a Spanish pronunciation, but also a Dominican intonation contour to communicate a summons. To get her classmate Frangelica's attention, Isabella called out *Frangelica!* with a pitch that started out lower than the corresponding English exclamation and did not rise as its English counterpart would. Isabella used a Dominican intonation contour for an interjection in a similar form of code switching, described in Chapter 3: "Where you going? Huh? *Eh? Woody!*" Even though Isabella did not engage in long Spanish conversations at school, her regular use of individual Spanish words or pronunciations made her Spanish ethnolinguistic identity more prominent than that of other English-dominant Dominican Americans.

7.6 Language and Ascriptions of Identity

The six students discussed in this chapter all identify themselves as Dominican, and they all share Dominican and American linguistic and cultural practices. At the same time that they identify themselves as members of one social group, they vary significantly among themselves in phenotype, linguistic and social experiences, and specifics of language use, all of which have significant implications for individual social identities. Language use reflects individual understandings of identity, and it also has a strong effect on the identities that others ascribe to individuals.

The ways in which language use affects other-ascriptions of identity vary with the particular phenotype and language style in question, so language use has different implications for each of these six individuals. Alejandro, for example, commonly uses vocabulary and structures associated with AAVE and socializes extensively at school with African-immigrant, African American, and Cape Verdean friends, in addition to Hispanic friends. No one ever mistakes him for African American, however, presumably because of his relatively European phenotype. His AAVE-influenced English correlates with the oppositional stances he expresses in interviews, and it may ease and reflect his access to non-Hispanic, African-descent social circles, but it doesn't lead to assignment to the category "African American."

Alejandro's AAVE-style English that includes Spanish phonological features, along with his frequent use of Spanish and code switching, does, however, contribute to Alejandro's successful enactment of a non-White identity. Alejandro's straight hair and relatively light skin make him phenotypically indistinguishable from many Americans who count as White, but peers do not teasingly accuse him of being White, but rather of being Guatemalan. Ascribing a Guatemalan identity to him is a way of making reference to his relatively European phenotype in a way that is congruous with his Spanish and Spanish-influenced language practices. Alejandro identified strongly as non-White, and in everyday interactions, his language is one factor that may prevent others from perceiving him as White.

Maria's phenotype, which is relatively European by Dominican standards, matches popular Caribbean Hispanic perceptions of Puerto Rican phenotype (Dominguez 1978), and she was sometimes perceived to be Puerto Rican until she spoke Spanish. Being perceived as Puerto Rican was compatible with her understanding of herself, however. She considered mainland Puerto Ricans and Dominicans to be very similar, and she once even referred to herself as "Mud," meaning Dominican-

Puerto Rican. Her birth-father had one Puerto Rican parent, like Puerto Ricans she was a United States citizen by birth, and she had lived for nine years in New York City where Puerto Ricans are the largest Hispanic group. Maria was highly conscious of discrimination by Whites against non-Whites in America, and she did not identify herself as White, although she possibly could have been perceived as White, based on phenotype alone. Maria's language contributed to her enactment of a non-White, Hispanic identity. Her regular use of Spanish at school, her Dominican and Puerto Rican social networks, and her active church membership served to mark an unambiguously Caribbean Hispanic identity. Her English language reflected this non-White, Spanish identity, including Spanish and AAVE patterns. Although she was born in the United States and had spent relatively little time in the Dominican Republic, her socialization in Hispanic communities resulted in her use of many convergent Spanish-English forms in addition to code switching.

For Janelle and Isabella, who are of similar phenotype, differences in language use contribute significantly to different attributions of identity by outsiders. Although both use AAVE grammatical structures and lexicon, Janelle uses a wider variety of such structures and her pronunciation, e.g. "ah" (/a/) for "I" (/ay/), more closely approximates popular notions of AAVE. Isabella also has a higher profile Spanish identity at school: she speaks more Spanish at school than Janelle and across a wider variety of contexts. Isabella reports that people think that she is African American only in contexts away from her school and neighborhood, e.g. at workshops on non-violence, and that such attributions are weak: "Some people might think that I look Black. Might." Isabella explained that if someone suggested that she was Black, she would simply speak Spanish: I'll be like, "Yeah, look," and I start talking and they be like "Okay."

Janelle's style of English was so authentically African American and her Spanish identity at school so inconspicuous that ascriptions to the category African American could be very forceful, even when she displayed evidence of Spanish speaking:

Janelle: There's a girl in my fifth period class, she thought I was Black the whole time. And I was like "No, I'm Spanish" and she was like (disbelievingly) "Yeah, right." and she was arguing with me, and I'm like, I am Spanish." She goes, "How are you Spanish? You look Black and you act Black." I'm like "How can you act Black? What is 'acting Black'." And she's like "Oh my god, I don't care what you say, you're Black to me." I'm like, "If you say so."

BB: Did you speak Spanish to show her that you knew Spanish?

Janelle: Oh, one day I was talking in Spanish, she was like, "Oh, you know Spanish," she just thought I knew. And then she was arguing, she wasn't really arguing, but she was like "Uh uh, I don't care what you say, you're just Black to me" and I'm like "I'm not," she says, "You are Black."

According to Janelle, when her peers say someone is "acting Black" they mean "talking Black." To this classmate, Janelle's English language and phenotype matched the criteria for assignment to the category "Black" so well that Janelle's Spanish fluency was immaterial. Even though Janelle was not categorized by Dominicans as belonging to the more African-phenotype Dominican color categories-- *indio oscuro* ['dark indian-colored'], *moreno/prieto* ['dark/black'], or *negro* ['black']--she was regularly and forcefully assigned by others to the category African American, in part because of her language practices.

For Wilson, like Janelle, phenotype and use of AAVE-style English combine to result in regular, unequivocal attributions of African American identity. Among teen-age Dominican Americans who speak English without apparent Spanish features, use features of AAVE, and are phenotypically indistinguishable from African Americans, attribution of an African American identity often continues until they are witnessed speaking Spanish. Those teen-agers who speak little Spanish with peers reported that some of their non-Hispanic friends did not realize they were Dominican/Hispanic (as opposed to Black/African American) until these peers visited their Spanish-speaking households or until they had known each other for months or years. For Wilson, attributions of African American, and sometimes Cape Verdean, identity followed this pattern even though he spoke Spanish in many contexts. Even when he was in the company of Dominicans, other Dominicans mistook him for African American:

Wilson: Like for example, like I told you before, a lot of people confuse me like I'm Black. Yesterday I got that comment, on Sunday. I was at the park playing basketball...there was this Spanish kid, he was Dominican, I was standing next to him and this other friend of mine, he's Dominican too, he was talking to me, and he heard me speaking Spanish to the other kid, he said, "Oh I could've sworn he was Black".... he asked me, "Yo, you Black? You're not Black, huh?" I was like, "Nah, I'm Spanish." He was like "I could've sworn you was Black."

Although both Wilson and Frangelica describe their skin color as *moreno/a* ['dark'], and both have been perceived to be African American, this occurs less frequently for Frangelica than it does for Wilson and Janelle, and it is less salient in her life. Her explanation of how she lets people know that she is Dominican rather than African American suggests this lack of salience and the ease with which she corrects such perceptions: "There have been a few cases where I actually had to speak Spanish so they would believe that I am Spanish." Janelle and Wilson must regularly use Spanish to show that they are "not Black," and for Janelle, speaking Spanish has not always been treated as sufficient evidence of Hispanic identity.

Language plays a central role in the difference in the experiences of identity ascription of Frangelica, Wilson, and Janelle. When speaking English, Frangelica uses few urban teen words and expressions that are associated with AAVE, and although she uses some AAVE grammatical structures, she does not use the highly salient habitual "be." She speaks English with readily apparent syllable timing and other Spanish phonological patterns. Because her English phonology suggests her Hispanic identity, it is sometimes non-native speakers who take her to be African American. One of the situations in which she was asked to speak Spanish to show that she wasn't Black was at her jewelry factory job, where there are no native speakers of English. Her colleagues, who immigrated as adults, presumably recognized her as a fluent English speaker and could not discern the effects of Spanish phonology in her English.

In school Frangelica regularly holds longer conversations in Spanish with Hispanic classmates, which makes publicly apparent her Spanish language. Her social networks are primarily Dominican and Hispanic, and she doesn't have African American friends. Based on phenotype, she can clearly be assigned to the category Black, but her language, behavior, and social networks fit much better into the widely recognized category "Hispanic." As described in Chapter 4, the social category "Black" is implicitly treated as an ethnically homogeneous category in America, so the conspicuousness of Frangelica's Hispanic ethnolinguistic identity is at odds with assignment to the category African American. The historical mutual exclusivity between these two categories in America creates ambiguity for those outsiders who would assign Frangelica to one category or the other. For Wilson and Janelle, whose English and social networks do not make their Hispanic ethnicity so immediately apparent, this ambiguity does not always arise, as they are assumed to be African American.

7.7 Conclusions

Categories such as "Dominican American" and "Dominican American language" are social and analytical constructions that can obscure the individuals whose diverse experiences and practices serve to constitute the categories. Individual Dominican Americans vary in language, phenotype, and life experiences, with the result that the issues of social identity, e.g. racial ascription and acculturation, that each individual faces are different. The relative balance of individual agency and social structural constraint in the enactment of identities is thus variable rather than constant among Dominican Americans. Attention to intra-group variation acts as an antidote to the homogenizing effects of abstract social theory building, and it better delineates the social processes that connect individual social actors to larger-scale social constellations.

CHAPTER 8
Concluding Remarks

> one and the same person may be considered white in the
> Dominican Republic....[and] a 'Negro' in Georgia (Hoetink
> 1967:xii)

In the thirty odd years since Hoetink made this observation, migration
has brought the societies to which he alludes closer together. The "one
and the same person" who "may be considered white in the Dominican
Republic" is increasingly likely to have immigrated to the United
States, where he or she may be seen in very different terms. The
available macro-social categories in the Dominican Republic organize
the identities of Dominican out-migrants, i.e. the ways that they think
of themselves, while the social categories available in America
determine the authorized identity options for immigrants upon arrival.
These differences in social organization, the result of disparate and
specific social histories, are confronted and negotiated at the micro-
social level by individual migrants in their everyday lives after
immigration. The ways in which this post-migration encounter is
negotiated make visible the interpenetrating micro- and macro-social
processes by which social/racial categories are enacted, challenged, and
transformed.

This negotiation is particularly evident in the lives of the second
generation, who are socialized in both Dominican and American
linguistic and cultural traditions, and who daily confront dominant
American discourses on race. Members of the Dominican second
generation have varying degrees of control over a bilingual repertoire
of language varieties, and varying achievement of the identities in the
Dominican American repertoire of identities. Because of intragroup
variation, individual Dominican Americans are variously assigned by

others to social categories that can include, among others, Black, White, Dominican, and Spanish.

There is frequently a disparity between the identities that individual Dominican Americans ascribe to themselves, and the ways in which they are seen by others. Phenotype-symbolized race is the preeminent criterion for social organization in America, but Dominican Americans define their race largely in terms of language, and unlike non-Hispanic African-descent immigrant groups, they maintain a distinctive, non-Black ethnolinguistic identity in the second generation.

Dominican American negotiation of this ambiguity focuses attention on social identity formation mechanisms and processes that are generally hidden from view and discursive consciousness. Although both language and social categories are characterized by internal variation and change in response to multiple influences, they are commonly constructed as if they were uniform and static. Categories of language, race, and identity in the United States are built not only on assumptions of purity, but also on an assumed unity of language/race/identity. Dominican Americans draw attention to contradictions in these assumptions through their explicitly heteroglossic language, their range of phenotypes, and their flouting of Black/White phenotype as a paramount social organizing principle.

Implicit purity and unity of categories is particularly evident in the construction "African American," in which race and ethnicity are treated as synonymous, and disparate linguistic phenomena are subsumed under a heading--African American English--defined implicitly (Mufwene et al. 1998) or explicitly (Morgan 1994a:327) by phenotype of speakers. It is this distinctive, totalizing characteristic of the linguistic/ethnic/racial category Black that makes it possible for so many Dominican Americans to successfully resist ascription to it. Dominican American heteroglossia and variation in phenotype are so salient in everyday life that they undermine this assumed unity, calling attention to the contradictions inherent in such constructed categories. Dominican American enactment of a "Spanish" racial identity reveals "the absence of any essential characteristics or fixed meanings in discourses on race" (Duany 1998).

The dominant American focus on phenotype, with its implicit biological basis, obscures the historical social relations out of which notions of race have grown. Smedley (1993), for example, argues that American notions of race have their roots in European colonial domination of the rest of the world, and it is the nature of this domination, rather than phenotypic differences, that are central to understanding race:

> It was only accidental, perhaps incidental, that the conquered and enslaved peoples were physically distinct, for this permitted social status to be linked with biophysical differences. At bottom, race was a social mechanism for concretizing and rigidifying a universal ranking system that gave Europeans what they thought was to be perpetual dominance over the indigenous peoples of the New World, Africa, and Asia. (Smedley 1993:303-4)

Like other diacritica of identity (Barth 1969), particular differences in phenotype have no meaning in and of themselves, but rather are *made* to matter in particular social and historical contexts. For Dominicans, whose recent social history differs from that of most United States residents, non-phenotype diacritica are the crucial markers of identity. Dominican American enactment of a language-based racial identity thus contextualizes both popular and social scientific (e.g. Omi and Winant 1994:55) United States notions of phenotype-race as specific, local constructions.

Dominican American enactment of identity in Providence, Rhode Island also shows that race, which is popularly treated as a static attribute of an individual, can be situational. In certain circumstances, Dominican Americans, as this paper has shown, can transform their race in the eyes of others, simply by speaking Spanish. While it has long been recognized that individuals count as members of different races in different societies (e.g. Hoetink 1967) and that one can "change one's race" with a plane ride between countries, this study shows that race can vary not only between geographical contexts, but also moment-to-moment across linguistically constituted contexts.

This power of language to situationally constitute transformative racial contexts is particularly notable given the rigidity and mutual exclusivity that have historically characterized American Black/White racial categories. Smedley (1993:9), for example, differentiates between the American racial system and racial systems in other societies precisely in terms of the impermeable nature of category boundaries: "one cannot transcend or transform one's 'race' status; in other words, no legal or social mechanism exists for changing one's race." Individual Dominican Americans, through speaking Spanish, *are* frequently able to transform their race status, from Black or White, to Spanish. In those situations in which the identity(ies) Spanish/Hispanic/Dominican are locally available, language has the constitutive power to overcome what are seen as static, natural boundaries.

Dominican American enactment of ethnolinguistic identities not only focuses attention on distinctive features of the American racial system, it serves to transform the system from within. Dominican American negotiation of identity thus illustrates the *reciprocal* relations between the communicative behavior of individual social actors and larger-scale social structures. While it is commonly recognized that larger-scale social constellations, e.g. racial categories, affect individuals' social actions, including language, such larger scale phenomena are themselves constituted through social action and relations at a smaller scale. When existing patterns of social relations and meanings are merely reproduced at the micro-level, it is difficult to discern the agency of individual social actors. The juxtaposition of social realities and contestation of meanings resulting from migration, in this case, make especially clear the agency of individual social actors because they are not merely reproducing pre-existing categories and meanings but turning hegemonic beliefs on their heads. The ongoing struggles of Dominican Americans with ambiguous ascriptions of identity in everyday life thus contribute to the transformation of existing social categories as well as the constitution of new ones where they might otherwise not have existed.[49]

The fact that Dominican Americans have had a transformative effect on local social categories suggests that more sweeping changes in American ethnic/racial categorization are imminent. Dominican Americans represent only a small fraction of the burgeoning second generation of post-1965 immigrants. Like Dominicans, the vast majority of post-1965 immigrants are not from Europe, i.e. they come from parts of the world that were once colonized and subjugated by Europeans, and many of these migrants do not count as White in the American phenotype-racial hierarchy. Dominican Americans show that ethnolinguistic practices and understandings can be used to resist hegemonic forms of ascription in ways that affect the American categorization system. Reproduced on a broader scale, post-1965 second-generation immigrant enactment of identities based on immigrant practices and understandings can speed and make more visible the ongoing transformation of American ethnic and racial categories.

Appendix A: Transcription Conventions

Wilson: The speaker is indicated with a name or abbreviation on the left of the page.

como   Italics indicate words spoken in Spanish.

['Jerk.']   Text surrounded by single quotation marks and brackets indicates a translation of the immediately preceding Spanish.

( )   Empty parentheses indicate material that couldn't be heard clearly enough to transcribe.

(I can)   Words in parentheses indicate uncertainty about accuracy of transcribed words.

((smiling))   Double parentheses indicate nonverbal, visual, or background information.

//I don't-
//He said   A double slash above another double slash indicates the onset of words spoken in overlap.

(1.5)   Numerals in parentheses indicate periods of time, in seconds, during which there is no speech.

e(s)to   Letters in parentheses within words represent phonemes that are not pronounced by the speakers (See Chapter Three).

Da::mn   A colon indicates that the preceding sound was elongated in a marked pronunciation

<u>rocking</u>   Text that is underlined is pronounced with emphasis, i.e. some combination of higher volume, pitch, and greater vowel length.

como l--   A hyphen or dash indicates that speech was suddenly cut
               off during or after the word preceding the hyphen or dash.

<If you're a junior or a senior- >
               Words inside of out-pointing arrows indicate speech that is
               spoken at a markedly slower tempo than surrounding
               speech.

>Yeah<   Words inside inward-pointing arrows are spoken at a
               markedly faster tempo than surrounding speech.

°Yeah   Words marked with '°' are spoken at markedly lower
               volume.

Hi   Speech between upward-pointing arrows is spoken at
               markedly higher pitch.

A: (bus)=
M: =No, okay
               Equal signs indicate that two turns are latched onto each
               other with no period of silence between them.

Appendix B: Grammatical Abbreviations for Interlinear Glosses and Descriptions of Language Structures

S	subject
DO	direct object
V	verb
1ST	first-person
2ND	second-person
REF	reflexive
NEG	negation
ART	article
POSS	possessive
SUB	subjunctive

References

Aarsleff, Hans. 1982. Introduction. in H. Aarsleff *From Locke to Saussure: Essays on the Study of Language and Intellectual History* (pp. 3-41). Minneapolis: University of Minnesota Press.

Alarcón, Antonio Menendez. 1994. Racial Prejudice: A Latin American Case. *Research in Race and Ethnic Relations* 7:299-319.

Alba, Orlando. 1990a. *Estudios sobre el español dominicano*. Santiago de los Caballeros, RD: Universidad Católica Madre y Maestra.

--------1990b. *Variacíon fonética y diversidad social en el español dominicano de Santiago*. Santiago de los Caballeros, RD: Universidad Católica Madre y Maestra.

--------1995. *El Espanol Dominicano dentro del Contexto Americano*. Santo Domingo, DR: Libreria La Trinitaria.

Alonso, Ana María. 1994. The Politics of Space, Time and Substance: State Formation, Nationalism, and Ethnicity. *Annual Review of Anthropology* 23:379-405.

Amastae, Jon and Lucía Elías-Olivares (eds.). 1982. *Spanish in the United States: Sociolinguistic Aspects*. New York: Cambridge University Press.

Anisman, P. 1975. Some aspects of code-switching in New York Puerto Rican English. *Bilingual Review* 2:(1-2):56-85.

Appel, R. and Pieter Muysken. 1987. *Language Contact and Bilingualism*. London: Arnold.

Auer, J. C. Peter. 1984a. *Bilingual Conversation*. Amsterdam/Philadelphia: John Benjamins Publishing Company.

--------1984b. On the meaning of conversational code-switching. in Peter Auer and A. di Luzio (eds.) *Interpretive Sociolinguistics* (pp. 87-112). Tübingen, Germany: Narr.

--------1988. A Conversation Analytic Approach to Codeswitching and Transfer. in Heller (ed.) *Codeswitching: Anthropological and Sociolinguistic Perspectives* (pp. 187-213). New York: Mouton de Gruyter.

--------1998. Introduction: Bilingual Conversation Revisited. in J. C. Peter Auer (ed.) *Code-Switching in Conversation: Language, interaction and identity* (pp. 1-24). New York: Routledge.

Austin, J. L. 1962. *How to Do Things with Words*. Oxford: Oxford University Press.

Austerlitz, Paul. 1997. *Merengue: Dominican Music and Dominican Identity*. Philadelphia: Temple University Press.

Badillo, Américo and Cassandra Badillo. 1996. Qué tan racistas somos: pelo bueno y pelo malo. *Estudios Sociales* Vol. 24, No. 103:59-66.

Bailey, Benjamin. 2000a. The Language of Multiple Identities among Dominican Americans. *Journal of Linguistic Anthropology* 10:2:190-223.

--------2000b. Language and Negotiation of Ethnic/Racial Identity among Dominican Americans. *Language in Society* 29:555-582.

--------2000c. Social and Interactional Functions of Code Switching among Dominican Americans. *Ipra Pragmatics* 10:2:165-193.

--------2001. Dominican American Ethnic/Racial Identities and United States Social Categories. *International Migration Review* Vol. 35, 2:677-708.

Bakhtin, M. M. 1981. *The Dialogic Imagination.* Austin: University of Texas Press.

Barth, Frederik. 1969. Introduction. in F. Barth (ed.) *Ethnic Groups and Boundaries: The Social Organization of Culture Difference* (pp. 9-38). Boston: Little Brown and Co.

Basso, Keith. 1979. *Portraits of the "Whiteman": Linguistic Play and Cultural Symbols among the Western Apache.* Cambridge: Cambridge University Press.

Bateson, Gregory. 1972. *Steps to an Ecology of Mind.* New York: Ballantine.

Baugh, John. 1983. *Black Street Speech: Its History, Structure, and Survival.* Austin, TX: University of Texas Press.

Beniak, E., R. Mougeon, and D. Valois. 1984-5. Sociolinguistic evidence of a possible case of syntactic convergence in Ontarian French. *Journal of the Atlantic Provinces Linguistics Association* 6/7:73-88. cited in Romaine 1995.

Blom, Jan-Peter and John Gumperz. 1972. Code-switching in Norway. in Gumperz and Hymes (eds.) *Directions in Sociolinguistics* (pp. 407-34). New York: Holt, Rinehart and Winston.

Bourdieu, Pierre. 1977. *Outline of a Theory of Practice.* Oxford: Oxford University Press.

Bourdieu, Pierre and Jean-Claude Passeron. 1977. *Reproduction in Education, Society, and Culture.* London: Sage.

Brown, Roger and Albert Gilman. 1960. The Pronouns of Power and Solidarity. in Thomas Sebeok (ed.) *Style in Language* (pp. 253-276). Cambridge, MA: MIT Press.

Bryce-Laporte, Roy Simón. 1972. Black Immigrants: The Experience of Invisibility and Inequality. *Journal of Black Studies* 4(1):29-56.

Bucholtz, Mary. 1995. From Mulatta to Mestiza: Passing and the Linguistic Reshaping of Ethnic Identity. in Kira Hall and Mary Bucholtz (eds.)

Gender Articulated: Language and the Socially Constructed Self (pp. 351-373). New York: Routledge.

Cambeira, Alan. 1997. *Quisqueya La Bella: The Dominican Republic in Historical and Cultural Perspective.* Armonk, NY: M.E. Sharpe.

Canfield, Lincoln. 1981. *Spanish Pronunciation in the Americas.* Chicago: University of Chicago Press.

Charles, Carolle. 1992. Transnationalism in the Construction of Haitian Migrants' Racial Categories of Identity in New York City. in Glick-Schiller, Basch, and Blanc-Szanton (eds.) *Towards a Transnational Perspective on Migration: Race, Class, Ethnicity and Nationalism Reconsidered* (pp. 101-125). New York: New York Academy of Sciences.

Chomsky, Noam. 1965. *Aspects of the Theory of Syntax.* Cambridge, MA: MIT Press.

Cleaver, Eldridge. 1973. As Crinkly as Yours. in A. Dundes (ed.) *Mother Wit from the Laughing Barrel: Readings in the Interpretation of Afro-American Folklore* (pp. 9-21). New Jersey: Prentice Hall, Inc.

Clyne, Michael. 1967. *Transference and Triggering.* The Hague: Martinus Nijhoff.

--------1987. Constraints on Code Switching: How Universal Are They? *Linguistics* 25, 739-64.

Cohen, Ronald. 1978. Ethnicity: Problem and Focus in Anthropology. *Annual Review of Anthropology* 7:379-403.

Davis, F. James. 1991. *Who Is Black?: One Nation's Definition.* University Park, PA: The Pennsylvania State University Press.

Davis, Martha Ellen. 1994. Music and Black Ethnicity in the Dominican Republic. in Gerhard Behague (ed.) *Music and Black Ethnicity: The Caribbean and South America* (pp. 119-155). New Brunswick: Transaction Publishers.

Del Castillo, Jose and Martin Murphy. 1987. Migration, National Identity and Cultural Policy in the Dominican Republic. *The Journal of Ethnic Studies* 15:3:49-69.

Diaz, Junot. 1996. *Drown.* New York: Riverhead Books.

Dominguez, Virginia. 1978. Show Your Colors: Ethnic Divisiveness among Hispanic Caribbean Migrants. *Migration Today* February 1978:5-9.

--------1986. *White By Definition: Social Classification in Creole Louisiana.* New Brunswick, NJ: Rutgers University Press.

Duany, Jorge. 1994. Ethnicity, Identity, and Music: An Anthropological Analysis of the Dominican Merengue. in Gerhard Behague (ed.) *Music and Black Ethnicity: The Caribbean and South America* (pp. 65-90). New Brunswick: Transaction Publishers.

--------1998. Reconstructing Racial Identity: Ethnicity, Color, and Class among Dominicans in the United States and Puerto Rico. *Latin American Perspectives* Issue 100, Vol. 25, No. 3, pp. 147-172.

Duranti, Alessandro and Charles Goodwin (eds.) 1992. *Rethinking Context: Language as an Interactive Phenomenon.* Cambridge: Cambridge University Press.

Duranti, Alessandro and Elinor Ochs. 1997. Syncretic Literacy in a Samoan American Family. in L. Resnick, R. Säljö, C. Pontecorvo, and B. Burge (eds.) *Discourse, Tools, and Reasoning: Essays on Situated Cognition* (pp. 169-202). New York: Springer.

Eastman, Carol. 1992. Codeswitching as an Urban Language-Contact Phenomenon. *Journal of Multilingual and Multicultural Development* Vol. 13, No.'s 1 and 2, pp. 1-17.

Ervin-Tripp, Susan. 1972. On Sociolinguistic Rules: Alternation and Co-occurrence. In Gumperz and Hymes (eds.) *Directions in Sociolinguistics: The Ethnography of Communication* (pp. 213-250). New York: Holt.

Evans-Pritchard, E.E. 1940. *The Nuer.* New York: Oxford University Press.

Feagin, Joe. 1991. The Continuing Significance of Race--Antiblack Discrimination in Public Places. *American Sociological Review* 56(1):101-116.

Fennema, Meindert and Troetje Loewenthal. 1987. *Construccion de Raza y Nacion en La República Dominicana.* Santo Domingo: Editorio Universitario.

Ferguson, Charles A. 1959. Diglossia. *Word* 15, 325-40.

Ferguson, Charles and John Gumperz. 1960. Introduction. in Ferguson and Gumperz (eds.) *Linguistic Diversity in South Asia: Studies in Regional, Social and Functional Variation* (pp. 1-26). Publication of the Research Center in Anthropology, Folklore, and Linguistics, No. 13. Bloomington: Indiana University Press.

Fishman, Joshua. 1989. *Language and Ethnicity in Minority Sociolinguistic Perspective.* Philadelphia: Multilingual Matters.

Fishman, Joshua, Robert L. Cooper, and Roxanne Ma. 1971. *Bilingualism in the Barrio.* Bloomington: Indiana University Press.

Foner, Nancy. 1987. The Jamaicans: Race and Ethnicity among Migrants in New York City. in Nancy Foner (ed.) *New Immigrants in New York* (pp. 195-217). New York: Columbia University Press.

Fordham, Signithia. 1996. *Blacked Out: Dilemmas of Race, Identity, and Success at Capital High*. Chicago: University of Chicago Press.

Foucault, Michel. 1972. *The Archaeology of Knowledge* and *The Discourse on Language*. New York: Pantheon Books.

--------1980. *Power/Knowledge*. New York: Pantheon.

Gal, Susan. 1979. *Language Shift*. New York: Academic Press.

--------1988. The political economy of code choice. in Heller (ed.) *Codeswitching: Anthropological and Sociolinguistic Perspectives* (pp. 245-264). New York: Mouton de Gruyter.

--------1989. Language and Political Economy. *Annual Review of Anthropology* 18:345-367.

Gans, Herbert. 1979. Symbolic ethnicity: the future of ethnic groups and cultures in America. *Ethnic and Racial Studies* 2:1:1-20.

--------1992. Second-generation decline: scenarios for the economic and ethnic futures of the post-1965 American immigrants. *Ethnic and Racial Studies* 15:2:173-192.

Garfinkel, Harold. 1967. *Studies in Ethnomethodology*. Englewood Cliffs, NJ: Prentice-Hall.

Gaskins, Bill. 1996. *Good and Bad Hair*. New York: Robert B. Menschel Photography Gallery.

Georges, Eugenia. 1990. *The Making of a Transnational Community: Migration, Development, and Cultural Change in the Dominican Republic*. New York: Columbia University Press.

Giddens, Anthony. 1984. *The Constitution of Society: Outline of the Theory of Structuration*. Berkeley: University of California Press.

Gilbert, Judy. 1993. *Clear Speech: Pronunciation and listening comprehension in North American English*. New York: Cambridge University Press.

Goffman, Erving. 1959. *The Presentation of Self in Everyday Life*. Garden City, NY: Anchor Books.

--------1974. *Frame Analysis: An Essay on the Organization of Experience*. New York: Harper and Row.

--------1981. *Forms of Talk*. Philadelphia: University of Pennsylvania Press.

Gonzalez, Nancie. 1975. Patterns of Dominican Ethnicity. in John Bennett (ed.) *The New Ethnicity: Perspectives from Ethnology* (1973 Proceedings of The American Ethnological Society) (pp. 110-123). New York: West Publishing.

Goodwin, Charles. 1981. *Conversational Organization: Interaction Between Speakers and Hearers*. New York: Academic Press.

Goodwin, Charles and Alessandro Duranti. 1992. Rethinking Context: An
    Introduction. in A. Duranti and C. Goodwin (eds.) *Rethinking Context:*
    Language as an Interactive Phenomenon (pp. 1-42). Cambridge:
    University of Cambridge Press.
Goodwin, Charles and M. H. Goodwin. 1992. Assessments and the
    Construction of Context. in A. Duranti and C. Goodwin (eds.) *Rethinking*
    Context: Language as an Interactive Phenomenon (pp. 147-189).
    Cambridge: University of Cambridge Press.
Gordon, Milton. 1964. *Assimilation in American Life: The Role of Race,*
    Religion, and National Origins. New York: Oxford University Press.
Grasmuck, Sherri and Patricia Pessar. 1991. *Between Two Islands: Dominican*
    International Migration. Berkeley: University of California.
--------1996. Dominicans in the United States: First- and Second-Generation
    Settlement. in S. Pedraza and R. Rumbaut (eds.) *Origins and Destinies:*
    Immigration, Race, and Ethnicity in America (pp. 280-292). Belmont, CA:
    Wadsworth.
Guarnizo, Luis. 1992. One Country in Two: Dominican-Owned Firms in New
    York and in the Dominican Republic. Unpublished Ph.D. dissertation,
    Johns Hopkins University.
--------1994. Los Dominicanyorks: The Making of a Binational Society. *The*
    Annals of the American Academy of Political and Social Science Vol. 533,
    pp. 70-86.
--------1997. Going Home: Class, Gender, and Household Transformation
    among Dominican Returned Migrants. in P. Pessar (ed.) *Caribbean*
    circuits: New directions in the study of Caribbean migration (pp. 13-60).
    New York: Center for Migration Studies.
Guitart, Jorge. 1982. Conservative vs. Radical Dialects in Spanish: Implications
    for Language Instruction. In J. Fishman and G. Keller (eds.) *Bilingual*
    Education for Hispanic Students in the U.S. New York: Teachers College
    Columbia.
Gumperz 1964. Linguistic and Social Interaction in Two Communities.
    American Anthropologist, 66(6):137-153.
--------1982. *Discourse Strategies.* New York: Cambridge University Press.
Gumperz, John and Jenny Cook-Gumperz. 1982. Introduction: Language and
    the Communication of Social Identity. In J. Gumperz (ed.) *Language and*
    Social Identity (pp. 1-21). Cambridge: Cambridge University Press.
Gumperz, John and Dell Hymes. 1986 [1972]. *Directions in Sociolinguistics:*
    The Ethnography of Communication. New York: Basil Blackwell.

Gumperz, John and R.D. Wilson. 1971. Convergence and creolization: a case from the Indo-Aryan-Dravidian border. In D. Hymes (ed.) *Pidginization and Creolization of Languages* (pp. 151-69). Cambridge: Cambridge University Press.

Haggerty, Richard (ed.). 1991. *Dominican Republic and Haiti: Country Studies.* Washington, D.C.: Library of Congress (U.S. Government Printing Office #550-36).

Halter, Marilyn. 1993. *Between Race and Ethnicity: Cape Verdean American Immigrants, 1860-1965.* Urbana and Chicago: University of Illinois Press.

Harris, Marvin. 1964. *Patterns of Race in the Americas.* New York: W. W. Norton.

Hatala, E. 1976. Environmental Effects on White Students in Black schools. Unpublished Master's Essay. University of Pennsylvania.

Heller, Monica (ed.). 1988. *Codeswitching: Anthropological and Sociolinguistic Perspectives.* New York: Mouton de Gruyter.

--------1992. The politics of code-switching and language choice. in Carole Eastman (ed.) *Codeswitching* (pp. 123-142). Cleveland, Avon: Multilingual Matters.

--------1995. Language Choice, Social Institutions, and Symbolic Domination. *Language in Society* 24:3:373-406.

Henríquez Ureña, Pedro. 1940. *El Español en Santo Domingo.* Buenos Aires: Biblioteca de Dialectología Hispanoamericana, Vol. 5.

Heritage, John. 1984a. *Garfinkel and Ethnomethodology.* Cambridge: Polity Press.

--------1984b. A change-of-state token and aspects of its sequential placement. in J. Atkinson and J. Heritage (eds.) *Structures of Social Action: Studies in Conversation Analysis* (pp. 299-345). Cambridge: Cambridge University Press.

Heritage, John and J. Maxwell Atkinson. 1984. Introduction. in Atkinson and Heritage (eds.) *Structures of Social Action: Studies in Conversation Analysis* (1-15). Cambridge: University of Cambridge Press.

Herskovits, Melville. 1937. African gods and Catholic saints in New World Negro belief. *American Anthropologist* 39:635-43.

Heskamp, Reade. 1959. La Enseñanza de los Idiomas, Según el Nivel Mental Lingüístio del Estudiante. Unpublished doctoral dissertation, Universidad Interamericana. Saltillo, Mexico.

Hill, Jane and Kenneth Hill. 1986. *Speaking Mexicano: Dynamics of Syncretic Language in Central Mexico.* Tucson: The University of Arizona Press.

Hoetink, Harry. 1967. *Caribbean Race Relations: A Study of Two Variants.* New York: Oxford University Press.

--------1985. "Race" and Color in the Caribbean. in Mintz and Price (eds.) *Caribbean Contours* (pp. 55-84). Baltimore: The Johns Hopkins University Press.

Hymes, Dell. 1974. *Foundations in Sociolinguistics: An Ethnographic Approach.* Philadelphia: University of Philadelphia Press.

Isajiw, Wsevolod. 1974. Definitions of Ethnicity. *Ethnicity* 1:111-124.

Itzigsohn, Jose and Carlos Dore-Cabral. 2000. Competing Identities? Race, Ethnicity and Panethnicity among Dominicans in the United States. *Sociological Forum* 15(2)225-247.

Jacobs-Huey, Lanita. 1997. Is There an Authentic African American Speech Community: Carla Revisited. *U. Penn Working Papers in Linguistics* 4:1:331-70.

Jefferson, Gail. 1978, Sequential aspects of story telling in conversation. In J. N. Schenkein (ed.) *Studies in the Organization of Conversational Interaction* (pp. 219-248). New York: Academic Press.

Jiménez Sabater, Max. 1975. *Más Datos Sobre el Español en la República Dominicana.* Santo Domingo: Ediciones Intec.

Kochman, Thomas (ed.). 1972. *Rappin' and Stylin' Out: Communication in Urban Black America.* Champaign, IL: University of Illinois Press.

Kraly, Ellen. 1987. U.S Immigration Policy and the Immigrant Populations of New York. in Nancy Foner (ed.) *New Immigrants in New York* (pp. 35-78). New York: Columbia University Press.

Kroskrity, Paul. 1993. *Language, History, and Identity: Ethnolinguistic Studies of the Arizona Tewa.* Tucson: University of Arizona Press.

Labov, William. 1966. *The Social Stratification of English in New York City.* Washington, D.C.: Center for Applied Linguistics.

--------1971. The notion of 'system' in creole languages. in D. Hymes (ed.) *Pidginization and Creolization of Languages* (pp. 447-72). Cambridge: Cambridge University Press.

--------1972a. *Language in the Inner City: Studies in the Black English Vernacular.*

--------1972b. *Sociolinguistic Patterns.* Philadelphia: University of Pennsylvania Press.

--------1979. Locating the Frontier Between Social and Psychological Factors in Linguistic Variation. in Fillmore, Kempler, and Wong (eds.) *Individual Differences in Language Ability and Language Behavior* (pp. 327-340). New York: Academic Press.

--------1980. Is There a Creole Speech Community?. in A. Valdam and A. Highfield (eds.) *Theoretical Orientations in Creole Studies* (pp. 389-424). New York: Academic Press.

Lambert, W. et al. 1960. Evaluational Reactions to Spoken Languages. *Journal of Abnormal and Social Psychology* 60:44-51.

Lee, Sharon. 1993. Racial classifications in the US census: 1890-1990. *Ethnic and Racial Studies* 16:1:75-94.

LePage, R.B. and Andrée Tabouret-Keller. 1985. *Acts of Identity: Creole-based Approaches to Language and Ethnicity.* New York: Cambridge University Press.

Lerner, Gene H. 1991. On the syntax of sentences-in-progress. *Language in Society* 20:441-458.

--------1996. On the 'Semi-Permeable' Character of Grammatical Units in Conversation: Conditional Entry into the Turn Space of Another Speaker. in E. Ochs, E. A. Schegloff and S. A. Thompson (eds.) *Interaction and Grammar* (pp. 238-76). Cambridge: Cambridge University Press.

Levinson, Stephen. 1983. *Pragmatics.* Cambridge: Cambridge University Press.

Levitt, Peggy. 2001. *The Transnational Villagers.* Berkeley and Los Angeles: University of California Press.

Lipski, John. 1985. *Linguistic Aspects of Spanish-English Language Switching.* Tempe: Arizona State University, Center for Latin American Studies.

--------1994. *Latin American Spanish.* New York: Longman.

Marx, Karl. 1976. *The German Ideology.* Moscow: Progress Publishers.

Massey, Douglas and Nancy Denton. 1989. Racial Identity among Caribbean Hispanics: The Effect of Double Minority Status on Residential Segregation. *American Sociological Review* 54:790-808.

McClure, Erica. 1977. Aspects of code-switching in the discourse of bilingual Mexican-American children. In M. Saville-Troike (ed.) Linguistics *and Anthropology*, Washington, DC: Georgetown University Press. GURT, 93-115.

Megenney, William. 1990. *Africa en Santo Domingo: Su Herencia Lingüística.* Santo Domingo, DR: Editorial Tiempo, S.A.

Milroy, James and Lesley Milroy. 1985. *Authority in Language: Investigating Language Prescription and Standardisation.* New York: Routledge and Kegan Paul.

Milroy, Lesley. 1987. *Language and Social Networks.* New York: Basil Blackwell Inc.

Mitchell-Kernan, Claudia. 1972. Signifying, loud-talking, and marking. In Kochman (ed.) *Rappin' and Stylin' Out: Communication in Urban Black America* (315-335). Champaign, IL: University of Illinois Press.

Mittelberg, David and Mary Waters. 1993. The process of ethnogenesis among Haitian and Israeli immigrants in the United States. *Ethnic and Racial Studies* 15:3:412-435.

Moerman, Michael. 1965. Ethnic Identification in a Complex Civilization. *American Anthropologist* 67:1215-1230.

Morales, Amparo. 1995. The Loss of the Spanish impersonal Particle *se* Among Bilinguals: A Descriptive Profile. in C. Silva-Corvalán (ed.) 1995. (pp. 148-162).

Morgan, Marcyliena. 1994a. The African American Speech Community: Reality and Sociolinguists. in Marcyliena Morgan (ed.) *Language and the Social Construction of Identity in Creole Situations* (pp. 121-148). Los Angeles: Center for Afro-American Studies, UCLA.

--------1994b. Theories and Politics in African American English. *Annual Review of Anthropology* 23:325-45.

--------1996. Conversational signifying: grammar and indirectness among African American women. in Ochs, Schegloff, and Thompson (eds.) *Interaction and Grammar* (pp. 405-34). New York: Cambridge University Press.

--------1998. More than a mood or an attitude: Discourse and verbal genres in African-American culture. in Mufwene, Rickford, Bailey, and Baugh (eds.) *African-American English: Structure, History and Use* (pp. 251-281). New York: Routledge.

Moya Pons, Frank. 1995. *The Dominican Republic: A National History*. New Rochelle, NY: The Hispaniola Book Corporation.

--------1996. Dominican National Identity: A Historical Perspective. *Punto 7 Review: A Journal of Marginal Discourse* 3(Fall):1:14-25.

Mufwene, Salikoko, John Rickford, Guy Bailey, and John Baugh (eds.). 1998. *African-American English: Structure, History, and Use*. New York: Routledge.

Myers Scotton, Carol. 1983. The negotiation of identities in conversation: A theory of markedness and code choice. *International Journal of the Sociology of Language* 44:115-36.

--------1993a. *Duelling Languages: Grammatical Structure in Codeswitching.* Oxford: Oxford University Press.

--------1993b. *Social Motivations for Codeswitching: Evidence from Africa.* Oxford: Oxford University Press.

Ochs, Elinor. 1992. Indexing Gender. in A. Duranti and C. Goodwin (eds.) *Rethinking Context: Language as an Interactive Phenomenon* (pp. 335-58). New York: Cambridge University Press.

Ochs, Elinor and Bambi Schieffelin. 1984. Language acquisition and socialization: Three developmental stories and their implications. In R. Shweder and R. LeVine (eds.) *Culture theory: Essays on mind, self and emotion* (276-320). New York: Cambridge University Press.

Ogbu, John. 1974. *The Next Generation: An Ethnography of Education in an Urban Neighborhood*. New York: Academic Press.

Omi, Michael and Howard Winant. 1994. *Racial Formation in the United States: From the 1960's to the 1990's*. New York: Routledge.

Oostindie, Gert (ed.). 1996. *Ethnicity in the Caribbean: Essays in Honor of Harry Hoetink*. London: Macmillan.

Oquendo, Angel. 1995. Re-imagining the Latino/a Race. *Harvard BlackLetter Law Journal* 12:93-129.

Ortner, Sherri. 1984. Theory in Anthropology since the Sixties. *Comparative Studies in Society and History* 26: 126-66.

Otheguy, Ricardo and Ofelia García. 1988. Diffusion of lexical innovations in the Spanish of Cuban Americans. In J. Orenstein-Galicica, G. Green, and D. J. Bixler-Marquez (eds.) *Research and issues and problems in U. S. Spanish* (pp. 203-237). El Paso: Pan American University at Brownsville/University of Texas-El Paso.

Otheguy, Ricardo, Ofelia García, and Mariela Fernández. 1989. Transferring, switching, and modeling in West New York Spanish: an intergenerational study. *International Journal of the Sociology of Language* 79:41-52.

Peirce, Charles Sanders. 1940. Logic As Semiotic: The Theory of Signs. In J. Buchler (ed.) *Philosophical Writings of Peirce: Selected Writings*. London: Routledge and Kegan Paul.

Pessar, Patricia. 1984. The Linkage between the Household and Workplace of Dominican Women in the U.S. *International Migration Review* 18:1188-1211.

--------1987. The Dominicans: Women in the Household and the Garment Industry. in Nancy Foner (ed.) *New Immigrants in New York* (pp. 103-129). New York: Columbia University Press.

Pfaff, Carole. 1979. Constraints on language mixing. *Language* 55:291-318

Poplack, Shana. 1981. Syntactic Structure and Social Function of Codeswitching. in Richard Durán (ed.) *Latino Language and Communicative Behavior* (pp. 169-184). Norwood, NJ: ABLEX.

--------1982 [1980]. "Sometimes I'll Start a Sentence in Spanish *y termino en español*": toward a typology of code-switching. in J. Amastae and L. Elías-Olivares (eds.) *Spanish in the United States: Sociolinguistic Perspectives* (pp. 230-263). New York: Cambridge University Press.

--------1988. Contrasting patterns of codeswitching in two communities. in Heller (ed.) 1988. pp. 215-244.

Poplack, Shana, David Sankoff, and Christopher Miller. 1988. The social correlates and linguistic consequences of lexical borrowing and assimilation. *Linguistics* 26(1):47-104.

Portes, Alejandro. 1995. Children of Immigrants: Segmented Assimilation and Its Determinants. in Portes (ed.) *The Economic Sociology of Immigration: Essays on Networks, Ethnicity, and Entrepreneurship* (pp. 248-279). New York: Russell Sage.

Portes, Alejandro and Ruben Rumbaut. 1996. *Immigrant America: A Portrait*. Berkeley and Los Angeles: University of California Press.

Portes, Alejandro and Min Zhou. 1993. *The New Second Generation: Segmented Assimilation and Its Variants*. The Annals of the American Academy of Political and Social Sciences Vol. 530 (November), 74-96.

Prince, Ellen. 1981. Topicalization, focus-movement and Yiddish-movement: a pragmatic differentiation. *Proceedings of the Seventh Annual Meeting of the Berkeley Linguistics Society* (pp. 249-64).

Psathas, G. (ed.). 1979. *Everyday language: Studies in Ethnomethodology*. New York: Irvington.

Quintero, Viviana. 1998. Linguistic and Racial Stereotyping among New York Latinos. Paper given at the 97th Annual Meetings of the American Anthropology Association, Philadelphia, PA.

Rampton, Ben. 1995a. *Crossing: Language and Ethnicity among Adolescents*. New York: Longman.

--------1995b. *Language Crossing and the Problematisation of Ethnicity and Socialisation*. Pragmatics 5:4:485-513.

Rodríguez, Clara. 1989. *Puerto Ricans: Born in the USA*. Boston: Unwin Hyman.

--------1994. Challenging Racial Hegemony: Puerto Ricans in the United States. in Gregory and Sanjek (eds.) *Race* (pp. 131-145). New Brunswick, NJ: Rutgers University Press.

Romaine, Suzanne. 1995 (2nd Edition). *Bilingualism*. Cambridge, MA: Basil Blackwell.

Romaine, Suzanne and Deborah Lange. 1998. The use of 'like' as a marker of reported speech and thought: a case of grammaticalization in progress. in

J. Cheshire and P. Trudgill (eds.) *The Sociolinguistics Reader, Vol. 2: Gender and Discourse* (pp. 240-77). London: Arnold.

Rout, Leslie. 1976. *The African Experience in Spanish America: 1502 to the Present Day*. New York: Cambridge University Press.

Royce, Anya. 1982. *Ethnic Identity: Strategies of Diversity*. Bloomington: Indiana University Press.

Sacks, Harvey, Emanuel Schegloff, and Gail Jefferson. 1974. A simplest systematics for the organization of turn-taking in conversation. *Language* 50:4:696-735.

Sanjek, Roger. *The Future of Us All: Race and Neighborhood Politics in New York City*. Ithaca: Cornell University Press.

Sankoff, D. and Poplack, S. 1981. A formal grammar for code-switching. *Papers in Linguistics* 14:3-46.

Sassoon, Anne. 1987. *Gramsci's Politics*. London: Hutchinson.

Schegloff, Emanuel. 1972. Sequencing in conversational openings. In Gumperz and Hymes (eds.) *Directions in Sociolinguistics: The Ethnography of Communication* (pp. 346-80). New York: Basil Blackwell.

Schegloff, Emanuel, Gail Jefferson, and Harvey Sacks. 1977. The preference for self-correction in the organization of repair in conversation. *Language* 53:361-82.

Schegloff, Emanuel and Harvey Sacks. 1973. Opening up closings. *Semiotica* 7:4:289-327.

Schenkein, J.N. (ed.). 1978. *Studies in the Organization of Conversational Interaction*. New York: Academic Press.

Schieffelin, Bambi B. (1994). Code-switching and Language Socialization: Some Probable Relationships. In J. Duchan, L. E. Hewitt and R. M. Sonnenmeier (eds.) *Pragmatics: From Theory to Therapy* (pp. 20-42). New York: Prentice Hall.

Schieffelin, Bambi B. and Rachelle Charlier Doucet. 1994. The "Real" Haitian Creole: Ideology, Metalinguistics, and Orthographic Choice. *American Ethnologist* 21(1), 176-200.

Schieffelin, Bambi, Kathryn Woolard, and Paul Kroskrity (eds.). 1998. *Language Ideologies: Practice and Theory*. New York: Oxford University Press.

Searle, John. 1969. *Speech Acts: An Essay in the Philosophy of Language*. Oxford: Oxford University Press.

Silié, Rubén. 1989. Esclavitud y Prejuicio de Color en Santo Domingo. *Boletín de Antropología Americana* 120:163-70.

Silva-Corvalán, Carmen. 1983. On the Interaction of Word Order and Intonation: Some OV Constructions in Spanish. in Flora Klein-Andreu (ed.) *Discourse Perspectives on Syntax* (pp. 117-40). New York: Academic Press, Inc.

--------1994. *Language Contact and Change: Spanish in Los Angeles*. New York: Oxford University Press.

--------(ed.). 1995. *Spanish in Four Continents: Studies in Language Contact and Bilingualism*. Washington, D.C.: Georgetown University Press.

Silverstein, Michael. 1976. Shifters, Linguistic Categories, and Cultural Description. in Keith Basso and Henry Selby (eds.) *Meaning in Anthropology* (pp. 11-56). Albuquerque: University of New Mexico Press.

--------1981. The Limits of Awareness. Sociolinguistic Working Paper, No. 84. Southwest Educational Development Laboratory.

Smedley, Audrey. 1993. *Race in North American: Origin and Evolution of a Worldview*. Boulder: Westview Press.

Smitherman, Geneva. 1977. *Talkin and Testifyin: The Language of Black America*. Boston: Houghton Mifflin.

--------1994. *Black Talk: Words and Phrases from the Hood to the Amen Corner*. New York: Houghton Mifflin Company.

Spicer, Edward. 1971. Persistent Identity Systems. *Science* 4011:795-800.

Stafford, Susan Buchanan. 1987. The Haitians: The Cultural Meaning of Race and Ethnicity. in Nancy Foner (ed.) *New Immigrants in New York* (pp. 131-158). New York: Columbia University Press.

Stepick, Alex. 1998. *Pride Against Prejudice: Haitians in the United States*. Boston: Allyn and Bacon.

Stevens, Thomas. 1989. *Dictionary of Latin American racial and ethnic terminology*. Gainesville: University of Florida Press.

Suárez-Orozco, Carola and Marcelo Suárez-Orozco. 1995. Migration: Generational Discontinuities and the Making of Latino Identities. in George DeVos (ed.) *Ethnic Identity: Creation, Conflict, and Accommodation* (pp. 321-347). Walnut Creek, CA: AltaMira/Sage.

Thomason, Sarah Grey and Terrence Kaufman. 1988. *Language Contact, Creolization, and Genetic Linguistics*. Berkeley: University of California Press.

Toribio, Almeida Jacqueline. 2000. Language Variation and the Linguistic Enactment of Identity among Dominicans. *Linguistics* 38 (6): 1133-1159.

Torres, Lourdes. 1997. *Puerto Rican Discourse: A Sociolinguistic Study of a New York Suburb*. Mahwah, NJ: Lawrence Erlbaum and Associates.

Torres-Saillant, Silvio and Ramona Hernández. 1998. *The Dominican Americans*. Westport, CT: Greenwood Press.

Ugalde, A., F. Bean, and G. Cardenas. 1979. International Migration from the Dominican Republic: Findings from a National Survey. *International Migration Review* 13(2):235-254.

Urciuoli, Bonnie. 1991. The Political Topography of Spanish and English: The View from a New York Puerto Rican Neighborhood. *American Ethnologist* 18:295-310.

--------1996. *Exposing Prejudice: Puerto Rican Experiences of Language, Race, and Class*. Boulder: Westview Press.

Vigil, Diego. 1988. *Barrio Gangs: Street Life and Identity in Southern California*. Austin: University of Texas Press.

Wallerstein, Imanuel. 1974. The Rise and Future Demise of the World Capitalist System. *Comparative Studies in Society and History* 16:387-415.

Warner, W. Lloyd and Leo Srole. 1945. *The Social Systems of American Ethnic Groups*. New Haven: Yale University Press.

Waters, Mary. 1990. *Ethnic Options: Choosing Identities in America*. Berkeley: University of California Press.

--------1991. The Role of Lineage in Identity Formation Among Black Americans. *Qualitative Sociology* 14:1:57-76.

--------1994. Ethnic and Racial Identities of Second-Generation Black Immigrants in New York City. *International Migration Review* 28:4:795-820.

Weinreich, Uriel. 1953. *Languages in Contact: Findings and Problems*. New York: The Linguistic Circle of New York.

Williams, Raymond. 1977. *Marxism and Literature*. Oxford: Oxford University Press.

Willis, Paul. 1977. *Learning to Labor: How Working Class Kids Get Working Class Jobs*. New York: Columbia University.

Woldemikael, Tekle. 1989. *Becoming Black American: Haitians and American Institutions in Evanston, Illinois*. New York: AMS Press.

Wolfram, Walt. 1974. *Sociolinguistic Aspects of Assimilation: Puerto Rican English in New York City*. Arlington, VA: Center for Applied Linguistics.

Wolfson, Nessa. 1982. *CHP: The Conversational Historical Present Tense in American English Narrative*. Dordrecht: Foris.

Woolard, Kathryn. 1985. Language variation and cultural hegemony: toward an integration of sociolinguistic and social theory. *American Ethnologist* 12:738-748.

Woolard, Kathryn and Bambi Schieffelin. 1994. Language Ideology. *Annual Review of Anthropology* 23:55-82.

Zack, Naomi. 1993. *Race and Mixed Race.* Philadelphia: Temple University Press.

Zentella, Ana Celia. 1990a. Lexical Leveling in Four New York City Spanish Dialects: Linguistic and Social Factors. *Hispania* V73 N4:1094-110.

--------1990b. Returned Migration, Language, and Identity: Puerto Rican Bilinguals in Dos Worlds/Two Mundos. in F. Coulmas (ed.) *Spanish in the USA: New Quandaries and Prospects. International Journal of the Sociology of Language* 84:81-100.

--------1993. The New Diversity: Bilingual and Multilingual Repertoires in One New York Puerto Rican Community. Paper presented at the American Anthropological Association Annual Meeting, Washington, D.C., November, 1993.

--------1997. Growing Up Bilingual: Puerto Rican Children in New York. Malden, MA: Blackwell Publishers.

Zephir, Flore. 1996. *Haitian Immigrants in Black America: A Sociological and Sociolinguistic Portrait.* Westport, CT: Bergin and Garvey.

Index

Notes

[1] I use the term "second generation" to refer both to the American-born children of Dominican immigrants, as well as to Dominican-born children who came to America by age 8. By their mid- to late-teens, such Dominican-born individuals are very similar to their American-born peers in terms of being English-dominant, seeing themselves as American minorities, and planning to spend their lives in the United States. I use the term "Dominican American" to refer to the same group, i.e. the second generation, rather than third- and fourth-generation Dominican Americans who experience a much more American than Dominican socialization.

[2] I use the term "phenotype-based race" to capture the popular perception in America that the form of social differentiation called "race" is based on phenotype. From a social scientific perspective, race is a form of social differentiation and domination that is not *based* on phenotype, but rather is *symbolized* by it (Smedley 1993).

[3] I use the terms "Africa" and "African" to refer specifically to those parts of sub-Saharan Africa from which individuals were taken as slaves in the trans-Atlantic slave trade.

[4] First-generation Dominicans in Providence are labor migrants who generally end up in what most Americans would consider low-paying, dead-end jobs, commonly in factories in the local costume jewelry industry. According to the 1990 census, 57.4% of employed Dominicans in Providence were in "Manufacturing." Generally, the economically most successful members of the community are the entrepreneurs serving the ethnic enclave (e.g. Guarnizo 1992), but they are a small minority of the overall population.

[5] Marilyn Halter (1993:18) makes a similar point about Cape Verdean Americans, who, like Dominican Americans, are of Iberian and West African descent and display a range of European/African phenotypes in a smooth continuum:

> Under the gaze of the person whose security and worldview depend upon a clear, state-sanctioned separation of black and white, the mestizo becomes a sexual transgressor. More than simply facing an individual of indeterminate racial background, what transpires in this case is an even more complex and unsettling clash of racial meanings. When significant numbers of people cannot be readily

categorized, it threatens to undermine the entire system of social classification.

[6] The census undercounts poor, non-Whites, in urban areas. This undercount is exacerbated among immigrants such as Dominicans who may lack official immigration documents and sometimes share one living unit among multiple families.

[7] United States immigration law, specifically the Family Reunification Act of 1965, favors certain close kin of United States legal residents and citizens in the visa application process. The presence of extended Dominican family networks in Providence is in part a function of this selective immigration process.

[8] A guidance counselor pointed out to me that this statistic is somewhat misleading because many of the students officially enrolled at the beginning of 9th grade have already stopped coming to school. Even if they have not been to school in years, however, they are technically enrolled because they cannot legally be defined as having dropped out until they reach high school age.

[9] Providence Journal-Bulletin, Metro Edition, September 22, 1997, page A1.

[10] Further interviews and observation in both Providence, Rhode Island and Santiago, Dominican Republic served as background for this study. In Providence, I interviewed adult Dominican community leaders who had grown up in Providence, students at three area colleges who had attended city high schools, students from three of the four main public high schools, and teachers and administrators at the school that was my main site. In Santiago, interviews of high school and college students, which were carried out in Spanish on the street and in three schools, focused on the meaning attached to European/African variations in phenotype, anti-Haitian feelings, and perceptions of White Americans, Black Americans, and Dominican migrants to the United States.

[11] I borrow the term "principal subjects" and this form of introducing them from Zentella (1997:20).

[12] These guaranteed admission programs represented an important avenue to higher education for Central High School students who generally do not qualify for admission to the two, public, four-year colleges, the University of Rhode Island and Rhode Island College, based on grades, and, particularly, test scores.

[13] Hill & Hill (1986:57) use the term "syncretic" in part because, they argue, "purism and degeneration theory have irrevocably tainted the term 'mixing'." While the term syncretic may have more technical and positive connotations than "mixing," it still suggests assumptions of discreteness that need to be

interrogated. Syncretism implies a less than successful union or fusion of differing systems, in which the analyst, from a position of privilege, defines individual components as having discrete heritage. All systems, whether language, philosophy, religion, etc., are syncretic, in that they are a function of multiple influences and histories. Beliefs or practices are most often termed syncretic, however, when they·violate (Western) analysts' implicit assumptions of purity, e.g. an implicitly "pure" Catholicism being integrated with implicitly "pure" African beliefs and practices (e.g. Herskovits 1937).

[14] The form of Isabella 's utterance "De pla:ne, de pla:ne" is drawn from the television show "Fantasy Island." A character on the show heralded the arrival of an airplane with these words at the beginning of each show.

[15] Although syllable-final /s/ elision is less prestigious in international Spanish contexts, it enjoys high status in many Dominican in-group contexts, in which the Castilian/conservative pronunciations (Guitart 1982) are disparaged. Pronunciation of syllable-final /s/ by Dominican males, for example, can be associated not only with putting on airs, but also with effeminacy (Zentella 1990a).

[16] Several consultants from Classical High School, the magnet college-preparatory school, did see Dominican Spanish as being "wrong." They noted that Dominican "eat their letters" (from the Spanish *se comen/cortan las letras*), e.g. they often elide syllable-final /s/. Several students from Classical used the standard Castilian form they learned in school to translate the English present perfect, i.e. *Hace un año que estoy aqui* rather than the popular Dominican Spanish *Tengo un año aqui* ['I've been here for a year'].

[17] According to Silverstein (1981), the ease with which speakers can characterize usage of forms depends on 1) the degree to which the forms are referential ("unavoidable referentiality"), 2) whether or not the form can be divided into overtly meaningful segments ("continuous segmentability"), and 3) the degree to which the pragmatic effectiveness of a form depends on (and is easily linked to) pre-existing, recognizable features of context ("relative presuppositional quality").

[18] Sometimes linguistic forms are transferred *and* shift in meaning and usage, e.g. the Dominican word *jebi* ['cool'], a phonologically assimilated version of English 'heavy.' In the mid-1990's, the word *jebi* was much more widely used by Dominicans to mean "cool" than the word "heavy" was used in English with such a meaning. This English usage may have been more common in the 1960's and 1970's. Poplack (1981:170) attests the usage *Tabanos en una nota*

bien jevi ['We were into a heavy vibe.'] in 1970's New York Puerto Rican
Spanish.

[19] The term *indio* in the Dominican Republic differs both in denotation and
connotation from the term *indio* in the many Latin American countries where it
refers to indigenous peoples and is pejorative. In the Dominican Republic it
does not refer to an ethnic/social group but to a range of skin
colors/phenotypes, and it is unmarked both as a phenotype and a term.

[20] While Isabella models her English expression on the Spanish one, research
among bilinguals more commonly cites the effects of English "like"
expressions on Spanish *gustar* ones (e.g. Zentella 1997:45; Silva Corvalán
1994:180).

[21] Portions of Chapter 3.7 previously appeared in Bailey (2000c).

[22] The common bipartite division of code switching studies--syntax vs. social
functions-- is neatly indexed by Myers Scotton's (1993a, 1993b) dual volumes
on code switching, one emphasizing grammatical structures, the other focusing
on social functions of code switching.

[23] The boundaries between code switching and switching among varieties or
styles to achieve particular conversational and social ends are not always clear.
Romaine (1995:170-1), for example, refers to switches to conversational
historical present tense in narratives (Wolfson 1982), as "monolingual code-
switching," and it has long been noted that speakers move among varieties as
they speak, e.g. between AAVE and other varieties of English (Labov
1971:462). Morgan (1996:414-5) describes how often-subtle differences
between unmarked American English and AAVE are exploited by speakers
alternating among forms to achieve discursive activities. Some of these
discursive activities, e.g. loud talking (relying on volume) or marking (relying
on pitch), do not rely on segmentable features such as lexicon, morphology, or
syntax that are frequently used to define AAVE and differentiate it from other
American English varieties.

[24] Some of Zentella 's (1997) 21 categories--those listed under the category
"Crutch-like Code Mixing" (1997:97-9)--are dominated by switches that others
would classify as forms of transfer rather than as switches. See, for example,
Auer (1984a:26).

[25] Appel and Muysken (1987:118-120) describe five functions of code
switching: 1) *referential* in which switches are used to make up for deficits in
one language or the other, 2) *directive* in which switching selects an addressee
or includes/excludes participants 3) *expressive* in which switching expresses a
dual identity, 4) *phatic* in which switches indicate a "change in tone of the

conversation", and 5) *metalinguistic* in which switching is used to "comment, directly or indirectly, on the languages involved." As with other taxonomies of code switching, these categories represent overlapping functions and disparate levels of analysis.

[26] Speakers of non-dominant varieties, however, are often judged to be superior in terms of traits related to solidarity, such as "friendliness."

[27] The available social categories are not just a function of socio-geographical or communicative context, but also of historical time period. The social categories available to Dominican Americans in Providence today are very different from those that were available just two decades earlier. A Dominican American consultant who had attended Central High School in the mid-1970's, for example, found herself identifying, as she grew up, at times as Puerto Rican, at times as Black, and, often, as something for which there was no available category:

> But high school was like, oh my god, it was so different. I went through the identity crisis of either "You're not Black, you're not White, so I guess you got to be Puerto Rican." And I was resentful, so I had to say that I was Puerto Rican, I couldn't even say that I was Dominican. And it was weird. They used to do the Puerto Ricans parade, I used to go and act like I was Puerto Rican....

> When I was younger, every time I used to fill out an application, I didn't know what to fill out, so I used to have to put Black, because I couldn't say White, because I'm not White, so I always used to put Black.

> The Black girls used to fight with me, "Well you can't be Black, because look at your hair, and you can't be White, because look at your skin color. So what are you?" "I'm Spanish, Dominican, you know, from another country." They couldn't understand. "What are you?" That's what I used to get. "What are you?"

[28] Dominican American high school students in Providence used "yo" frequently. Alejandro, who considered himself authentically Dominican, was discussing with classmates the possibility that he might be labeled a *yo* during his upcoming summer in the Dominican Republic, when he stated, with no apparent intended irony:

> "Yo, if they call me a 'yo', yo...."

[29] Kroskrity 's (1993) repertoire of identity among trilingual Tewa and Zentella's (1993, 1997) emphasis on the multi-variety linguistic repertoire of New York Puerto Ricans represent exceptions to this tendency.

[30] Portions of Chapter 4.10 previously appeared in Bailey (2000a).

[31] Alejandro pointed out that differences between life in the Dominican Republic and Providence were largely a function of whether one's Dominican origins were rural or urban:

> It depends on where they come from, if they come from the *campo* or the farm or whatever, it's kind of different than if you're over there from a city. If you come from the *campo*, from the farm, it's different, cause you live with the cows and everything. I used to go to the *campo*, but I wasn't from there. When I came over here I was kind of used to it...there's people over there from the *campo* farm...even over there if they go to a city...there's gonna be a lot of difference.

[32] Thus, Isabella referred to Alejandro , for example, as being like a hick   , because of his extensive use of Spanish in school. Paradoxically, Isabella herself is of relatively poor, rural origins near the town of Barahona, an area that is semi-arid, less economically developed, more African in phenotype, and closer to disparaged Haiti than other parts of the country. Alejandro, in contrast, came from an educated upper-middle class family in the historical cultural capital and second-largest city, Santiago. Alejandro said that he got along with both new immigrants and longer established ones: "Some people call them hicks, but I don't think that's right. When it happens, I say 'Look at yourself first' before you call somebody something else." He noted specifically that some individuals from the *campo* became conceited and looked down on more recent immigrants after some acculturation in Providence.

[33] The visual and prosodic features of Isabella 's hick enactment vary in English and Spanish. In English she uses a deep pitch with a blank stare and slack face.

In Spanish she uses a nasal voice with slightly high pitch and a tensed face, i.e. squint, wrinkled nose, and lifted upper lip.

[34] Weinreich might not have made this statement had he had access to audiotapes made in ethnographic contexts. Even in contexts of supposed diglossia or in cases in which strict compartmentalization of codes is valued-- and consultants deny code switching in nominally unchanged contexts-- individuals *do* code switch (e.g. Kroskrity 1993).

[35] Auer (1988:209) found that such intrasentential switching was characteristic of only a "few, insulated, and dense networks." This matches my finding that repeated intrasentential switching between varying constituents was typical of only a few speakers in a few situations. Janelle, for example, engages in this type of code switching primarily with one particular friend, Jose, with whom she spends considerable time.

[36] Language socialization of newcomers *to* and *through* peers' code switching has not been studied. Schieffelin (1994) examines language socialization-- socialization *through the use* of language and socialization *to use* language (Ochs & Schieffelin 1984)--specifically through code switching, but she focuses on a 2-3 year-old Haitian American child in interaction with adult caregivers.

[37] Compartmentalization of language could actually have a negative effect on Dominican American socioeconomic mobility. It would increase the ascription by others to phenotype-racial categories, and could thereby encourage eventual acculturation to longer established non-White groups, e.g. African Americans, who have faced enormous obstacles to socioeconomic mobility (Gans 1992).

[38] Portions of Chapter 5 previously appeared as Bailey (2001).

[39] Even recent, constructionist social science definitions of race focus on phenotype differences, as if the current, dominant United States notion of race were universal:

> race is a concept which signifies and symbolizes social conflicts and interests by referring to different types of human bodies (Omi & Winant 1994:55)

[40] Dominicans engaged in public soul searching when a relatively dark-skinned Dominican immigrant to Italy won the Miss Italy contest in 1996. She was phenotypically representative of Dominicans in that she appeared to be of both European and African descent, but contestants as dark as she were typically not contenders for the title in the Dominican Republic.

[41] "Mirrors of the Heart: Race and Identity," video produced by WGBH/Boston and Central Television Enterprises in the "Americas" series.

[42] According to Moya Pons   (1996:24), Dominican notions of race and treatment of African descent began to broaden in the 1970's as a result of "returning migrants [from the United States] who went back to their communities transformed into new social agents of modernity, capitalism, and racial emancipation." Particularly significant in this incipient transformation are "the younger generation who have been raised in the cities of the East and have grown up with colored Puerto Ricans, West Indians, and black Americans." Such returned migrants have learned to think of themselves as non-White, and they have been exposed to American-style racial politics and seen that one's African descent can be a source of pride rather than stigma.

[43] A version of this chapter previously appeared as Bailey (2000b).

[44] The phrase "At what time?" is a standard form in American English but typical of more formal registers. It is common in the speech of Dominican Americans as it better matches the structure of the equivalent phrase *A qué hora* in Spanish.

[45] Smitherman (1994:69) defines "word!" as an interjection of affirmation and "break you up" as an AAVE basketball term meaning "to fake out the defense and create scoring opportunities in such a way as to break the defender's spirit and embarrass him."

[46] Zentella (personal communication) points out that these two identities, Haitian and African American, are not equally valued in teen-age Dominican circles, whether on the island or in urban America. There is prestige in urban African American youth identities for other low-income, non-White, urban teen-agers, but not in Haitian/Haitian American identities. Economic sociologists of immigration (e.g. Waters 1994, Portes 1995) and many adult migrants, in contrast, emphasize the superior social capital of African-descent immigrants over African Americans, and African-descent immigrants' greater chances for social and economic mobility.

[47] Dominican Americans of relatively African phenotype explained to me that one way they know that they're being perceived as African Americans is their treatment in informal, playground basketball games. In such informal games, teams are frequently formed by two "captains," who alternately pick players, with the best players being chosen first. Relatively African-phenotype Dominican Americans report that they are often chosen relatively early during such team selection when the captain has not seen them play and does not know that they are Dominican.

[48] Alejandro expressed strong loyalty to his Dominican heritage, e.g. by enumerating activities that showed he was true to his roots:

> I don't forget my roots, man? I like speak Spanish all the time, I eat my food, I eat rice and beans, you know what I'm saying? I listen to my music, so I'm still there, man. Like people, some people change, they forget about all that. They forget about rice and beans and the *platanos* ['plantains'], and they start eating burgers, so that's it. Not me, yo. Rice and beans that's it, that's what I like, I can't live without rice and beans. Every time I get home, my rice and beans got to be there, even though I work at Burger King, rice and beans, man, that's all I want, rice and beans.

Key diacritica (Barth 1969) used by Dominican Americans to characterize degrees of acculturation are language (control over varieties of Spanish and English), clothing and hairstyles, musical tastes (*merengue*, *bachata*, and *salsa* versus hip hop, reggae, and rhythm and blues), and food (stereotypical American fast foods versus rice and beans and plantains). Central High School graduate Nanette, like Alejandro, uses the criteria of language and food to differentiate between herself and her relatively more acculturated older brother:

> My brother, he speaks really bad Spanish, Junior. He doesn't really speak really good Spanish. I think he's the most Americanized of all of us. He'll prefer pizza over rice and beans. That's not me. Please. I cannot live without my rice and beans. I can live without pizza, I can live without hamburgers. That's him, hamburgers and pizza.

Dominican Americans in Providence use the Dominican staple of *platanos* ('plantains') as a particularly Dominican symbol of identity. At the annual Dominican Independence Day festival in Providence, Dominicans tape *platanos* to their vehicles, hold them aloft, and wave them along with their Dominican flags.

[49] This transformation of social categories and meanings is occurring not only in the United States, but also in the Dominican Republic. Individual return- or circular-migrants, through their micro-level social behavior, become agents of social transformation (Moya Pons 1996). Experiences in America of ascription to the category Black have led many such migrants to consider their African descent from new perspectives, and living in America has exposed

them to phenotype-racial identity politics, in which African descent can be a source of pride. According to Moya Pons (1996:23), being of African descent became a "positive existential option" for Dominicans for the first time in the 1970's, a result of returned-migrants' contact with negritude in America.